Advance praise for *In Defiance*

"*Laced with grit and goodness, these are powerful stories that must be told, and they are recounted by graceful and faithful storytellers. These deeply moving and historically significant narratives, hidden and suppressed for too long, are shared with vivid and heart-wrenching detail. In Defiance is a book to inspire us, fortify us, and energize us to heed the clarion call—in our own times, in our own ways—for freedom and justice, liberty and dignity for all.*" —**The Rev. Dr. Andrea Ayvazian**, Founder and Director of Sojourner Truth School for Social Change Leadership

"*This wide-ranging and well-structured anthology offers a critical contribution to the constant* sankofa *retrieval of and engagement with the concepts, history and practice of abolitionism in achieving and expanding the realm of African and human freedom. It provides not only some of the most important voices and practices of abolitionism, but also critical interpretations that reaffirm their valuable insights and activist models useful in reimagining and achieving racial and social justice in our time. The texts collected here will serve as a continuously relevant and useful resource in the current and ongoing vital resistance to proposals and practices of erasure, removal, banning, and reversals of gains in order to escape the truth and judgment of history and to narrow the horizon of radical imagination and initiatives to achieve a just and good society and world.*" —**Dr. Maulana Karenga**, Professor and Chair, Department of Africana Studies, California State University-Long Beach

"*In Defiance is the book we need in every classroom. It is the raw inspiration and truth telling that is so necessary for this particular moment in U.S. history.*" —**Dr. Marcella Runell,** Vice President for Student Life & Dean of Students, Mount Holyoke College, co-author *Uncommon Bonds: Women Reflect on Race & Friendship*

"*Tom Weiner and Amilcar Shabazz have given the heterogeneity of abolitionism a fresh veneer of race and gender, and none of those profiled is more illustrative of this process than Belinda X. This eighteenth century Black woman typifies the depth and sweep of the writers' research, and reparations activists should study her resolve and ingenuity. In Defiance is indispensable!*" —**Herb Boyd** is the co-author with Don Rojas of *Malcolm X, The CIA, and Other Blacks*, and a journalist with the *New York Amsterdam News*.

T0413281

IN
DEFIANCE

20 ABOLITIONISTS YOU WERE
NEVER TAUGHT IN SCHOOL

By Tom Weiner and Dr. Amilcar Shabazz

OLIVE
BRANCH
PRESS

An imprint of Interlink Publishing Group, Inc.
Northampton, Massachusetts

First published in 2025 by

Olive Branch Press

An imprint of Interlink Publishing Group, Inc.

46 Crosby Street, Northampton, MA 01060

www.interlinkbooks.com

All images without attribution are public domain.

Library of Congress Cataloging-in-Publication data available.

ISBN-13: 978-1-62371-661-5

Printed and bound in the United States of America

To all those who defiantly and courageously sought freedom, justice and equality and to those who continue to do so...

Contents

Preface in Two Voices: . . . . *ix*

 Tom Weiner. . . . . *ix*

 Dr. Amilcar Shabazz . . . . *xiii*

Introduction: Defying the Infernal System of Slavery . . . . *xv*

Chapter 1: Belinda X and the Fight for Reparations 1

Chapter 2: Paul Jennings and the Pearl Incident. 17

Chapter 3: Sarah Mapps Douglass: Against Patriarchy 27

Chapter 4: Mary Ellen Pleasant: A Constant Soldier Never Unready,
 Even Once 39

Chapter 5: Henry Highland Garnet: Before Malcolm X 49

Chapter 6: Mary Ann Shadd Cary: So Visible and So Vocal. 75

Chapter 7: Robert Morris: Crusader for School Integration,
 circa 1849, Boston. 85

Chapter 8: John Stewart Rock: First Black Supreme Court
 Lawyer and Always Supreme Spokesman for His People 101

Chapter 9: Sarah Parker Remond: Firebrand Defying Limits of
 Age and Sex 115

Chapter 10: The Anguish of Abraham Galloway 125

Chapter 11: Francis Pastorius: and the Germantown Petition
 of 1688 135

Chapter 12: Benjamin Lay: A Small Man with An Outsize
 Passion for Justice 145

Chapter 13: Anthony Bénézet: Celebrant of African Culture and
 Educator of African American Youth. 159

Chapter 14: Moses Brown: Defying Family and Convention to Honor
Those He Had Once Enslaved. 169

Chapter 15: Elizabeth Buffum Chace: Memoirist of the Anti-Slavery
Movement 181

Chapter 16: Jane Swisshelm: Staunch Abolitionist Refusing to Accept
Gender Limitations. 193

Chapter 17: John Gregg Fee: Using Religion to Advance Justice
for the Oppressed. 205

Chapter 18: Delia Webster: Accepting Imprisonment as the Price for
Demanding Freedom 223

Chapter 19: Sallie Holley: Recognizing the Centrality of Black
Women's Freedom 231

Chapter 20: Graceanna Lewis: Abolitionist and Natural Scientist . 245

Conclusion in Two Voices: 253

Tom Weiner 253

Dr. Amilcar Shabazz 256

Appendix. 261

Belinda Sutton's Reparations Petition 1783 261

Germantown Friends' Protest Against Slavery, 1688. 264

Henry Highland Garnet's Address to the Slaves of the United
States of America, delivered on August 16, 1843 267

Endnotes 275

Works Cited 295

Acknowledgements 313

Tom Weiner. 313

A final blue note from Dr. Amilcar Shabazz 316

Preface in Two Voices:

Tom Weiner

I began working on this book over forty-five years ago. My determination to tell little-known or unknown stories of people who fought for freedom, justice, and equality for African Americans arose from my work in the classroom. Whereas my prior book—*Called to Serve: Stories of the Men and Women Confronted by the Vietnam War Draft*—was concerned with whether the stories for which I wanted to act as conduit might otherwise be forever lost, with *In Defiance* I was concerned with whether the stories could even be found to begin with. Over the decades, I kept searching for such stories and found that, though they were there, they were not readily accessible.

In lieu of something more ideal, I drew on a book in my sixth grade classroom called *Meeting the Challenge*, which included approximately thirty African Americans who had made contributions to American culture—from Dr. Charles Drew, known as the father of the blood bank, to Jackie Robinson, from Mary McLeod Bethune, educator, civil and women's rights leader to Wilma Rudolph, renowned track athlete. I used the short biographies in a unit titled African American Contributors to American Culture. Many of those featured were unknown to me. Like most people of my age and background, I had gone to public schools during a time when African American history and culture were routinely left out of the curriculum, and though I had tried, through my reading and contacts, to educate myself, I was still woefully lacking.

As an example of that, I would start the unit by asking my students to guess the score I had gotten on a test I had taken at the beginning of a graduate course on African American history at the University of Massachusetts in 1973. I told them I'd received the second highest score in the class. They were flabbergasted when I told them I'd gotten 22 percent, a measure of my ignorance at the time I began that course.

In order to teach my students the actual history of our country, I continued searching for the stories of white Americans, allies in the struggle, who had fought for the freedom and equality of Black Americans. There were rich sources for stories about William Lloyd Garrison, John Brown, and Harriet Beecher Stowe. But I knew there were others whose stories should be included in history books and in an inclusive curriculum. That was the initial conception of the book back in the mid-seventies, and I carried that goal with me until I began writing in 2017.

It was at that point that my two younger children, Madeline and Stefan, hearing about my project, let me know that it was not the right time to center white people in a book about racism. In fact, their point was that there is never a right time to do so. I considered their criticism and came to fully agree with them. Such a book, no matter what my intention, would be perceived by many as accentuating white people while neglecting Black people's roles in fighting for their own freedom. Thus the decision was made to include Black men and women alongside white men and women, starting in 1688 with the story of Daniel Pastorius and the Germantown petition and covering the next two centuries up to and including the decade following the Civil War.

My decision to include Black men and women in the book was reinforced by the words of Manisha Sinha, the author of *The Slave's Cause*. She spoke of the failure of our education system to honor their contributions in an interview that appeared in the *Boston Globe* on February 13, 2016, titled "The Forgotten Abolitionists":

> Ignoring the Black presence in the abolitionist movement was important for slaveholders because their whole philosophy was based on the idea that African-Americans weren't resisting slavery. That continued at the turn of the century, when the American

academy had completely excluded African-Americans and did not do African-American history. It became as entrenched in American historiography as views about the Civil War being a needless conflict between brothers.[1]

There was another motivating factor that was affirmed in a visit to the River Road African American Museum in Donaldson, Louisiana, in 1993. Kathe Hambrick, the museum's founder and curator, has been trying for the past twenty-five years to inform people about the history of African American contributors to American culture who have been forgotten. When she visited plantations along the Mississippi River in the early 1990s, she discovered that enslaved people were still referred to as "servants" by tour guides.

She told me that one night she had a vision of her ancestors floating on a barge on the Mississippi River, calling out to her, "Don't let them forget us." She was both appalled at the plantation tours and inspired by her vision and subsequently founded the museum to honor those who came before. She told me of an African proverb that she said clarified her quest: "Until the lion tells the tale, tales of the hunt will glorify the hunter."

So it has all too often been with the teaching of American history. Like Ms. Hambrick's museum, this book will enable the lion's tale to be told. Ultimately, those asserting that the movement should not be called Black Lives Matter, but instead All Lives Matter, will hopefully come to the realization that all lives will not matter until all Black lives do. This book will show how this has been true since before 1619—now 404 years ago—and how there have always been Black people and white people who were willing to risk their lives *in defiance* to ensure freedom and equality for *all* people.

Dr. Shabazz has chosen to collaborate with me to the betterment of this work. His scholarship and acquired wisdom from the life he has led inspire me. His own efforts *in defiance* of the status quo at the universities he has worked, in the communities in which he has lived, and within his chosen field of African American studies are evidence of his commitment, the range of his intellect, and his determination to undo racism. We see this work as a contribution to those efforts and as another means of accomplishing the relentless truth-telling so essential to overcoming centuries of lies and distortions about America's true history. In the words of James Baldwin when he spoke at a program called Project Awareness, sponsored by the Nonviolent Action Group at Howard University in 1963: "We must tell the truth 'til we can no longer bear it..." This book contains that truth. It is our hope that you find it within yourself to bear it and then spread it and be inspired to act *in defiance* of racism and all its pernicious effects.

Dr. Amilcar Shabazz

In 2019, the authors of this book met upon land in the historical native care of the Pocumtuck. As the leaves changed from green into golds, reds, browns, and yellows, we gathered in the town square of Springfield, Massachusetts, to consciously build, together with a small group of activists and creatives, an interracial dialogue group known as Bridge for Unity. It was an act *in defiance* against narratives of racism, anti-black structural violence, political polarization, and ideological strife that had reached a maddening level in the middle of the Trump presidency. We decided to turn to people who were willing to make a space where we would engage in profound listening and deep discussions with each other about this enemy of us all: white supremacy.

That night we opened with our eyes meeting the eyes of each and every person in the circle. From our hearts, we each began to share bits of our personal histories of racial awareness, the joy and the pain of it, where it haunted and shielded us, its myriad manifestations in all its perplexing complexities. The key word in this experience was history. From our interaction in that space grew the trust and struggle that has produced *In Defiance.*

As a professional academic historian I was immersed in Africana historical research, teaching, and service. I had writing projects underway like a biographical series called Little Known Seekers of Racial Justice, the original subtitle of this book. I had the stewardship of the National Council for Black Studies as its elected president, meeting in Atlanta the moment a global pandemic was declared. What Tom was writing sounded interesting and I remained a supporter from afar. Curiosity and Tom's persistence led me to read what he had written, and, in a quiet moment in my mind, local figures from history like Sojourner Truth, whose statue in Florence, Massachusetts, I've stood beside, and John Brown, whose Bible I've held at Springfield's Historic St. John's Congregational Church, appeared in a dream and encouraged me to believe that the persons in this book demanded space, screen time, and voice to communicate their truth in this post-George Floyd/Breonna Taylor moment, along the color line in this first quarter of the twenty-first century. These venerable ancestors, in the broadest sense, have a way of compelling our vision, our listening, our imagination. And so I began to work with Tom to write their stories into the urgency of our now. How they might engage you begins another personal story.

Defiant, rebellious lives against slavery, and the anti-Black racism that justified such an infernal institution, are the result of certain factors and patterns in the course of human events. A collective biography can reveal the patterns that enable ordinary people to do extraordinarily courageous acts for peace, human rights, and justice. That is the aim of this book: to introduce readers to people not so widely known but who should be, and to show how they made a history worth looking at, honoring, and learning from today. Sometimes these lives tell stories that raise more questions than answers, but perhaps there is a lesson in that imbalance that is worth the ambiguity it may leave us with. At the end of the book, we provide a select set of resources and recommendations for further study that the curious and the eager student of history alike can consider as part of a deeper investigation of the past as well as of making that past meaningful in our present struggles against racial domination and exclusion.

Some of our "defiant ones" have begun to find their way onto historical markers, bas reliefs, statues, and plaques, even while various public monuments and tributes to historic slave traders and plantation masters are being redefined into special museum areas or at the bottoms of rivers and seas. With these stories we embrace and add to the radical revising of our collective human history. With these stories we endeavor to sing another song of freedom and to listen carefully, as Abraham Lincoln prescribed, to the natural "mystic chords of memory ... touched by the better angels of our nature."

INTRODUCTION:

Defying the Infernal
System of Slavery

Susan Neiman, author of the important work *Learning from the Germans: Race and the Memory of Evil,* connects the dots between the experiences of East and West Germany's responses to the Holocaust and the divergent responses in the United States to the enslavement and killing of African Americans for nearly two and a half centuries, as well as the subsequent oppression of Black people since the Civil War. She interviewed Bryan Stevenson. His work with the Equal Justice Initiative, which is "committed to ending mass incarceration and excessive punishment in the United States, and to challenging racial and economic injustice," as well as his writing of *Just Mercy* (made into a film with the same title), inspired the title of this book.

During the interview, Stevenson suggested that buildings named for advocates of the Lost Cause of white supremacy be renamed after white abolitionists and anti-lynching activists:

> You should be proud of those Southerners in Mississippi and Louisiana and Alabama who argued in the 1850s that slavery was wrong. There were white Southerners in the 1920s who tried to stop lynchings, and you don't know their name[s]. The fact that we don't know their names says everything we need to know.[2]

Neiman continues the prescription Stevenson has recommended: "If those names were commemorated, the country could turn from shame to pride." She then quoted Stevenson again:

> We can actually claim a heritage rooted in courage, and defiance of what is easy, and preferring what is right. We can make that the norm we want to celebrate as our Southern history and heritage and culture.[3]

We have chosen to use the words "in defiance" for the title because defiance was what was required to act against the social norms that promoted the acceptance of the enslavement of one group of human beings by another. Every person we have included acted in defiance of society. Bryan Stevenson endorsed this title in response to an email requesting permission to use his words. He said he was honored that our book would derive its title from the ideas he put forward in his interview with Neiman and his lifelong efforts.

Stevenson lives in the South and his work to combat racism has been centered there. But the work to undo racism is not limited to the South. As the protests in all fifty US states that occurred after the deaths of George Floyd and Breonna Taylor reveal, systemic racism is a national problem, and it is our hope that this book will contribute to dismantling that racism among all who read it, regardless of where you are on the map.

Researching the men and women in these pages was certainly a challenge. Piecing together their profiles from a variety of sources was painstaking, but always gratifying. There were websites and occasional book references to many of them, but definitely most satisfying was coming upon letters or even books and memoirs written by these individuals, in which they or others documented the obstacles and supports they encountered in their efforts to undo enslavement.

The twenty subjects of this work comprise a small fraction of those who deserve similar study and commemoration. The accomplishments they represent are awe-inspiring, as are those of the people we did not choose. Someone—a Quaker to be sure—actually helped write a petition against enslavement in 1688. But there were Quakers who owned enslaved people and who vigorously resisted acknowledging that to do so was wrong. In 1731, another man used street theater to penetrate the resistance of his fellow Quakers and to arouse his fellows to condemn enslavement. A Black woman sued for and won reparations in 1783. Virtually every chapter contains surprises and dazzling displays of creative resistance to the status quo. The friendships between Black and white people are an additional revelation and inspiration.

It is our hope that reading this work will inspire students of history to keep digging to find others who richly deserve to be in the forefront of our collective consciousness. One could do worse than starting with Harriet Forten Purvis, an African American abolitionist and suffragist who helped establish the first women's abolitionist group for Blacks and whites, the Philadelphia Female Anti-Slavery Society. Or Myrtilla Miner, a white woman who founded a school for African American girls against enormous opposition in Washington, DC, that is now the only public university in the city, the University of the District of Columbia. Or Samuel Green, an African American who escaped enslavement, became a religious minister, and was jailed in 1857 for possessing a copy of *Uncle Tom's Cabin*. Or Rabbi David Einhorn who, in 1861, delivered a sermon where he called Rabbi Morris Jacob Raphall's support of enslavement a "deplorable farce" and argued that the institution was inconsistent with Jewish values, asking:

> Does the Negro have less ability to think, to feel, to will? Does he have less of a desire [for] happiness? Was he born not to be entitled to all these?...Slavery is immoral and must be abolished.[4]

These and the others contained herein just represent a few of the brave men and women who richly deserve our appreciation and emulation. In the famous words of Lincoln's Gettysburg Address, from these honored dead may "we take increased devotion to that cause for which they here, gave the last full measure of devotion," that enslavement and the anti-Black ideas and actions that came from it be forever buried.

To fathom and fully appreciate these stories of people who confronted the enslavement of human beings, what follows is a brief overview of the origins of that which they so vehemently fought to end. We shall show how enslavement of human beings became institutionalized in the English colonies of North America. We will examine the factors that contributed to its terrible power and prolonged duration. We will explore how a racist system of oppression flourished to the point where, when an American republic emerged in 1776, it had warped the new country into a slave society that could see the mote in the eye of King George III as regards taxation without representation, but could not see the beam in its own eye of building its wealth and security on raped and whipped Black bodies forcibly kept in ignorance of who they were and had a right to be.

A fitting place to begin such an examination is with David Walker, who, though born free in 1796, after America had won its freedom from Great Britain (the same year Ona Judge escaped from the home of George and Martha Washington when she learned she was about to be handed over to Martha's granddaughter after two decades of servitude), came into a world where men and women like himself were everywhere in chains. His father had been enslaved and was already deceased by the time his son was born in Wilmington, North Carolina—the site of one of the first insurrections in American history, when white men violently overthrew elected Black officials in 1898.

Walker lived for a time as a free person of color in the slave port city of Charleston, South Carolina, where more Africans in the United States passed through upon entering North America than any other city. He also lived in Philadelphia, the so-called City of Brotherly Love, where he learned to read and write and where enslavement remained firmly entrenched. By the time he moved to Boston, Massachusetts, in 1825, he was able to comment on the world the enslavers made in a way that we can learn a great deal from.

Walker published his *Appeal, in Four Articles; Together with a Preamble, to the Coloured Citizens of the World, but in Particular, and Very Expressly, to Those of the United States of America*, in Boston, Massachusetts, September 28, 1829. In it he speaks of Indigenous people of North and South America, Greeks, Irish, Jews, and the inhabitants of the islands of the sea, as being regarded as human beings who "are, and ought to be free." All people's lives mattered, as it were, except for the sons and daughters of Africa. In the eyes of a racist world, African people and their children "are brutes!!"

Despite the way many other groups of people are oppressed, only Africans were regarded in Walker's depiction as fit only "to be SLAVES to the American people and their children forever!! to dig their mines and work their farms; and thus go on enriching them, from one generation to another with our blood and our tears!!!!"[5]

Thus, from Walker we learn three basic points about the kind of slavery that emerged in the Americas. First, in order for it to make any sense and be sustainable, the institution demanded the dehumanization of African people. Second, it is a system that enriched the owning class at the expense of the enslaved. Third, the institution was designed to go on forever, from one generation to the next, that is to say, it was a system of perpetual bondage. If you are enslaved, then the only time when you can ever expect that your condition will change is when you die.

So while the practice of enslaving people was widespread across the Atlantic world, involving Arabs, Berbers, Italians, Portuguese, Spaniards, Dutch, Jews, Germans, Swedes, French, English, Danes, Indigenous peoples in the Americas, along with a plethora of African ethnic groups, there are unique features of the kind of slavery in the Americas from how it had been practiced in Africa, Asia, and Europe before 1500. The so-called New World of the Western Hemisphere is new in the sense that it was in the Americas that all the people of the world came together at the advent of what economic historians refer to as the first phase of capitalism, known as merchant capitalism. In this phase, the goal was to maximize profits from the first ever system of production for an international mass market involving the growing of sugar, tobacco, coffee, chocolate, rum, dyestuffs, rice, spices, hemp, and cotton.

The year 1619 is often cited as the beginning of the slave trade in the English colonies with the arrival on the James River in Virginia of the *White Lion*, an English privateer vessel. John Rolfe, a colonist, documented the arrival of the ship and "20 and odd" Africans in his journal, and the August 20 date is featured in many textbooks as a starting point for the story of enslavement in North America.[6]

In fact, the origins of slavery and the bringing of enslaved Africans into the North American continent go back at least a hundred years before 1619. Author Michael Guasco, who has written extensively on the subject, warns against placing too much emphasis on 1619. "To ignore what had been happening with relative frequency in the broader Atlantic world over the preceding 100 years or so understates the real brutality of the ongoing slave trade," he writes. The 1619 story "minimizes the significant African presence in the Atlantic world to that point. People of African descent have been 'here' longer than the English colonies."[7]

The evidence is clear that Africans were taken against their will and enslaved dating back at least to 1441, when the Portuguese captured twelve Africans in modern-day Mauritania and brought them to Portugal. Eighty-five years later, men from Spain brought the first enslaved Africans to settlements in what would become the United States. It was on land in today's Florida where the enslavement of Africans began in the early sixteenth century. Thus, as early as a 1526 expedition that King Charles V of Spain endorsed, African captives were part of the making of a Spanish outpost in what is now South Carolina.

The settlement was named San Miguel de Gualdape and its founder was Lucas Vázquez de Ayllón, a wealthy sugar planter on Hispaniola and magistrate of a colonial royal appeals court, the Real Audiencia. Bad luck and worse fortune caused the settlement to flounder and ultimately fail. Many of the original six hundred settlers perished, including Ayllón. In the ensuing conflict among his subordinates to determine what to do, one of them, Captain Francisco Gómez, took over the leadership and along with members of the ruling council, chose to stay and await supplies from a ship from Hispaniola. Another faction led by Gines Doncel wanted to head home to Spain. Doncel managed to have Gómez placed under house arrest.

It was at this point that a rebellion of the enslaved occurred—the first documented on American soil. There had been an unknown number of enslaved Africans among the six hundred settlers. Gonzalo Fernández de Oviedo y Valdés, the contemporary scribe of the expedition, said that there were "some" captive Africans aboard the ship. Historians hypothesize that they were likely household servants or craftsmen rather than field workers. Oviedo offers no specific account for their actions, he just writes that they "had their reasons," and that they set fire to Doncel's home. In the confusion that resulted, Doncel and his fellow mutineers were placed under arrest. It is not documented whether the enslaved succeeded in escaping and finding succor with local Indigenous people, but what is clear is that this was the first documented occurrence of African slavery in all its problematic and rebellious dimensions in North America.[8]

In its colonization efforts, the British also enslaved Africans long before 1619. Sir Francis Drake and his cousin John Hawkins made three voyages to Guinea and Sierra Leone that resulted in the capture and enslavement of 1,200 to 1,400 Africans. Some enslaved Africans may have been aboard one of Drake's ships when he landed at Roanoke Island in 1586. While 1619 is a key date in the history of slavery in the English colonies, historians emphasize that slavery developed gradually, elaborating a racist economic system under the pretext of the "rule of law" in which colonial legislatures drew upon English common law traditions.

For instance, slavery was widespread in the English colonies by the end of the seventeenth century, but its establishment as a fully articulated legal practice did not occur in any of the colonies until 1705, with the passage of the Virginia slave codes. These laws stripped Africans of all legal rights and officially legalized their enslavement and mistreatment. As Guasco puts it, the Spanish, Portuguese, and English were "co-conspirators in what we would now consider a crime against humanity."

In *African American Voices: The Life Cycle of Slavery*, Steven Mintz has noted that Europeans used enslaved Africans and Russians on Italian sugar plantations as early as 1300. "During the 1400s, decades before Columbus' 'discovery' of the New World," Mintz writes, "Europeans exploited African labor on slave plantations on sugar-producing islands that lay off the Wet African coast. With European colonization of the New World came a dramatic expansion of slavery." The reason for this has been a major concern of historians from as far back as 1896, when W.E.B. Du Bois's PhD dissertation was published by Harvard. He wrote:

> We must face the fact that this problem arose principally from the cupidity and carelessness of our ancestors. It was the plain duty of the colonies to crush the trade and the system in its infancy: they preferred to enrich themselves on its profits. It was the plain duty of a Revolution based upon "Liberty" to take steps toward the

abolition of slavery: it preferred promises to straightforward action. It was the plain duty of the Constitutional Convention, in founding a new nation, to compromise with a threatening social evil only in case its settlement would thereby be postponed to a more favorable time: this was not the case in the slavery and the slave-trade compromises; there never was a time in the history of America when the system had a slighter economic, political, and moral justification than in 1787; and yet with this real, existent, growing evil before their eyes, a bargain largely of dollars and cents was allowed to open the highway that led straight to the Civil War. Moreover, it was due to no wisdom and foresight on the part of the fathers that fortuitous circumstances made the result of that war what it was, nor was it due to exceptional philanthropy on the part of their descendants that that result included the abolition of slavery.[9]

Cupidity and carelessness, promises, and compromises are the factors that led otherwise decent people into the criminally inhuman behavior of creating slave societies in the Americas. Church and state, pulpit and press all bent their backs to support slavery. The Catholic church through its "Doctrine of Discovery" played a role. The doctrine emerged from a papal decree set by Pope Nicholas V in 1452 that approved and encouraged the conquest, colonization, and exploitation of non-Christian territories and peoples. The decree called for "perpetual servitude" for infidels. Also in the doctrine was the idea that if a person converted to Christianity they would receive their freedom. In practice, however, wealthy planters in the Caribbean quickly closed this loophole.

Thus the second and much more permanent guise. No longer was there to be a religious exemption for those conquered in war or believing in a different religion if they converted. Skin color became the key distinction the enslavers used to rationalize and sustain the enslavers' world. By making color difference the key element enabling enslavement, native people and then Africans brought to work in silver mines and on sugar plantations could be enslaved for life. The next step was to make enslavement hereditary, meaning the children of an enslaved mother would automatically inherit the same status.

This diabolical, self-perpetuating system did not immediately take hold in North America. When King Charles II was restored to the British throne in 1660, he soon created the Royal African Company so he could enter the slave trade much more aggressively. The king rewarded those who had helped him regain power and greatly boosted the profits of some of his loyal subjects in the New World. He was determined to compete with the Spanish in Florida and the Caribbean, both economically and militarily, so he chartered the colony of Carolina. Many of the first English settlers who came to this new home after 1670 came from Barbados and, not surprisingly, brought their enslaved Africans with them. Far more significantly, they brought the beginning of a set of laws and a conception of society that accepted enslavement.

Difficult as it might be to believe, given what is known about the duration and horrors of enslavement, there was a brief period in the mid-seventeenth century when those arriving from Africa could hope to become free. The arriving Africans often mixed with other unfree laborers on small plantations. Regardless of their country of origin—European or African—these workers could eventually either work long enough to fulfill their obligations or be freed so they could purchase their own land and enjoy the independence that goes with private property. One example offered by historian Peter Wood will suffice:

> In 1645, in Northampton County on Virginia's Eastern Shore, Captain Philip Taylor, after complaining that "Anthony the negro" did not work hard enough for him, agreed to set aside part of the cornfield where they worked as Anthony's plot. "I am very glad of it," the black man told a local clerk, "but now I know myne owne ground and I will worke when I please and play when I please."[10]

Anthony eventually became free, though how or when is undocumented, and moved to the Eastern Shore. Known there as Anthony Johnson, he married "Mary a Negro Woman." She had arrived in 1622, and together they raised four children, gaining "respect for their hard labor and known service," as indicated by the court records of Northampton County.

Tragically, within thirty years of Mary's death in 1672, their grandson,

John Jr., died without an heir, and the entire Johnson family disappeared from colonial records. The reality was that the window was closing, and a terrible transformation was occurring that ended the hopes of Black men and women to earn their freedom and to be independently success-ful in the colonies. A line had emerged dividing the life chances of the indentured from the enslaved—such was the dawn of a white-over-black, racist world.

Labor shortages in the colonies resulted from the English Civil War in (1642–1651) as well as the Great Plague of 1665–1666. Due to the Great Fire of London in 1666, workers were required to remain at home. Penalties were increased for sea captains who stole young people in England and sold them as indentured servants in the colonies. The term "kidnapping" originated from this practice. "Kid" was an underworld reference to a child, while "nap," a variation of "nab," means "to seize or steal." English people already working in the colonies as indentured servants demanded shorter indentures, better conditions, and farmland when their contracts ended. These demands had to be met to the great-est extent possible to avoid losing even more recruits if word got back to England that conditions were not improving.

Native American laborers were no solution. Those captured in war could easily escape given their familiarity with the region and the proxim-ity of the frontier where they could find support from other Indigenous communities. There was a limited number of them, and though the Spanish exploited them for more than a century, especially missionaries in the Southwest, for the English it was much more profitable to bring African Americans, whose numbers were enormous and who were thousands of miles from their homes, making escape and a return to the continent of their origin virtually impossible.

The slave trade increased dramatically as European countries com-peted with one another and West African leaders were more willing to participate in the sale of their people to make profits. The planters in the New World obviously could afford to pay for these new workers in greater and greater quantities. "Every decade the ships became larger, the contacts more regular, the departures more frequent, the routes more familiar, the sales more efficient," writes Wood.[11]

The competition had the desired effect. The numbers of enslaved Africans rose exponentially, which caused the cost of an individual slave to decrease just as the cost of European labor was rising. North America was at the edge of the expanding system of trade and was an enormous potential market. Instead of the small ships with twenty people, large ships coming directly from Africa were arriving daily on the eastern shores. The monopoly on slave trading that the Royal African Company had for almost forty years came to an end in 1698, opening the floodgates to independent slave traders from England, resulting in far more voyages for purposes of capturing a share of the profits.

In summary, by 1700 there were 27,817 enslaved Africans in British North America. In 1740, there were 150,024. By 1770, the number of slaves had grown to 462,000, about one-fifth of the total colonial population.

It should be noted that the numbers of enslaved people in North America between 1620 and 1780 are dwarfed by those in the Caribbean and South America. The total figure of 462,000 in North America represents only 2 percent of the more than six million people brought from Africa. Because life expectancy in Brazil and the Caribbean was so short, a staggeringly higher number were brought into that part of the hemisphere.

Since the Middle Passage—the journey from Africa to the Americas—was so cataclysmically atrocious and caused such enormous loss of life, it is even more disturbing to realize that many more were captured than arrived in the Americas. Such was the horror that confronted men and women who would defy slavery. It would take many defiant acts in opposition to slavery to begin to delegitimize and dismantle the infernal institution. With so much money and power lined up to create and back a slaveholder society in North America, it would not be a crystal stair to disrupt that society and to make a better world. Still, some tried, and you are about to learn of the deep-seated convictions, willingness to take enormous risks, alliances across the color line, and ultimately achievements of men and women whose stories must be told if we are to become a more whole, more compassionate, and more united nation.

of freedom; compelled her Master to fly—and to breathe away his Life in a Land, where, Lawless domination, sits enthroned, pouring bloody outrage and cruelty, on all who dare to be free.

The face of your Petitioner, is now marked with the furrows of time, and her frame feebly bending under the oppression of years, while she, by the Laws of the Land, is denied the enjoyment of one morsel of that immense wealth, apart whereof hath been accumulated by her own industry, and the whole augmented by her servitude.

~~Wherefore prostrating~~

Wherefore casting herself at the feet of your honours, as to a body of men, formed ~~for the extirpation~~ of vassalage, for the reward of virtue, and the just returns of honest industry—she prays, that such allowance may be made her out of the Estate of Colonel Royall, as will prevent her, and her more infirm daughter, from misery in the greatest extreme, and scatter comfort over the short and downward path of their Lives—

and she will ever Pray

Boston 14th February 1783   the   X   mark

Belinda

A page from the Petition of Belinda, signed with an X.
Massachusetts Archives. Boston, Mass.

CHAPTER 1

Belinda X and the Fight for Reparations

"The reason Black people are so far behind now is not because of now... It's because of then."
—Clyde Ross, quoted in "The Case for Reparations" by Ta-Nehisi Coates, *The Atlantic*, 2014.

How humbling it is to write about a person when you do not even know the name she was given at birth. All we know is that around 1725, when this African girl was twelve years old, she was ripped from her home and her family, her people and her continent, by men she later remembered as having faces like the moon. Shackled below decks, a phenomenon we call capitalism takes her through the Middle Passage across the Atlantic Ocean to America. Somewhere along the way she was branded with the unlikely name Belinda—derived as it is from Italian or Old High German. Added to that dynamic of domination, being renamed, she is owned by the surname of her master, Isaac Royall, one of the wealthiest slave owners in Massachusetts Bay Colony history. When the spirit of independence began to rise in Massachusetts, Royall was so loyal to the British crown that he fled to England in 1775, leaving behind much of the wealth that he had primitively accumulated. Belinda, and the other eleven enslaved Africans he left behind, were manumitted (freed immediately).

Worried how she would live at seventy years of age with an "infirm" daughter, what Belinda X did over 225 years ago is a story for right now. An eighteenth-century woman of African descent who felt fully justified in demanding unpaid wages from her former owner's estate, a fraction of what she was owed for her years of labor, is a story of defiant struggle that teaches us the justness of the unfinished business of reparations still relevant to us today.

Much of what we know about Belinda's enslaved life comes from an extraordinary document. It is in the form of a petition to the Massachusetts General Court, which names the seat of legislative power in the new state that became a leader in so many ways of the newly emerging United States. In the petition, the first of its kind to be successful, she recounted the story of her life and demanded a pension from the estate of Isaac Royall Jr., the man who enslaved her. For her heroic efforts and determination, Belinda richly deserves a place in history and in public memory as well as credit for inspiring the fight for reparations for African enslavement.

At the start of this chapter is a copy of the third page of the original petition that was presented to the Massachusetts General Court in 1782. It features her mark, an X, which is why we have chosen to refer to her as Belinda X. The complete text is in the appendix.

This bold petition was one of six she submitted for consideration by the Massachusetts General Court. Its existence has been known for many years, but it took until 2015, when a digital database of the historical anti-slavery petitions was launched, for four additional petitions to be uncovered. Belinda's petitions over the course of a decade are compelling evidence, both of her determination to receive compensation she was promised by the legislature for her lifetime in slavery, as well as how easy it has always been in America to elude reparations.

Belinda's defiant appeal makes in five paragraphs a deeply moral and intellectual argument. It also reveals a story that invites solidarity. It brings to life what she experienced as well as what she richly deserved. Stolen from Africa, brought to America. Violently captured at the age of twelve, this daughter of the Volta River region "received her existence" in today's Ghana around 1713.[12]

The petition introduces us to twelve-year-old Belinda's life, and the moment of her social death as the trauma of capture and the enslavement process begins, flash bangs exploding in her mind:

The mountains Covered with spicy forests, the valleys loaded with the richest fruits, spontaneously produced; joined to that happy temperature of air to exclude excess; would have yielded her the most compleat felicity, had not her mind received early impressions of the cruelty of men, whose faces were like the moon, and whose Bows and Arrows were like the thunder and the lightning of the Clouds.[13]

Her mind is tormented even as she is driven away from everything she has known into bondage without end—from Africa to American chattel slavery:

The idea of these, the most dreadful of all Enemies, filled her infant slumbers with horror, and her noontide moments with evil apprehensions!—But her affrighted imagination, in its most alarming extension, never represented distresses equal to what she hath since really experienced—for before she had Twelve years enjoyed the fragrance of her native groves, and e'er she realized, that Europeans placed their happiness in the yellow dust which she carelessly marked with her infant footsteps – even when she, in a sacred grove, with each hand in that of a tender Parent, was paying her devotions to the great Orisa who made all things—an armed band of white men, driving many of her Countrymen in Chains, ran into the hallowed shade!—could the Tears, the sighs and supplications, bursting from Tortured Parental affection, have blunted the keen edge of Avarice, she might have been rescued from Agony, which many of her Country's Children have felt, but which none hath ever described,—in vain she lifted her supplicating voice to an insulted father, and her guiltless hands to a dishonoured Deity! She was ravished from the bosom of her Country, from the arms of her friends—while the advanced age of her Parents, rendering them unfit for servitude, cruelly separated her from them forever![14]

The petition effectively shows us how Belinda's life is torn apart in the captivity event she lives through, but also where a part of her dies.

The narrative continues onto the slave ship that cruelly transports the cargo across the Atlantic of Africans who were also victims of slave raids:

> Scenes which her imagination had never conceived of—a floating World—the sporting Monsters of the deep—and the familiar meetings of Billows and clouds, strove, but in vain to divert her melancholly attention, from three hundred Affricans in chains, suffering the most excruciating torments; and some of them rejoicing, that the pangs of death came like a balm to their wounds.[15]

Belinda the individual is at war with the horrendous spectacle of Africans chained to bodies that are no longer their own. Then the scene shifts to terra nova and new terrors:

> Once more her eyes were blest with a Continent—but alas! how unlike the Land where she received her being! here all things appeared unpropitious—she learned to catch the Ideas, marked by the sounds of language only to know that her doom was Slavery, from which death alone was to emancipate her.—What did it avail her, that the walls of her Lord were hung with Splendor, and that the dust troden underfoot in her native Country, crowded his Gates with sordid worshipers—the Laws had rendered her incapable of receiving property—and though she was a free moral agent, accountable for her actions, yet she never had a moment at her own disposal![16]

Learning the language of her oppressors only brings doom. She comes to realize that the wealth of her owner is legally predicated upon her being penniless, and so it goes for the next half century, from 1725 to 1775. But what happens when a new nation arises, in all its armed terrors, and her Empire-loyal owner flies away?

> Fifty years her faithful hands have been compelled to ignoble servitude for the benefit of an Isaac Royall, untill, as if Nations must be agitated, and the world convulsed for the preservation of that freedom which the Almighty Father intended for all the human

Race, the present war was Commenced—The terror of men armed in the Cause of freedom, compelled her master to fly—and to breathe away his Life in a Land, where, Lawless domination sits enthroned— pouring bloody outrage and cruelty on all who dare to be free.

The face of your Petitioner, is now marked with the furrows of time, and her frame feebly bending under the oppression of years, while she, by the Laws of the Land, is denied the enjoyment of one morsel of that immense wealth, apart whereof hath been accumilated by her own industry, and the whole augmented by her servitude.[17]

Belinda the free moral agent, homo economica, is age seventy now. She has a daughter who is unable to work who she must take care of, and faces a bare life under a state of exception that reveals itself on three moral levels:

WHEREFORE, casting herself at the feet of your honours, as to a body of men, formed for the extirpation of vassalage, for the reward of Virtue, and the just return of honest industry—she prays, that such allowance may be made her out of the estate of Colonel Royall, as will prevent her and her more infirm daughter from misery in the greatest extreme, and scatter comfort over the short and downward path of their Lives—and she will ever Pray. [18]

The petition argues on three grounds. First, her impoverished condition is a byproduct of a monarchy that is being overthrown. Thus in the revolutionary process she should be paid what she is owed from the confiscated property (that she was once a part of) her departed loyalist master left behind and has forfeited. Second, she worked hard and produced part of the wealth the state now owns and should get what she is owed because that is justice. Third, reparations in the form of monetary support will reduce the harm that has her and her daughter on a short, downward path to the grave—in other words, as a matter of poverty reduction or, in our contemporary parlance, the extension of a social safety net.

The petition is thus one of the earliest recorded statements we have of a demand for reparations, but it is obviously more than that. It is a defiant cry for help, for justice, and for the belief that Black lives matter. The mention of "visiting a sacred grove" to pay "devotion to the great Orisa, who made all things" is a remembrance of a life, an African way of life, that slavery murdered. You cannot repay that, but you can repair the damage done, or die trying. Belinda chose to die trying and therein lies her defiance.

The great historian, W.E. Burghardt, also from Massachusetts, whose great-great-grandfather, Tom, born circa 1736 in West Africa served in the 1st Berkshire County Militia Regiment of the Continental Army during the war for independence from Britain, observed the following about his native region: "It can be safely asserted that since early Colonial times the North has had a distinct race problem."[19]

That "problem" emerged from slavery and from a triangular relationship—West Africa, where Belinda's journey begins, to Antigua, to Medford, Massachusetts, where Antiguan sugar cane is made into Medford rum that is paid to raiders and traders in exchange for enslaved Black bodies from Africa. Historian Lorenzo Greene identified the year 1638 as the start of the enormously profitable New England slave trade, which at first was "confined almost wholly to Massachusetts." This lasted until the end of the seventeenth century, when factors like the Royal African Company losing its monopoly and other diplomatic treaties being signed opened up opportunities for entrepreneurs in other New England states to build the trade in enslaved Africans into "New England's greatest industry."[20]

With rum as the main ingredient of the slave trade, millions of gallons were manufactured and the resulting distillery industry flourished in New England. Between 1700–1750, the Bay State had the most—sixty-three rum distilleries—followed by Rhode Island with thirty. Medford, Massachusetts, became the rum capital due to the high quality of its "Old Medford" rum. The region's leading slave ports of Boston and Newport were the dominions of the chief slave merchants like the Fanueils, Pepperells, and Royalls of Massachusetts, and the Browns, Champlins, and Wantons of Rhode Island. The Eastons held it down in Connecticut, and the Whipples in New Hampshire. Great Ivy League institutions like Harvard and Brown owe their survival and the success of their finances and endowments to slave merchants like the Royalls of Old Medford.

Enslaved Africans were in every northern state, and in 1790 there were forty thousand enslaved and seventeen thousand free Africans in New England. The "better conscience of Puritan and Quaker" had "a chance to be heard," writes Du Bois, and so developed processes of "gradual emancipation" early in the nineteenth-century northern United States. This is how Du Bois, whose great grandfather fought in the American Revolution, framed the context of Belinda's claim against a portion of Royall's estate. Courthouse historical records from 1765 to 1783 reveal eighteen "freedom suits" in Massachusetts. Between 1773 and 1777, the legislative record of the commonwealth has six different petitions for the general emancipation of Africans.

Records housed at the Royall House and Slave Quarters museum in Medford, Massachusetts, give a clear indication of how Isaac Royall Jr. considered Belinda. His will, dated May 26, 1778, and written during his years in self-imposed exile in England, mentions her: "I do also give unto my said daughter (Mary Royall Erving, who fled with her husband to England as well) my negro Woman Belinda in case she does not choose her freedom; if she does choose her freedom to have it, provided that she get Security that she shall not be a charge to the town of Medford." Did Royall know so little about Belinda that he could even conceive of the possibility that she would not choose freedom over continued bondage when offered the choice? Documents also indicate that Willis Hall, a friend of Royall's and Medford's town clerk who was the executor of his will, was instructed to pay Belinda "for 3 years, £30" ($6,300 in today's dollars). Presumably, this payment was made commencing with Royall's death in 1781.

The petitions that were discovered in 2015 revealed that Belinda had been married. In the 1788 petition she wrote, "Belinda Sutton of Boston in the County of Suffolk Widow." She used the same name in her 1793 petition.

There are two additional documents that help us to establish her identity—one, another petition in 1785, and the other, a receipt. In these she is identified as Belinda Royall. This was the common practice—assigning an enslaved person the surname of their former master. Documents related to her efforts to receive reparations are preserved and interpreted at the Royall House and Slave Quarters. But there is much more to the story that deeper digging brings to light. In fact, in light of the historical significance of Sutton's petition, it was the subject of a comprehensive article in the *William and Mary Quarterly* written by Roy E. Finkenbine.

After the discovery of the lost petitions in 2007, Finkenbine chronicled the events and people directly and indirectly involved in Belinda's quest for reparations and made key points about her identity. In Finkenbine's opening paragraph, he points out that "history never records that she adopted a surname."[21] Royall was a surname that was forced upon her by her master. Sutton was a product of societal conventions and legal customs arising from her marriage. Just as we may never know her original African name, we also do not know the name that she called herself in her own mind. Her use of the word *Orisa* in one of her petitions suggests a remembrance of things past still mattered to her. She signed the petition with an X that indicates not only her distance from being literate in the English language, but of the unknown value of her original African name and identity.

Belinda's owner, Isaac Royall of Medford, was the largest slave owner in the colony, and one of the wealthiest, but the decision to flee to England in 1775 meant abandoning his Georgian mansion in Medford, as well as the two dozen enslaved people he owned. The resulting manumission of Belinda and several others gave them their freedom, but meant they had to fend for themselves. Belinda chose to leave the place where she'd lived for over fifty years in enslavement and headed to Boston, home of a thriving free Black community. Of course, being over sixty, having no sources of support, caring for an invalid daughter, Prine, and having a son, Joseph, likely sold away from her, left her in a desperate state. It was under these circumstances that she presented her petition to the Massachusetts General Court on February 14, 1783. She asked the court for an annual pension to be paid to her and Prine from the proceeds of the Royall's estate, to compensate her for the decades of free labor she had performed while in bondage. After Finkenbine describes Belinda's plight, he makes sure to point out a common misconception concerning Belinda's motivation:

Divergent sources have misrepresented Belinda's plea as a plea for freedom. These publications include An Enquiry Concerning the

Intellectual and Moral Faculties, and Literature of Negroes (1810), among the first positive assessments of black ability in the literature of the modern West; Freedom's Journal, the first African American newspaper; The Colored Patriots of the American Revolution, one of the earliest works of African American history; and a poem by Rita Dove, the former poet laureate.[22]

Finkenbine follows this list of sources that got the plea wrong with these words:

Actually the petition is a systematic but subtle statement of the right of reparations and a plea for a specific form of reparations, a very personal one...As a call for personal compensation for slavery, the petition offers evidence of a radical thread in African American thought and writing in the era of the Founding Fathers.[23]

It is worth noting that there was a context for Belinda's petition. Numerous appeals to the legislature of Massachusetts occurred in the years prior to her effort, though these were suing for freedom. Often the language used was that of the impassioned colonists seeking their liberation from the oppression of Britain. From 1765–1783, at least eighteen freedom suits were initiated in the Massachusetts courts. One petition even resulted in a bill to abolish slavery completely, though it failed to gain passage. These lawsuits definitely set the stage for Belinda's petition by "pricking the conscience" of legislators, and in the process, the enslaved of Massachusetts gained invaluable knowledge of the legal process.

Belinda's petition was not the first attempt by a formerly enslaved person to receive compensation for their time spent in bondage. According to Theodore Lyman, a nineteenth-century legislator, as early as 1770, enslaved Africans in Massachusetts sued for payment of all work after the age of twenty-one. Some of these requests succeeded. Cesar Hendrick of Newburyport, for example, sued his owner, Richard Greenleaf, for illegally keeping him enslaved. He was awarded £18 ($5,400 in today's dollars) and his freedom.[24]

Another noted advocate for reparations used the Bible to build his argument. James Swan's pamphlet on the subject, "A Dissuasion to Great Britain," was subsequently used by several enslaved people from Boston in their petition to the legislature in June 1773. Swan was a member of the Sons of Liberty and a participant in the Boston Tea Party. His writing attacked slavery on moral and economic grounds and acknowledged that "Mosaic law required not only the freeing of slaves in the sabbatical year (every seventh year in the calendar of ancient Judaism), but also compensation for the slaves being freed." He proceeded to quote Deuteronomy 15:13–14 to prove his point: "Thou shall not let him (the slave) go away empty…Thou shall furnish him out of thy flock, and out of thy floor, and out of thy wine press, of that wherewith the Lord thy God hath blessed thee, thou shalt give him. This is in token that thou dost acknowledge the benefit thou hast received by his labors." Swan was asked to revise his pamphlet so it could accompany subsequent petitions to the legislature.

There was an even more direct connection between Belinda and another formerly enslaved man who sought reparations. She almost certainly knew the story of Anthony Vassall of Cambridge. Mr. Vassall had also been enslaved by a loyalist, John Vassall, who also owned his wife, Coby, and their children before fleeing for England. In 1781 when his master's estate was confiscated, he petitioned the Massachusetts legislature seeking title to a plot of land that he felt entitled to for having been enslaved for fifty years. He used a similar argument to that of Belinda two years later—that he and his wife were no longer able to work due to their age and infirmity. Instead they were forced to swallow their pride and beg for bread. They did not receive the land they sought, but the legislature did award them with an annual pension of £12 ($2,200 in today's dollars) from the sale of the estate. Their pension petition included these words:

> … though dwelling in a land of freedom, both himself and his wife have spent almost sixty years of their lives in slavery and that though deprived of what makes them now happy beyond expression yet they have ever lived a life of honesty and have been faithful in their master's service…. [One hopes] that they shall not be denied

the sweets of freedom the remainder of their days by being reduced
to the painful necessity of begging for bread.[25]

The likelihood of Belinda knowing about the Vassalls and their plight
is increased by the fact that they had also been enslaved in Medford and
Vassal's wife was Royall's sister, Penelope.

Yet another aspect of Belinda's petition was that it was almost certainly
crafted by a copyist since Belinda was most likely illiterate. In the first three
versions of her petition "her authorship is merely indicated by her mark, an
X." In addition, the language of the petition indicates that the writer was
someone who had knowledge of previous petitions seeking redress from
the Massachusetts legislature. Mr. Finkenbine conjectures that Prince Hall
is the likeliest author. He was one of the most prominent African American
activists in Boston at the time. There is considerable evidence to support
this theory, including Hall's having gotten fully immersed in all aspects
of the community after being freed from bondage in 1770 at the age of 35.
He even voted in state and national elections. The franchise was allowed
for free black men as indicated in the dissent by Supreme Court Justice
Benjamin Robbins Curtis in *Dred Scott v. Sandford* (1857):

> Of this there can be no doubt. At the time of the ratification of the
> Articles of Confederation, all free native-born inhabitants of the
> States of New Hampshire, Massachusetts, New York, New Jersey,
> and North Carolina, though descended from African slaves, were
> not only citizens of those States, but such of them as had the other
> necessary qualifications possessed the franchise of electors, on
> equal terms with other citizens.[26]

Did this include women, as the quote implies? *All* free native-born
inhabitants? Probably not, and certainly not Belinda X. Nevertheless,
someone of the stature of Prince Hall would likely have recognized
the legitimacy of her petition and agreed to use his knowledge and
experience to support her efforts. Hall founded and guided an African
Masonic Lodge, which has been described as the NAACP of its time,
and he also penned several petitions from 1777 to 1788. Here is how the

earliest of these petitions concludes:

> They therefore humbly beseech your Honors, to give this Petition its due weight & consideration, & cause an Act of the Legislature to be passed, whereby they may be restored to the enjoyment of that freedom which is the natural right of all Men—& their Children (who were born in this land of Liberty) may not be held as Slaves after they arrive at the age of twenty one Years—So may the Inhabitants of this State (no longer chargeable with the inconsistency of acting, themselves, the part which they condemn & oppose in others) be prospered in their present glorious struggles for Liberty; & have those blessings secured to them by Heaven, of which benevolent minds cannot wish to deprive their fellow-Men.[27]

Subsequent petition submissions asked for full emancipation, equal access to public education, financial assistance for those who wished to settle in West Africa, and protection against kidnapping into slavery, a never-ending fear for all Black men, women, and children.

Thanks to either Hall himself or someone of his skill and erudition, the legislature awarded Belinda an annual pension of £15,12 shillings ($2,766 in today's equivalence) from the Royall's estate. It certainly helped turn the decision in her favor that Royall chose the wrong side in the American struggle for independence. But despite her victory, it was not smooth sailing. She received the allotted payment only for the first year, and when informal requests for payments to resume failed, she was forced to create a second petition in 1787. This resulted in the resumption of payments until 1790, but the executor of the estate then refused, and no action was taken by the legislature. Belinda, in her third petition, claimed to be "perishing for the necessities of life." A committee investigated her case and determined that the pension—Belinda's personal reparations—was still fully enforceable and ordered that the payments should resume.

We have no record that this occurred. But thanks to the Quaker anti-slavery network, the original petition went on to great renown. Just months after its original appeal, readers in Europe and the US learned of the petition. It was printed verbatim in the June 18, 1783, issue of the *New*

Jersey Gazette. With its editor, Isaac Collins, a Quaker, the *Gazette* was an exponent of anti-slavery sentiment. By August 9, the petition was printed by an English Quaker, Samuel Bonner, in Bonner and Middleton's *Bristol Journal* under the title "The Complaint of Belinda, an African." It also appeared with the same title in the September 1 issue of the British magazine *Weekly Miscellany.* There were ulterior motives for this particular publication. A British abolitionist editor had remade Belinda's story into an archetypal slave narrative to generate sympathy and support for the growing British anti-slavery movement.[28]

As a result of this repurposing, three major differences can be seen between the original and the British versions of Belinda's petition. First and perhaps foremost, the British version is in the first person, thus purporting to be the voice of Belinda herself. No mention is made of Royall, to avoid his being viewed favorably as a result of his loyalist views. Instead it notes that Belinda was enslaved "for the benefit of a cruel, ungrateful master." Most powerfully, it went on to identify enslavement as a rape culture by inserting a paragraph that lays claim to this occurrence: "One of her master's meanest servants robbed me of my innocence by force, and at an age when my youth should have been my security from pollution."[29] Given the unlikelihood of any contact between Bonner and Belinda, this version of events was "almost certainly invented to serve anti-slavery purposes," since it portrays her assailant in a most unfavorable light.

The general public's initial surge of interest in the petition began to wane until 1787, when *American Museum Magazine* reprinted the 1783 petition in its June issue. Its editor, Mathew Carey, added his own forceful anti-slavery piece to her efforts, though his critique was in the spirit of the American Colonization Society that sought the emigration of all enslaved people back to Africa. His essay used Belinda's story to condemn slavery as "an extensive and inveterate evil," but he also saw emancipation as problematic, because "universal immediate emancipation would be the greatest curse not merely to the masters, but to the slaves, utterly unfit as they are for such a novel situation."[30]

What Belinda's petition does above all is to force scholars "to expand the boundaries of abolitionist studies to include reparations arguments and practices, which were part of the African American struggle for justice in the U.S. nearly a century before Reconstruction's forty acres and a mule." Could her petition have influenced Black abolitionists like David Walker of Boston? In his *Appeal* (1829), he declared that whites must "reconcile us to them, for the cruelties with which they have afflicted our fathers and us." He was passionate in expressing that Black people should only begin to be satisfied when whites "raise us from the condition of brutes to that of respectable men, and...make a national acknowledgment to us for the wrongs they have inflicted on us."[31]

The minister and abolitionist Hosea Easton, also of eastern Massachusetts, added fuel to the argument for reparations in his *Treatise on the Intellectual Character and Civil and Political Condition of the Colored People* (1837). He wrote that "the emancipated must be placed back where slavery found them, and restore to them all that slavery has taken away from them. Merely to cease beating the colored people, and leave them in their gore, and call it emancipation, is nonsense."[32]

The Quakers deserve a special place in this story of the earliest efforts at reparations. Hundreds of eighteenth-century Quakers freed their enslaved people and "personally compensated them for their unpaid time in bondage." But there were also "dozens of penitent masters in the upper South who set their slaves at liberty (most often in their wills) as acts of retribution and gave them plots of land, at first in the South and later in the emerging free states north of the Ohio River."[33]

In addition, there was a small group of anti-slavery Evangelicals who supported freedom as well as "some recompense for slavery." Timothy Dwight, president of Yale University, was another strong advocate for reparations. In an 1810 sermon, he asserted the essential role of reparations to former enslaved people:

It is in vain to allege that *our ancestors* brought them hither, and not we.... We inherit our ample patrimony with all its incumbrances; and are bound to pay the debts of our ancestors. *This* debt, particularly, we are bound to discharge: and when the righteous Judge of the Universe comes to reckon with his servants, he will rigidly exact the payment at our hands. To give them liberty and stop here, is to entail upon them a curse.[34]

Dwight deals head on with the objection to reparations that many continue to make: that it was our ancestors who enslaved black people and it should not be the responsibility of descendants to atone for their errors. He shreds this argument with his conviction that it is the right action to take while invoking the "righteous Judge of the Universe" to take his words to an even higher plane.

This forceful, passionate, and articulately expressed sentiment would doubtless have met with Belinda's strong approval. It is past time to pay homage to this determined woman who recognized that she was entitled to just compensation for her unpaid labor and fought for justice. Here is the poem by Rita Dove, United States Poet Laureate in 1993, to honor Belinda Sutton:[35]

"Belinda's Petition"
(Boston, February, 1782)
To the honorable Senate and House
of Representatives of this Country,
new born: I am Belinda, an African,
since the age of twelve a Slave.
I will not take too much of your Time,
but to plead and place my pitiable Life
unto the Fathers of this Nation.
Lately your Countrymen have severed
the Binds of Tyranny. I would hope
you would consider the Same for me,
pure Air being the sole Advantage
of which I can boast in my present Condition.
As to the Accusation that I am Ignorant:
I received Existence on the Banks
of the Rio de Valta. All my Childhood
I expected nothing, if that be Ignorance.
The only Travelers were the Dead who returned
from the Ridge each Evening. How might
I have known of Men with Faces like the Moon
who would ride toward me steadily for twelve Years?

The E.C. Perry Photograph Co.

139 S. BROAD ST. PERMANENT PHILADELPHIA, PA.
473 PENNª AVE. PHOTOGRAPHS WASHINGTON, D.C.

Courtesy of The Estate of Sylvia Jennings Alexander

CHAPTER 2

Paul Jennings
and the Pearl Incident

If only for his part in saving a portrait of George Washington by Gilbert Stuart on the night the White House was set aflame during the War of 1812, Paul Jennings deserves some sort of historical acknowledgment. Writing the first inside account of life in the White House, let alone doing so as an enslaved person, is an additional reason for him to be celebrated, but Jennings's role in the largest attempted escape of enslaved people surely merits a place in the historical record. Nevertheless, the story of this courageous figure is not well known.

In its biography of Paul Jennings, which begins with an acknowledgment of "one of the most grievous aspects of slavery...that it stripped human beings of their own stories," the website for James Madison's home, Montpelier, states, "Regular records weren't kept on enslaved individuals' births, deaths, or marriages with nearly the regularity as those of white Americans and the discouragement or prevention of literacy among slaves (in many cases, it was even illegal to teach a slave to read) meant that far fewer letters or other written documents remain today to give us insight.."[36]

The biography cites Jennings as one of the very few Africans to receive an education among the countless Black people who were deprived of the right. That he was permitted to learn to read and write is an acknowledgment that enslavement was "a system at odds with its perpetrators' values." As the website points out:

Paul Jennings, an enslaved African American who served the Madison family both at Montpelier and in Washington, D.C., made the incredible journey from slavery to freedom to memoirist. His brief volume, entitled *A Colored Man's Reminiscences of James Madison*, is considered the first memoir about life at the White House. It's also a rich firsthand account of the relationship between slave and slaveholder—even more valuable for its insight into a system that was at odds with its perpetrators' values.[37]

Jennings was born in 1799 at Montpelier. His mother was enslaved and little is known about her beyond that her grandmother was Native American. His father, Benjamin Jennings, was a British merchant, living in Chesterfield, Virginia. Paul learned this from his mother, and it makes sense given the frequency of white men taking advantage of Black women. Paul was a friend of Payne Todd, Dolley Madison's son from her first marriage. Her previous husband and younger son had died of yellow fever, on the same day, during the epidemic that gripped Philadelphia in 1793. During his servitude at Montpelier and throughout his life, Paul was an avid learner. He eventually became literate, well versed in mathematics, and even studied the violin—all extremely rare privileges for enslaved Africans.

When Madison was elected the fourth president of the United States, Paul became his personal manservant, affording the ten-year-old house slave a unique perspective on one of the world's most powerful men. The new capital, still in the initial stages of becoming a city during Madison's eight-year incumbency, was a "dreary place," according to Jennings. Entirely at the mercy of the elements, DC was a mess of mud and dust, and several rooms of the White House remained unfinished. "It must have felt chaos to one used to plantation life," wrote Jennings, but Dolley Madison, began "establishing a sense of order, a precedence of graceful hospitality and signature presidential style that still characterizes the White House to this day."[38] As he performed the assigned tasks of a butler, setting the table for official events, he was likely unaware of the historical scope of events to which he was privy.

In recounting his years in the White House through his *Reminiscences*,

Jennings offers a unique perspective on the Madisons during that time. In his memoir, primarily concerned with the War of 1812 and its effect on the president and his family, Jennings depicts himself as remarkably independent in his movements. In his account of the night of Dolley Madison's flight from the capital, August 23, 1814, he recounts how word arrived that British troops had landed just as he and other house slaves were preparing the dinner. He writes that Dolley Madison, understandably frantic, carried off only "the silver in her reticule, as the British were thought to be but a few squares off, and were expected at every moment."[39]

One additional item was rescued, and though Dolly receives acknowledgment for this accomplishment, here is how Paul recounts what actually took place:

> It has often been stated in print, that when Mrs. Madison escaped from the White House, she cut out from the frame the large portrait of Washington (now in one of the parlors there), and carried it off. This is totally false. She had no time for doing it. It would have required a ladder to get it down. All she carried off was the silver in her reticule, as the British were thought to be but a few squares off, and were expected every moment. John Susé (a Frenchman, then door-keeper, and still living) and Magraw, the President's gardener, took it down and sent it off on a wagon, with some large silver urns and such other valuables as could be hastily got hold of. When the British did arrive, they ate up the very dinner, and drank the wines, &c., that I had prepared for the President's party.[40]

Jennings does not follow the Madisons and instead appears to choose his own route, walking "on to a Methodist minister's," where he would witness the burning of the Navy Yard from afar.

When Madison's two terms concluded in 1817, the former president and his wife returned to Montpelier with Jennings accompanying his master. He continued to be enslaved as a manservant or valet until Madison died in 1836. Madison's correspondence with friends and family reveals that Jennings was renowned for his table-waiting skills, so much so that some of Dolley's friends asked to borrow him for their homes.

There is some evidence to suggest that Jennings helped runaway slaves escape during his time with the Madisons in Washington. Here's one account:

> Thurston Hern, once owned by Thomas Jefferson who gave him to his grandson Thomas Jefferson Randolph, ran away in 1817. "He is supposed to have gone to Washington," Jefferson wrote in a letter to an associate of his in the capital, on June 14, 1817. Jefferson's overseer, Edmund Bacon, reported that the runaway "went off with Mr. Madison's servant," who might have been Paul Jennings.[41]

This story is consistent with his family's oral tradition. Jennings used his White House position and his literacy to forge passes and emancipation papers. Given his subsequent exploits there is no reason to discount the validity of this account.

In 1822, Jennings married Fanny Gordon, who was enslaved on a nearby plantation. Together they had five children: Felix, Frances, John, Franklin, and William. Despite their twenty-two years of marriage, Fanny and Paul were never able to be together for more than a weekend at a time. As was so often the case, little else is known about their private life or their children.

In his will, Madison bequeathed the enslaved people he owned to his wife to protect her from debt, but he explicitly required that "none of them be sold without consent, especially when it involved children or families." Unfortunately, the Panic of 1837 wiped out the paper value of her inheritance and coupled with the enormous cost of her troubled son's gambling and drinking habits, she had to sell Montpelier and its historical papers to the federal government. When the proceeds from these sales were exhausted, she overrode her husband's wishes and sold slaves without their consent. Thankfully for the Jennings family, their children could not be sold since they lived on a neighboring plantation with their mother.

Though this prevented a disastrous separation, what followed were indeed trying times for the Jennings family. Desperately in need of money, Dolley Madison ordered Paul back to Washington, where she hired him out to President James Polk and First Lady Sarah Polk, but during a visit back to Virginia to see his family in the spring of 1844, Paul discovered his wife was in grave condition with an undiagnosed illness. In a letter to Dolly Madison dated April 23, 1844, Jennings wrote, "I found faney vary porley but she says she is better then she was in the winter." A few weeks later, he wrote a letter addressed to "Sister sukey," detailing Fanny's deteriorating condition: "I am looking every day to see the last of her." Madison allowed Jennings to remain in Virginia during his wife's illness. Fanny Gordon Jennings died on August 4, 1844.

But Jennings also took responsibility for communicating news and greetings between those enslaved by the Madisons in Montpelier and Washington. Many of these people had been separated for months from their families. In this particular letter to Sukey, Jennings conveyed his blessings to "Beckey Ellen Ralph and sister jane Bell" back in Washington. In addition, he informs Sukey that "Cattey an the Boys & peater is well." "Cattey an the Boys" were Catharine Taylor and her sons, who were separated from her partner Ralph Taylor while he served Dolley Madison in Washington. Similarly, "Beckey," or Rebecca Walker, must have appreciated receiving the news that her husband Peter was doing well back at Montpelier. Paul's literacy was thus used to maintain connections among his fellow enslaved people. He very purposely performed this essential role with distinction.

Jennings returned to DC after his wife's death, but even renting out Jennings couldn't turn around Dolley Madison's financial fortunes. In September 1846 she sold him to a local insurance agent, who sold him after about six months to Daniel Webster, the former secretary of state, then a senator for Massachusetts. On March 19, 1847, Webster put the arrangement in writing:

> I have paid $120 for the freedom of Paul Jennings. He agrees to work out the same at $8 a month, to be furnished with board, clothes & washing...His freedom papers I gave to him: they are recorded in this District.[42]

Here is a facsimile of the original document:

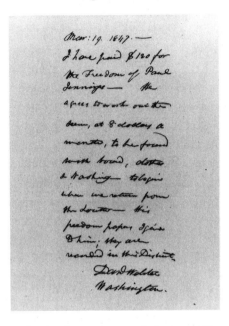

Courtesy of Moorland-Spingarn Research Center at Howard University

Paul thus worked as a dining room servant for Webster as a free man. Upon completing his contract, he lived with three free Black men near the White House. Webster had kept his word and went even further, recommending Jennings for a job at the Pension Office in the Department of the Interior. He described Jennings as an "honest, faithful and sober" home servant.

While working for Webster in Washington, Jennings helped plan and organize a significant slave escape in April of 1848. In a letter that first appeared in a book by John H. Paynter (a relative of three of the escapees) *Fugitives of the Pearl*, but has not been authenticated, Paul wrote:

Honored Friend,
A deep desire to be of help to my poor people has determined me
to take a decided step in that direction. My only regret is that I shall
appear ungrateful, in thus leaving with so little ceremony, one who

has been uniformly kind and considerate and had rendered each moment of service a benefaction as well as pleasure. From the daily contact with your great personality which it has been mine to enjoy, has been imbibed a respect for moral obligations and the claims of duty. Both of these draw me towards the path I have chosen.

According to Paynter, Jennings returned to Webster's home and took back the unread letter, evidently thinking it would be dishonorable to be ending his service before his debt was repaid.

The Pearl Incident was the single largest recorded escape attempt by enslaved people in US history. The mass escape plan was organized by Black and white abolitionists in Washington. Former slaves Paul Jennings and Paul Edmonson, whose wife and fourteen children were still enslaved, initiated the plot and persuaded William Chaplin, a white abolitionist, to join them. He contacted Philadelphia abolitionist Daniel Drayton, captain of *The Pearl,* and the captain in charge of the cargo, Edward Sayres, who agreed to participate. Financial backing came from Gerrit Smith of New York, another white abolitionist.

Jennings's involvement in the plot may have come through his connection to Chaplin, a member of the New York State Anti-Slavery Society and the Washington correspondent for the *Albany Patriot.* Chaplin had printed two reports that included Jennings's role in another escape of an enslaved person—Ellen Stewart (referred to in the article as Helen), a fifteen-year-old girl, daughter of Sukey, owned by Dolly Madison who, instead of accepting being sold, chose to run away. Jennings was reported to have assisted her in her original escape. This time he made sure she was included among the thirty-eight men, twenty-six women, and thirteen children hidden below decks on *The Pearl.*

The plan called for the escapees to sail south along the Potomac River and north up the Chesapeake Bay. They would then cross overland to the Delaware River until they reached the free state of New Jersey, a total distance of 225 miles.

Washington's free Black community risked their lives to assist these enslaved men, women, and children from across the city in slipping away from their workplaces and residences. On the evening of April 15th, they boarded *The Pearl* at a wharf on the Potomac. Everything went according to plan as they sailed down the Potomac and made the left turn into the Chesapeake Bay, but then the wind intervened and forced *The Pearl* to anchor for the night, which tragically contributed to what followed.

The slaveholders soon discovered that their slaves were missing, and so was *The Pearl*. A posse of thirty-five men was dispatched on the steamboat *Salem*, which caught up to *The Pearl* near Point Lookout, Maryland. They boarded the vessel and recaptured all seventy-seven escapees. *The Pearl* then sailed back to Washington.

As frequently occurs in the wake of slave revolts and escapes, a violent response followed. An angry mob attacked suspected white abolitionists, and no one in the free Black community was safe from the mayhem of what would come to be known as the first Washington Race Riot. Much of the vitriol was focused on Gamaliel Bailey, editor of the anti-slavery newspaper *The New Era*. The rioters were convinced that Bailey helped plan the escape, though he had not done so. Police only stepped in after the mob smashed several office windows, to prevent Bailey from being killed.[43]

As for the seventy-seven who had courageously risked their lives in the effort to attain freedom, after the Washington Riot was quelled, their owners sold them to Georgia and Louisiana slave traders—"down the river"—who took them to New Orleans. Two of Edmonson's children, Mary and Emily, were purchased and freed with funds from Henry Ward Beecher's Plymouth Congregational Church in Brooklyn, New York.

The men who made *The Pearl* available, Drayton, Sayres, and Chester English, the ship's cook, were arrested and indicted for abetting the escapees. Despite securing the legal services of Horace Mann, the noted education reformer and Massachusetts congressman, Drayton and Sayres were found guilty on all seventy-seven counts of aiding the enslaved to escape and transporting them illegally to do so. English was released since the jury decided he played no part in the escape.

Because the captain and pilot were unable to pay the $10,000 (approximately $400,000 in today's dollars) in fines and court costs, they were four years into their sentences when Massachusetts senator and well-known abolitionist Charles Sumner successfully petitioned President Millard Fillmore to release them. Thanks to Drayton's refusal to provide the names of the plot's conspirators, Jennings managed to escape the consequences that would have befallen him had his participation been discovered.

The story of *The Pearl* did not end there, however. The attempted escape by so many enslaved people is said to have contributed to a major debate on the floor of the Senate and then to a provision in the Compromise of 1850 that ended the slave trade in Washington, DC. Slavery was not abolished in the capital, but the new law made the sale of enslaved individuals illegal. In addition, Harriet Beecher Stowe is believed to have been inspired by the incident in writing *Uncle Tom's Cabin*, especially the horrible experience that her enslaved characters dreaded of being sold "down South."

Jennings thus epitomizes the ultimate contradiction among some enslaved people. He could only speak positively about his time with the Madisons, yet he actively participated in the largest attempted slave escape in American history through his planning and organizing efforts. He chose not to participate in the exodus because he felt obligated to Daniel Webster for enabling his freedom and decided instead to fulfill their agreement. Jennings's staunch opposition to enslavement assuredly influenced his three sons. They all enlisted to fight for the Union.

In 1849 in Alexandria, Virginia, Jennings met and married his second wife, Desdemona Brooks, a free woman whose mother was white. In the 1850's he bought two wood-frame houses on L Street near 18th Street. Each cost $1000 ($40,800 in today's dollars). The law at the time required children to take the status of their mother. Having secured his freedom and over the next several years that of his sons and daughters, Jennings "firmly established himself and his family in Washington's free black community, which was at that time three times as large as its enslaved community."[44]

To support his family, he worked at the job Webster had helped him secure in the Pension Office, encompassing various clerk-like duties. The office handled claims of veterans' and soldiers' families. While working at this office, he encountered John Brooks Russell, an antiquarian who, upon hearing Jennings' stories about his time in the White House, persuaded him to publish his memoir in a magazine entitled *Historical*

Magazine and Notes and Queries Concerning the Antiquities, History and Biography of America.

Two years later, the magazine's editor, John Gilmary Shea, privately published Jennings's work as a book titled *A Colored Man's Reminiscences of James Madison.* Shea ordered seventy-five copies and placed in each one an inlaid facsimile of the document Webster had signed giving Jennings his freedom.[15]

Although numbering fewer than three thousand words, including a two-paragraph preface by Mr. Russell, the book is nonetheless considered a crucial resource as a depiction of life inside the Madison White House.

Jennings lived at 1804 L St. with Desdemona. His daughter, Frances and his two grandsons lived next door. John, Franklin and William survived their service in the Civil War. After Desdemona's death, Jennings prepared his will on September 13, 1870, and in it he mentions the wife whom he plans to marry the next day.

The Montpelier website does an excellent job in concluding their article about the significance of Jennings' life:

> Throughout his remarkable life, Paul Jennings witnessed firsthand the paradox that's so startling for today's Americans. How could one of our greatest advocates of liberty take such an active part in the institution of slavery? And why would a once-enslaved human being act so loyally to his former mistress while at the same time helping slaves escape? In 1874, at age 75, Paul Jennings departed this world, leaving behind him property in Washington, an increasing number of descendants, and a story that would become legend in the decades and even centuries to come.

A man of contradictions in a time filled with them, Jennings demonstrated great loyalty to a president's family while showing great resolve in his quest to bring freedom to those enslaved by the very same president and many others. His words and deeds validate his life's work.

CHAPTER 3

Sarah Mapps Douglass
Against Patriarchy

"A token of love from me, to thee." Watercolor and gouache
by Sarah Mapps Douglass, ca. 1833.

Well, children, where there is so much racket there must be something out of kilter. I think that 'twixt the negroes of the South and the women at the North, all talking about rights, the white men will be in a fix pretty soon. But what's all this here talking about?

—Sojourner Truth, "Ain't I a Woman?"
Women's Rights Convention, Akron, Ohio, 1851

The reason this chapter begins as it does with a black and white photograph of a painting is because there is no authenticatable photograph of Ms. Douglass. The two photographs that were considered came from reputable sources—the Black newspaper, The Amsterdam News in New York City and a Massachusetts history website—but upon deeper investigation we learned that neither were of Sarah. Our research did reveal as you will soon learn, that Sarah was a gifted painter and became the first Black woman to have her paintings reproduced in books. The painting in brilliant color along with several others can be seen on-line at https://www.themarginalian.org/2021/06/16/sarah-mapps-douglass-flowers/

Sarah Mapps Douglass was a womanist, a Black feminist activist for equal rights and justice, at a time when new ideas of reforming government, human beings, and human relations were flooding the scene like a long drink of whiskey. Sister Sarah was a member of the Religious Society of Friends, a Quaker, in a state with deep Quaker roots, until her defiance put her at odds with her so-called friends. She is not a simplistic microcosm of a bigger picture. Her life begins in a space that was not the norm for people of African descent, and her lifetime will be marked by the shattering of norms, especially those established by a racist and capitalist patriarchy.

Sarah was born free just as her mother, her mother's mother, and her father had been. Her father was already a wealthy barber before Sarah or any of her five siblings were born. She was born in 1806 in Philadelphia, America's second-largest city, in a country that was still mostly rural. Relatively wealthy, urbane, and educated, she fully utilized these advantages to become a radical, transgressive woman in nineteenth-century North America in disruptive ways. In 1996, noted scholar Sarah Grayson wrote:

The most prominent images of Black women in antebellum America depicted in classes across the United States are of passive victims as opposed to active agents of change. The names and deeds of Black women like Frances E. W. Harper, Maria Stewart, Sarah Mapps Douglass, and Sarah Jane Giddings are not an integral part of American education. Further, most history books overlook Black women's roles in antebellum America—oversights which can be considered suppression through historical omission. How indeed do the name and deeds of Sarah Mapps Douglass become an integral part of American history education? Where is the curriculum guide that puts her in what we teach our grade school students? Where does she fit into our social and racial justice, and worker and gender equity courses? Let us start at the tertiary level.[46]

There is one Douglass you now find in college-level African American history courses, especially those covering the transatlantic slave trade era to the Civil War: Frederick Douglass (no relation). But Sarah Douglass should be there, too, as well as in African American art and culture classes encompassing the nineteenth century. She's a must for a Black women's history class and should be studied in courses on womanism or women's studies or US and African American religious history. Unlike Frederick she did not leave us a slave narrative because she was never a slave.

When Sarah dared to expose the racist hypocrisy among members of the Society of Friends, Arnold Buffum, a Quaker from Providence, Rhode Island, showed up to support her. He charged that a "woman had been denied membership" in the Society of Friends in Philadelphia and cited Sarah's story of how her mother, Grace Douglass, was obliged to sit under the stairs or on a separate back bench at services at the Arch Street Philadelphia Meeting. Someone who used the initials P.R., tried to refute Buffum's charges in *The Friend*, a Quaker publication. Sarah responded to the stereotypical arguments presented there:

> P. R. says very few of them incline to attend our meetings. Friends' mode of worship does not suit their dispositions. They are fond of music and excitement, and hence prefer their own meetings, where

they regularly hear singing and preaching. In this, I think P. R. is mistaken. I have frequently heard my mother say that very many of our people inclined to Friends' mode of worship; she lamented the unchristian conduct that kept them out. I myself know some, whose hearts yearn for the quiet of your worshiping places, and who love the "still small voice" better than harp or viol. Some have gone out from "Friends," not because they prefer their own meetings, "where they regularly hear singing and preaching" but because they could not bear the cross of sitting on the "black bench." Ah, there are many poor stray starving sheep, wandering in this world's wilderness, who would gladly come into your green pastures, and repose them by your still waters; did not prejudice bar the entrance! I am persuaded the Lord has a controversy with "Friends" on this account. Let them see to it.[47]

Sarah was very outspoken in her criticism of what she saw as a serious blind spot for many of her white fellow Quakers. Her Quaker roots extended to her grandparents. Cyrus Bustill was the child of a slave-owning Quaker lawyer, Samuel Bustill of Burlington, New Jersey, and an enslaved African woman, Parthenia. This was a master-slave relationship, and little is known about the extent of coercion that was involved. We do know that upon his death, Bustill's wife, Grace, sold Cyrus to Thomas Prior, also a Friend, who instructed Cyrus in the baking trade, took him to Quaker meetings, and freed him after seven years of enslavement. Or did he? There is some uncertainty as to whether Cyrus saved up enough money to purchase his own freedom in 1774, or if Thomas manumitted him in 1769. Regardless of the way in which Cyrus became free, he baked bread for the Revolutionary Army and settled in Philadelphia after the war. He attended the monthly meeting of Friends at Arch Street and taught at a school supported by the Pennsylvania Abolition Society. He is also the great-great grandfather of Paul Robeson, twentieth-century renaissance man—singer, actor, lawyer, orator, and activist who, 180 years later encountered much prejudice regarding both his race and his political beliefs.

Meanwhile Sarah's grandmother, Elizabeth Morey was also becoming a Quaker. Her father was Richard Morey, but her path to being a Friend was via her mother, Satterwait, a Delaware Indian woman. Satterwait was a maid in the household of Nicholas Wain, a Quaker, with whose family she attended meetings. Thus, even before her marriage to Cyrus, Elizabeth had experienced the Quaker religion.

Cyrus and Elizabeth married and had eight children, the fifth of whom, Grace, was Sarah's mother. Grace attended meetings with her parents at the Old North Meeting. She married Sarah's father, Robert Douglass, who had a hairdresser business next door to Grace's milliner business, both on Arch St. They married in 1803 and had six children. Grace also ran a school and was a founding member of the Philadelphia Female Anti-Slavery Society (PFASS).

Sarah was born in 1806 in Philadelphia and grew up in an educated, middle-class family. Her Bustill family adopted a Quaker lifestyle—attending meetings, speaking the Quaker language, and wearing Quaker clothing. Sarah was aware that her mother wanted to become an official member of the faith but was "warned in a kindly fashion by a Friend not to apply, because she would only get her feelings hurt."

Sarah attended schools either run by Quakers or informed by Quaker principles, including the school organized by her mother alongside sail-maker and abolitionist James Forten, when she was thirteen. Six years later, in 1825, Sarah became a teacher at her mother's school. In 1833 Sarah left for New York to teach at the Free African School for several years, but she missed Philadelphia and returned to start her own school for girls. She earned a reputation as an excellent teacher partly due to her skill in teaching both the sciences and arts. She had high standards for her pupils. Her collection of shells and minerals was noteworthy at the time, and she used them to great advantage in teaching basic science to the girls under her tutelage. She also excelled at drawing, many of which appeared in her written letters and are thought to be the first and/or earliest surviving examples of signed paintings by and African American woman.

After a bit of back and forth as to who would be in control of the school Sarah started, the PFASS that Sarah's mother had helped found in 1833 took Sarah's school "under its care" in 1838. In 1841, Sarah chose to run her school independently, although PFASS continued to provide assistance. Sarah was deeply committed to the Philadelphia Female Anti-Slavery Society. The endeavor included Black and white women who worked together to educate one another through writing, reading, listening to speakers and working ceaselessly to end enslavement via petitions and boycotts. They wanted freedom for all of the enslaved with no compensation for their owners.

The next big change occurred in 1853 when Sarah had the school moved to the third floor of the building owned by the Institute for Colored Youth on Lombard Street. Sarah became the head of the primary department, which she continued for 24 more years until her retirement in 1877 at the age of 71.

The advancement of education in the African American community, especially schools like the Institute for Colored Youth, played a significant role in developing defiant women like Sarah Douglass. The institute was founded by the philanthropist Richard Humphreys. The legend goes that Humphreys had been a slave trader who converted to the Society of Friends and was persuaded to use part of his extensive, ill-gained fortune for the education of Black children. The theory also suggests witnessing violent race riots throughout the city added to his conviction that education was essential if African Americans were to make progress in the so-called City of Brotherly Love. Whatever inspired him, he bequeathed $10,000 ($328,000 in today's dollars) to establish the Quaker-controlled African Institute, which had been renamed the Institute for Colored Youth by the time it opened in 1840.

Much of the credit for the school's prominence goes to Fanny Jackson Coppin, whose freedom was purchased by an aunt while she was still a young girl. Fanny's determination to become educated led to her attending the Rhode Island State Normal School while working as a domestic servant at the same time. Not content to end her formal education upon graduating high school, she learned of the opportunities available to Black students at Oberlin College and enrolled there. Upon completion of her undergraduate degree in 1865, she taught Latin, Greek, and mathematics at the Institute for Colored Youth and also worked in administration as principal of the girls' high school department.

In 1869, Coppin became the school principal, making her the first

Black woman in the US to hold such a position. Once she assumed her leadership position, she began making innovations with the curriculum. Within the first two years of her tenure, Jackson created a teacher training program that attracted many more enrollees than the school's classics courses. By 1878, Jackson added a practice-teaching component. Ultimately, she transformed the institution at every level, expanding and modernizing the curriculum and improving the school's outreach and fund-raising. Despite the widespread racial prejudice that followed Reconstruction, Coppin succeeded in earning friendly benefactors nationwide. In her autobiography, she wrote, "However brilliant a person may be intellectually, however skillful in the arts and sciences, he must be reliable; he must be trustworthy." Fanny lived up to these notions. Her example inspired many outstanding African American teachers who strengthened the school's mission throughout her administration.

In 1881 at age forty-four, Jackson slowed down long enough to marry the Reverend Levi J. Coppin. He became a bishop of the African Methodist Episcopal Church, while Coppin focused her efforts on developing an industrial-training department within the school. She deeply valued vocational training and saw it as equally important to an academic education in the struggle to overcome racism. After a decade-long effort, the school offered training in ten trades.

Fanny Coppin retired from teaching in 1902 after thirty-three years of service. The school relocated to Cheyney, Pennsylvania, and eventually became Cheyney State Teacher's College in 1951. With its origins dating to 1837 and renamed in 1983, Cheyney University is considered the first historically Black college in America. After leaving the school, Coppin and her husband set their sights on Cape Town, South Africa. For the next ten years, she organized mission societies there and promoted temperance among the Black women. The Coppins then returned to Philadelphia, where Fanny Coppin died in 1913. Coppin State University in Baltimore is named in her honor.

Teaching was certainly a centerpiece of Sarah's life, but there were numerous other strands that she developed concurrently. One was her involvement with the Grimké sisters, Sarah and Angelina, with whom she sustained a long and meaningful friendship. The sisters were the daughters of South Carolina enslavers and later joined the Quaker community's abolitionist movement.

In her letters to Sarah Grimké, Sarah opened up about the pain she experienced as a result of the racial discrimination she encountered with the Philadelphia Quakers. Black people were required to sit on separate benches at the Arch Street meeting she and her mother had attended. Sarah ultimately chose to leave the meeting, though her mother remained loyal despite the mistreatment.

Another strand was Sarah's anti-slavery activism. She was twenty-five when she sent money that she had helped raise in Philadelphia to William Lloyd Garrison to support his publication, *The Liberator*. Poetry and prose also captured her imagination, and her writing was frequently published in the Ladies' Department section of Garrison's newspaper as well as in *The Colored American* and the *Anglo-African Magazine*. She used the pseudonym Zillah and possibly also "Sophonisba." Here is an excerpt she wrote as Zillah, which we know was her work, based on an analysis of the characters, all of whom correspond to her siblings:

> O, children, did you know the bitterness of having the finger of scorn pointed at you wherever you appear, at school, in the streets, and even in the Lord's house; could you feel for one moment the anguish of being despised merely for your complexion, surely you would throw this unholy prejudice from you with disdain.[48]

Sarah helped found two important organizations promoting the dignity and centrality of Black women. The first was the Female Literary Association (FLA), which she helped start in 1831. Such Black literary societies had begun in northern cities in the 1820s. The main objectives of these groups of free African American women was to both improve their intellectual skills and to deepen their identification with their enslaved sisters. The underlying premise of the FLA and other such groups was that becoming better educated would undermine the white conviction that Black people were intellectually inferior. The belief that Douglass and her comrades in the FLA shared was that the "cultivation of intellectual powers was the greatest human endeavor since the powers and talents of the mind were bestowed upon ALL people by God." Thus it was their "duty as women and African Americans to use those talents to try to break down the existing divides between African Americans and whites and to fight for equal rights to advance their race."

We can experience the call to activism that Sarah expressed in her address to the FLA in 1832 at a "mental feast," which she described as intended to "feed our never-dying minds, to excite each other to deeds of mercy." The event was reported by an unnamed writer for the *Liberator*, which credits one Simeon Jocelyn for providing the idea for mental feasts to the Philadelphia community. He encouraged meetings where women would participate in "moral and religious meditation, conversation, reading and speaking, sympathizing over the fate of the unhappy slaves, improving their own minds, &c. &c.; and, in order to make the meeting truly a Mental Feast and unburthensome to the entertainer, that the visitors should receive the simplest fare."

> One short year ago, how different were my feelings on the subject of slavery! It is true, the wail of the captive sometimes came to my ear in the midst of my happiness, and caused my heart to bleed for his wrongs; but, alas! the impression was as evanescent as the early cloud and morning dew. I had formed a little world of my own, and cared not to move beyond its precincts. But how was the scene changed when I held the oppressor lurking on the border of my peaceful home! I saw his iron hand stretched forth to seize me as his prey, and the cause of the slave became my own. I started up, and with one mighty effort threw from me the lethargy which had covered me as a mantle for years; and determined, by the help of the Almighty, to use every exertion in my power to elevate the character of my wronged and neglected race. [49]

It is true that Sarah was understating her commitment to ending enslavement, which she describes as "evanescent as the early cloud and morning dew," but the scene change she is referring to is the Nat Turner rebellion of 1831, which resulted in efforts to restrict the entry of free Black people even in the northern states. Thus her reference to the "iron hand" alludes to the even more oppressive treatment of African Americans that Turner's rebellion inspired in whites throughout the country.

Sarah also participated in efforts to end enslavement on the national level. With the urging of the Grimké sisters, she attended the Anti-Slavery Convention of American Women that took place in New York from May 15–18, 1838. It was the first such convention to integrate Black and white women opposed to slavery. Sarah served on the ten-member committee that made the arrangements for the convention.

We need to remember that, throughout this period of her life, Sarah was teaching and eventually administering schools. She did choose to marry in 1855, when she was almost fifty. William Douglass, also fifty, was rector of the African Episcopal Church of St. Thomas. He had proposed to her the previous year, but it was a colossal decision for Sarah since it meant becoming stepmother to Douglass's nine children from his first marriage. The marriage was not a happy one for Sarah. The responsibilities she took on for her new instant family forced her to cut back on the anti-slavery work to which she was so devoted.

When her husband died six years into their marriage, Sarah returned to the work that was so crucial to her being—the freedom of her people. But once again, that was not all that drew her to her lifelong focus. Two years before her marriage, in 1853, Douglass began taking basic medical courses at the Female Medical College of Pennsylvania. She was the school's first African American student, and she continued her studies at the Ladies' Institute of Pennsylvania Medical University with the goal of using the knowledge she gained to teach African American women in the subjects of hygiene, anatomy, and health. The lectures and teaching that she offered her students at the Banneker Institute were considered by the authorities to be a more proper endeavor for a married woman than practicing medicine, which may have been at least part of what motivated her to become stepmother to her husband's many children.

During the Civil War, Sarah worked to promote the cause of southern freedmen and freedwomen. Along with delivering lectures, she served as vice president of the Women's Freedmen's Relief Association, helping to raise funds for books, tools, and teachers to be sent to the South to assist the newly emancipated. In 1864 she co-founded the Philadelphia Home for Aged and Infirm Colored Persons, which was among the first such institutions in the country.

Sarah was finally forced to retire in 1877, due to rheumatism. The institute's board was deeply saddened by her departure. It continued paying her for several months and went on to purchase the set of minerals that she had used so effectively in her teaching, as a means of augmenting her income. Two members of the board left her a small legacy in their wills, further indicators that Sarah was struggling at the end of her life. She died five years later, in the fall of 1882, having directed her next of kin to destroy all of her correspondence. The letters that she wrote to others reveal that Sarah did ultimately become reconciled with her Quaker religion. Since she was able to eventually return to the Arch Street meeting, it is safe to assume that "her protest against segregated seating within the Society of Friends had at last been heard." Here is further proof:

> But one can read in these latter-day letters the evidence of the depth and strength of Sarah's spiritual life which made it possible for her to forgive the past, and continue in fellowship if not membership, with the Religious Society of Friends.[50]

Thus we have evidence that once again Sarah's commitment to human equality had a dynamic impact, which in this case enabled her to experience her deep and abiding faith in the power of the Holy Spirit working in silence. Yet another polymath to add to the list of those whose multi-talents, whether artistic or scientific, and in Sarah's case both, served to enrich their own lives and add to what they brought to their abolitionist endeavors. Sarah refused to take a backseat to any man or men or to rein in either her voice or her spirit when justice required that it ring out.

Courtesy of UCLA Library

CHAPTER 4

Mary Ellen Pleasant
A Constant Soldier Never Unready,
Even Once

On December 2, 1859, the day abolitionist John Brown was set to be hanged for leading a daring raid in Virginia, he found a note in his pocket. It read, "The ax is laid at the foot of the tree. When the first blow is struck, there will be more money to help.—MEP."

There was little doubt that someone with considerable funds and sympathetic to Brown's cause of liberation had written the message "to incite and arm an enormous slave uprising...taking over an arsenal at Harpers Ferry." No one suspected that the author of the note was a Black woman named Mary Ellen Pleasant. More than forty years later, when she told the journalist Sam Davis about her life, an amazing story of defiance would emerge. "Before I pass away," Pleasant revealed, "I wish to clear the identity of the party who furnished John Brown with most of his money to start the fight at Harpers Ferry and who signed the letter found on him when he was arrested."

The MEP signature on the note was misread as WEP and the authorities sought a northern white man instead of the southern woman of color who actually contributed $30,000 to Brown's antislavery activities, or what would be worth nearly $900,000 in today's dollars. The kind of proofs that historians like to have when they make a conclusive statement about persons, places, or events—such as multiple, independent, corroborating accounts, physical artifacts, official records, and the like—are not often available for people who actively sought to conceal their real identity and activities. Those who fought against slavery when it was the law of the land, those operators on the Underground Railroad, those who were the comrades of outlaws like Nat Turner and John Brown, do not leave us the kind of material evidence about their lives to make claims with a high degree of certainty and confidence. As Veronica Chambers has noted in her obituary that appeared in the NYTimes Overlooked tribute, Mary Ellen "live her life between the lines of legitimacy and infamy, servitude and self-invention."[51]

Notwithstanding these difficulties and complexities, we have to try to reconstruct Mary Ellen's life because she is that important and, in all the complicated facets that she presents, she is an even more compelling figure for our times. Thus, we set out after a child some say was born in slavery in Georgia, another source says it was in Virginia, while a third says she was born in Philadelphia on August 19, 1814. Can we know the truth about this woman, impoverished and degraded by a system of racial capitalism, who becomes a millionaire? Is there a truth that is knowable about this antislavery warrior who led many enslaved persons to freedom and then may have become a capitalist who exploited people and circumstances to amass great wealth but who lost her fortune in the end?

Comparing Mary Ellen to Harriet Tubman, W.E.B. Du Bois described her this way in *The Gift of Black Folk* (1924):

> [Pleasant was] quite a different kind of woman and yet strangely effective and influential...Here was a colored woman who became one of the shrewdest business minds of the State. She anticipated the development in oil. She was the trusted confidante of many of the California pioneers such as Ralston, Mills and Booth, and for years was a power in San Francisco affairs...Throughout a life that was perhaps more than unconventional, she treasured a bitter hatred for slavery and a certain contempt for white people.[52]

So who was Mary Ellen Pleasant? Born from the union of a free "full-blooded Negress from Louisiana" and a wealthy Hawaiian planter, she started working at a young age as a domestic in Nantucket, Massachusetts. According to her obituary in the *New York Times*, her experience of living in a Quaker home transformed somehow by Pleasant into "a kind of finishing school." Here's what she had to say about this period in her life in her unpublished autobiography:

> I often wonder what I would have been with an education...I have let books alone and studied men and women a good deal...I have always noticed that when I have something to say, people listen. They never go to sleep on me.[53]

Yet another mystery pertains to Mary Ellen's first husband. Was James Henry Smith a white man or of mixed ancestry? No evidence conclusively convinces historians. No matter. What does matter is that when he died in the 1840s, he left Mary Ellen with a sizable inheritance. There is no doubt as to the identity of her second husband, John Pleasant. Though she evidently never confided how they met, her biographers are convinced John and Mary Ellen became acquainted in New Bedford, Massachusetts, one of the many destinations of the Underground Railroad.

The California Gold Rush of 1848 soon beckoned Mary Ellen and, since Black people were free to try to seek their fortune on the West Coast, Pleasant left for San Francisco. From this point on there is considerable mystery surrounding her movements, her choices, her accomplishments and those with whom she became involved. There is even some controversy over whether she and her second husband passed for white.

One of Mary Ellen's strengths throughout her life was the ability to make the most of opportunities. A key to this approach was her capacity to multi-task. While working as a cook - theoretically both invisible and unimportant in the households of the affluent people she served - she would eavesdrop and learn information that proved critical in the successful investments of her inheritance that she made. In the census of 1890, she listed her profession as "capitalist." Who could question such a designation upon learning that she was the owner of restaurants, boarding houses rumored to be brothels, and had shares in a variety of businesses from dairies and laundries to a Wells Fargo Bank?

Mary Ellen's biographer, Lynn Maria Hudson, in telling the story of this part of Mary Ellen's life explains that:

> One of the reasons that she's not known to students of U.S. history and Americans is because a lot of the activities that she was involved in were either controversial or secret...Her legacy is not the pure, selfless freedom fighter or heroine as how Harriet Tubman is described. Pleasant does not fit that mold.[54]

Nowhere is the "zigzag of fortune and power, infamy and blame"[55] more in evidence than in her relationship with Thomas Bell, a white man. It was upon the occasion of his death that the public learned that much of Mary Ellen's "portfolio," including the mansion she designed and had constructed, were in Bell's name. This was likely done strategically. What were the chances of a woman, let alone a Black woman, successfully obtaining the business interests she was able to acquire? Tragically for Mary Ellen, Bell's widow sued her. The court record is incredibly complex and reflective of the racism of the period as well as of the degree to which Mary Ellen had penetrated the white power structure, which inevitably came crashing down upon her. She lost control of the Bell estate, and with the verdict, the fortune she had worked so assiduously to accumulate was greatly diminished.

But being a capitalist was only one dimension, albeit a remarkable one given the times, of Mary Ellen's endeavors. While the Black men of California were holding conventions to assert their rights to suffrage and education, Black women were leaders in the fight against segregation in public places. Mary Ellen was in the center of this movement and appeared in court to demand equal access. She affirmed her belief in the significance of these efforts in her unpublished autobiography. The paradox is that her power and status were most visible in her attempts to gain recognition for Black women, and yet they resulted in her losing both.

The fight against segregation on public transportation affords a window into a city's racial, class, and gender politics. Historians have used the evolution of public transportation in various cities as a barometer to measure the resistance of African Americans to segregation. For example, James MacPherson, a Civil War historian, described the Reconstruction-era fight in Philadelphia for equal access to transportation as a microcosm of Black people's seemingly endless struggle for equal rights and dignity.

Black communities nationwide monitored and cheered on such struggles. In 1862, Philip Bell, editor of the west coast's first major Black newspaper in San Francisco, *Pacific Appeal,* denounced segregation in a fiery op-ed that saw the exclusion of Black people from the railroad as a form of "barbarism" in a city that was supposed to have outgrown such racial prejudice.

San Franciscans relied on streetcars during and after the Civil War. Cable cars didn't start replacing carts pulled by horses or mules until the late 1870s. Black people were prevented from accessing these cars regardless of how they were powered. If they did succeed in boarding, they were harassed and forced off. The motivation to segregate was the same as it always is—to keep Black people "in their place" and thus prevent them from mingling with white people and "mongrelizing" their superior race. The degree to which Black people were traveling throughout the country, leaving the South and plantation life as far behind as possible, was a "dangerous transgression in the minds of many white Americans."[56]

The streetcar cases in San Francisco, in which Black women took the leadership roles, are indicative of the significance of their involvement. Since Black women had jobs that required then to use public transportation, the effort to integrate streetcars was a logical site where women "stake out claims to public space, articulate their class privileges and also insist on treatment afforded to 'ladies,' a term reserved for elite white women."[57]

Of course, such transgressive behavior was not without risks. The parallel can be made to the way in which Black women shaped the discourse and strategies of Reconstruction in their campaigns against the lynching of Black female bodies.

It will come as no surprise, given her assertiveness and her ongoing quest to be treated equally, that Mary Ellen eventually came up against the prejudice of the streetcar system. In the lawsuit she brought in 1866 regarding being removed from a streetcar, she took two approaches: one pertaining to her bodily mistreatment and one in which she adopted a strategy frequently used by the abolitionist movement—having an upper-class white woman testify in support of her case. As regards the former approach, she called forth the notion that enslaved women did not own their own bodies, which was a key element in the approach taken by 19th century abolitionist women. This is summed up well here:

> As Elizabeth B. Clark argues, this rhetoric of sympathy for pained Black bodies also signaled shifts in rights discourse and legal reasoning. When abolitionists commandeered an "identification with suffering others," they shaped not only the literature of the period, but the legal argument as well.[58]

Mary Ellen had employed these abolitionist strategies as part of her Underground Railroad endeavors, so it is understandable that she would revise them skillfully to fit the Reconstruction era.

In the early days of his career as an orator, Frederick Douglass called upon William Lloyd Garrison to introduce him. Slave narratives often made use of white abolitionists to validate their accounts in introductions. So, too, did Mary Ellen appreciate the value of a white person on her side. In her lawsuits, she enlisted Lisotte Woodworth, wife of Selim Woodworth and her former employer, with whom she had lived in the early 1860s.

When Mary Ellen told her story of being refused service by both the driver and conductor of the streetcar, Woodworth's testimony served to confirm the occurrences, since she was present when the conductor denied Mary Ellen service solely because of her race. Woodworth went on to testify in considerable detail:

> I was in the car when she hailed it. I saw her hail it, and the conductor took no notice of her and walked into the car. Said I to the conductor, "Stop this car; there is a woman who wants to get in." He took no notice of what I said…I said, "I want her to get in." His answer was, "We don't take colored people in the cars." I then said, "You will have to let me out."[59]

It is notable that there had already been a lawsuit demanding the integration of streetcars in San Francisco, and the plaintiff, Charlotte Brown, had been successful in her suit. The conductor, a man named Dennison, was convicted in criminal court of assault and battery. The case was tied up in appeals for two years, but Charlotte eventually won with Judge Orville C. Pratt upholding the earlier verdict, ruling that excluding passengers from streetcars because of their race was illegal. He had no desire, he said in his ruling, to "perpetuate a relic of barbarism."[60]

Clearly the ruling of the district court carried little weight with those supposedly in the position to enforce it. Instead Mary Ellen took on the establishment and made use of a white woman to substantiate her claim. Even though the ban on testimony from Black people in San Francisco had been repealed, there was no assurance that testimony in their own defense would be believed, just that they had the right to speak in court. She knew that, despite her achievements, the position of Blacks in San Francisco and beyond was tenuous at best. Still, she won the case and was awarded monetary damages only to have an appeals court overturn the award, saying it was excessive.

Nevertheless, this was a most significant moment in Mary Ellen's life and was the first of several court appearances. It was also the first time the public heard her referred to as "Mamma." Fanned by the press, the nickname "Mammy Pleasant" became popular among the white public. Although she detested the name due to its association with enslaved Black woman caring for white children, she continued to make use of it. She knew that such a nickname, although abhorrent to her, would be considerably less threatening to the judges, juries, and lawyers with whom she would be interacting.

The lawsuits referenced earlier did much to call Mary Ellen's reputation into question and diminish her fortune. Some lawyers tried to tarnish her integrity by accusing her of practicing voodoo or of using her wiles to deceive her colleagues and friends. She was feisty up until the end, though, and had this to say in response to being called Mammy Pleasant:

> I don't like to be called mammy by everybody. Put that down. I am
> not mammy to everybody in California. I got a letter from a minister

in Sacramento. It was addressed to Mammy Pleasant. I wrote back to him on his own paper that my name was Mrs. Mary E. Pleasant. I wouldn't waste any of my paper on him.[61]

Mary Ellen died in 1904, and though it has taken several generations, she has received some recognition. San Francisco commemorated a Mary Ellen Pleasant Day, and a Mary Ellen Pleasant Park (the smallest in the city) where she is praised as the Mother of Civil Rights in California. She was the inspiration for Michelle Cliff's novel *Free Enterprise* and tours of the city often mention her on the corner of Octavia and Bush Streets, where her mansion once stood.

"Mammy Pleasant: Angel or Arch Fiend in the House of Mystery?"
from the May 7, 1899, issue of the *San Francisco Call*.
Courtesy of National Woman's Historical Society

Ms. Hudson began her book with this poem that touches amusingly and poignantly on some of the various controversies surrounding Mary Ellen:

"Mary Ellen Pleasant?"

"Wasn't she a voodoo queen?"

"A madam?"

"A mammy?"

"Didn't she run a whorehouse for white businessmen in
  San Francisco?"

"Wasn't she Mammy Pleasant?"

"Didn't she work voodoo on that white woman and
  Send her off her head?"

"Wasn't she Haitian?"

"Didn't she have a witchmark on her forehead?"

"A cast eye?"

"One blue eye and one brown eye?"

"Wasn't she ebony?"

"Yellow?"

"Wasn't she so pale you'd never know?"

"Didn't she come back as a zombie?"

"Didn't she have a penis?"

"Couldn't she work roots?"

"Didn't she make a senator's balls fall off?"

"Didn't she set fire to her own house?"

"Never heard of her."

Sixty years after her death, her gravestone was amended with a line that she had asked for on her deathbed: "A Friend of John Brown." As Pleasant herself once put it, "I'd rather be a corpse than a coward," words that now even adorn a t-shirt![62]

It has taken far too long, but Mary Ellen Pleasant has finally received at least some of the recognition she so richly deserves. The *New York Times* has created a site that honors those whom it did not acknowledge when they died. Here's how the tributes are introduced:

These remarkable Black men and women never received obituaries in *The New York Times*—until now. We're adding their stories to our project about prominent people whose deaths were not reported by the newspaper.[63]

The sub-heading of the obituary that shares key aspects of her life tells us this: "Born into slavery, she became a Gold Rush-era millionaire and a powerful abolitionist." These would be reasons enough for her inclusion in this project, but as shown in this chapter, there was so much more to her extraordinary life.

There are additional posthumous honors worth mentioning. The ghost of Mary Ellen Pleasant is a character in the 1997 novel *Earthquake Weather,* by Tim Powers. Karen Joy Fowler's historical novel *Sister Noon,* published in 2001, features her as a central character and Thomas Bell and Teresa Bell as secondary characters. She has also been discussed in film and television. The 2008 documentary *Meet Mary Pleasant* covered her life, as did a segment of a 2013 episode of the Comedy Central series "Drunk History," with Pleasant portrayed by Lisa Bonet. We think Mary Ellen would have enjoyed the portrayal. Now you can judge for yourself. ("Mary Ellen Pleasant Becomes a Rich, Black Abolitionist") We, of course, now know how much she contributed to our country's history.

CHAPTER 5

Henry Highland Garnet
Before Malcolm X

Courtesy of National Portrait Gallery

El Hajj Malik Shabazz, commonly known as Malcolm X, is considered the twentieth century's most uncompromising and resolute enemy of the evil system of white supremacy. All over the planet his example of fierce determination to call out racism and to prod people to action against it has endured far longer than the short thirty-nine years of his life. In the century before him there rose another warrior who never achieved the acclaim of Brother Malcolm, but who is certainly as deserving. Henry Highland Garnet is his name.

In 2018, a *Time* magazine article celebrated Henry's life and called attention to him as an overlooked but crucial figure in the anti-slavery movement. The article echoed the sentiment expressed by William M. Brewer, an associate of the eminent Dr. Carter G. Woodson, who founded what is today called Black History Month, as well as *The Journal of Negro History*. In the January 1928 edition of the journal, Brewer wrote that Henry "deserves front rank as the radical forerunner of Frederick Douglass."

We will argue here that the key to unlocking Henry's importance is to understand how he was a champion, not of the freedom and human rights of individuals, but of a new African people. His genealogical and historical roots return us to a time before US chattel slavery, before the transatlantic slave trade, and before the existence of the Euro-American colony, nation, or people. He was the grandson of a chief or king within what had once been the Mali Empire. It was in the 1500s that tens of thousands of Mandinka children, women, and men began being captured and shipped to the Americas to be chattel slaves, meaning slaves for life. The Mandinka (a Mande ethnic group) were first heard of in the 1970s when the author Alex Haley traced his "Roots" back to the village of Juffure in the Gambia, and the grandfather of his great-grandfather, Kunta Kinte, was severed from their Mandinka roots. Henry's grandfather was also captured and his life's brand as a Mandinka leader was renamed to slave, a thing not a person, not a part of a people but a piece of someone else's capital stock.

On December 23, 1815, in New Market, Maryland, a Colonel William Spencer listed Henry's body, under the color of law, as a new addition to his financial property and physical assets. Within the system of slavery,

Spencer would provide "food, clothing and other comforts" in exchange for a lifetime of unwaged labor and the passing on of that condition to all children he might produce. The African prince "brought moral and religious power with him to New Market, which *won* for him the significant name of Joseph Trusty – JOSEPH from his gifts in exhorting, praying and praising the Lord and TRUSTY from his unbending integrity of character." Joseph became father of eight—two daughters and six sons.[64]

One of the six sons was George. According to James McCune Smith, who wrote a detailed and vivid introductory biography of Henry, George was "the son who most resembled his father, Joseph, in person and character." George was blessed to unite with "a woman of extraordinary energy, industrious, pious and holding at the highest value that education from which her condition had debarred her and continued to debar her children."[65] Henry was born December 23, 1815.

A few words about Mr. Smith, Henry's lifelong friend, are in order and richly deserved. A former slave, Smith was the first African American to become a medical doctor. Because of his race he was refused admission to American universities and acquired his degree at the University of Glasgow.

In 1824, Colonel Spencer, who never married, died and left his estate to his brother, Isaac, and numerous nephews. Humans the colonel once enslaved now became the property of his heirs. In the face of impending change, George called a meeting of the Trusty family, and a plan to seek freedom in the North was born.

It took subterfuge to obtain permission to attend a funeral eleven miles away and to take that as the chance to escape. As Smith tells it, "They started on that sad errand, but really with hearts which the North Star lit up with its wondrous joys."[66] In a "covered market wagon" hidden in the woods, nine year-old Henry, together with his father, mother, sister, and others, slept in woods and swamps by day and traveled through the night. When Henry could not keep up with the older refugees, his father and uncles took turns carrying him upon their backs. When they reached Wilmington, Delaware, a Quaker philanthropist named Thomas Garrett offered his barn as a rest stop.

Freedom-loving people would eventually memorialize Quakers and others who provided refuge in hidden, safe spaces for African people who escaped from slavery via the Underground Railroad. Alternatively, monuments erected in the South paid homage to the Lost Cause while essentially refusing to acknowledge that the South had fought to maintain enslavement and that it had lost the war legitimately. These monuments are finally being called into question, though much work remains to be done. For example, in 2019, Governor Bill Lee of Tennessee was compelled by a state law to set aside a day to honor Nathan Bedford Forrest, a Civil War general and the first grand wizard of the Ku Klux Klan. Tennessee law requires that governors proclaim six dates, including Nathan Bedford Forrest Day, Memorial Day or Confederate Decoration Day, Robert E. Lee Day and Jefferson Davis Day. Finally, in June of 2020, both houses of the Tennessee legislature passed a bill that stopped compelling the governor to honor Forrest, but the other days are still set aside.

It was in Wilmington that the fugitives separated. Henry's family went to New Hope, Pennsylvania, where he began to attend school. After a few months, in 1825, the family relocated to New York, which was still two years away from ending enslavement, whereas Pennsylvania had been a free state for forty-five years.

In 1780, Pennsylvania's legislative body passed An Act for the Gradual Abolition of Slavery, the first of its kind in the US and the first in human history adopted by a democratic body. It was deemed a "gradual" act because its component parts laid out a plan that, as opposed to the "instant abolition" enacted in Massachusetts three years later, unfolded over time. It prohibited the importation of enslaved Africans, required the annual registering of the enslaved (forfeiture was the price for noncompliance, as was manumission for the enslaved) and provided for the freedom of all children born in Pennsylvania, regardless of their parents' status. It also kept those enslaved prior to the passage of the 1780 law enslaved for life. It would take another act of the Pennsylvania legislature, in 1847, to finish emancipation completely.

Regardless of the differing laws involving the condition and status of African Americans in the two states, Smith offers an explanation for George's decision to relocate from Pennsylvania to New York: "There was something gladdening in the State (of New York) in which freedom was newly entering, than in the other State[67] whose so-called free border was in poisoned contact with the direful institution of slavery."[68]

Soon after moving to New York City in 1825, George called the family together. Here is how Smith captures what must have been a triumphant moment:

> Gifted and fervent in prayer, he poured out his whole soul at this homely altar, in which he felt freedom united with religion for the first time in his sojourn on this earth. He then rose from his knees, and said to Henry's mother: 'Wife, they used to call you Henny (Henrietta), but in future your name is Elizabeth.' Placing his hand on his daughter's head: 'Your name is not Mary any longer, but Eliza. And, my dear little boy,' he continued, taking him on his knees: 'Your name is Henry. My name is George Garnet.' With these new names, they started anew on the journey of life.[69]

George supported his family with his shoemaking skills, and with his gifts as a preacher he became a leader in the African Methodist Episcopal Church. Henry began his formal education at the New York African Free School in 1826. Smith offers a brief description of young Henry that he credits to "the recollections of this writer, and all the contemporary evidence he has been able to gather up from school-fellows yet surviving." He asks us to "picture out the schoolboy Henry Garnet as quite the opposite of the nice, good, quiet little fellow, in whose mouth 'butter would not melt.'"[70] Some of these traits would hold Henry in good stead as the opposition to his cause intensified.

At the New York African Free School, No. 1, Henry was surrounded by a who's who of extraordinary classmates. Among them were Alexander Crummell, an Episcopal priest and a leading Black intellectual, who was Henry's neighbor and close boyhood friend; Samuel Ringgold Ward, a celebrated abolitionist and Henry's cousin; James McCune Smith, the pioneering Black physician and author of the introduction to Henry's congressional speech; Ira Aldridge, the celebrated actor; and Charles Reason, the first Black college professor in the United States.

Together these young men formed their own club, the Garrison

Literary and Benevolent Association. Named for William Lloyd Garrison in an era when abolitionist meetings in New York City frequently led to mob violence, the group's name was met with displeasure by school authorities. In response, the members kept the name and conducted their meetings off school property. These young African American residents of New York City, although still living in a slave state, often acted as if they were free men. As a result, their friends were at times alarmed by their boldness.

One example occurred in 1809 at an event commemorating the first anniversary of the New York African Society for Mutual Relief, which worked to address the needs of the free Black community of Manhattan. It was a secular, charitable, and cooperative organization, unique at the time. The founders met at the Rose Street Academy, a school for Black children in Manhattan, to begin planning the organization. There were strong ties to the Black churches of the city. Eight ministers were members. In addition to assisting the sick, widowed, and orphaned with burial expenses, the society provided financial support for Black schools like the one Henry attended.

The society purchased a building on Orange Street (now Baxter Street) in Lower Manhattan for the purposes of holding meetings and renting out space to build a budget. "The building also helped the organization fulfill its abolitionist goals. A secret trap door in the building served as a gateway to freedom for slaves who had escaped from the south."[71]

Even after just a year, the society had much to celebrate. The members celebrated with painted silk banners, one of which contained a full-length portrait of one of them, along with the words "AM I NOT A MAN AND A BROTHER?" The plaque by Josiah Wedgewood, a noted abolitionist famous for revolutionizing pottery techniques, upon which this phrase originally appeared in 1787, depicted a kneeling, chained, and supplicant enslaved man. These words, once part of a Quaker plea to end enslavement, became a source of considerable controversy, with the accompanying image being seen as demeaning and thereby reinforcing the view that Black men were inferior.

However, it was a similar phrase used in a speech on May 29, 1851, by Sojourner Truth—"And ain't I a woman"—that has come down through

history, some of the most poignant and powerful words that capture the spirit of a woman seeking freedom and recognition of her humanity. More than a century later, on April 4, 1968, Martin Luther King Jr. marched alongside striking sanitation workers carrying placards that read "I AM A MAN." Later that day, he was assassinated.

On the day the State of New York abolished slavery, July 5, 1827, Smith sought to capture the jubilance of the celebration:

> A real, full-souled, full-voiced shouting for joy, and marching through the crowded streets, with feet jubilant to songs of freedom! It was a living proof of the poet's words:

> "Oh yield him back his privilege, no sea
> Swells like the bosom of a man set free."

> The sidewalks were crowded with the wives, daughters, sisters, and mothers of the celebrants, representing every State in the Union, and not a few with gay bandana handkerchiefs, betraying their West

Indian birth: neither was Africa itself unrepresented, hundreds who had survived the middle passage, and a youth in slavery joined in the joyful procession. The people of those days rejoiced in their nationality, and hesitated not to call each other "Africans," or "descendants of Africa;" it was in after years, when they set up their just protest against the American Colonization Society and its principles that the term "African" fell into disuse and finally discredit. It was a proud day in the City of New York for our people...It was a proud day, never to be forgotten by young lads, who, like Henry Garnet, first felt themselves impelled along that grand procession of liberty, which through perils oft, and dangers oft, through the gloom of midnight, dark and seemingly hopeless, dark and seemingly rayless, but now, through God's blessing, opening up to the joyful light of day, is still "marching on.[72]

Sadly, the festive mood and the dreams of freedom and equality that characterized the day were short-lived. Thirteen-year-old Henry became a cabin boy in 1828, traveling twice to Cuba and then sailing on an American schooner, serving as a cook and steward. Upon his return he learned that his family had scattered due to the threat of slave catchers. His father somehow survived after making his escape by leaping from the upper floor of their home. A grocer who lived nearby offered shelter to Henry's mother.

The slave catchers did capture his sister, but she managed to convince them that she was not a fugitive slave, but rather had always lived in New York. Again, at a mere fourteen years old, Henry had the foresight to purchase a large clasp-knife with the idea of defending himself and seeking revenge. Fortunately, before anything untoward could come to pass, he was discovered by friends in Jericho, Long Island, who managed to hide him.

At this point, Henry was left to his own devices once again, and since he was self-supporting he was "bound out" to Epenetus Smith of Smithtown, Long Island. Smith's son, Samuel, became his tutor, but Henry suffered a horrible injury to his knee playing sports. It did not heal properly, leaving him reliant on crutches for the remainder of his life. After thirteen years of suffering, Henry had to have his leg amputated at the hip. Unable to support himself, he returned to his family, which had successfully reunited, and in 1831 he attended high school alongside his friend Alexander Crummell.

His leg injury might well have had an effect on Henry's subsequent turn towards studiousness and eventually towards religion. He participated in the Sunday School of the First Colored Presbyterian Church and became the protégé of the minister Theodore Sedgewick Wright, a noted abolitionist. Wright deserves his own chapter, but for now it is worth noting that he was the first Black graduate of Princeton's Theological Seminary, and his home was a station on the Underground Railroad. He was instrumental in Henry's conversion to Presbyterianism from the African Methodist Episcopal Church of his father and encouraged him to become a minister.

The next stop on Henry's educational journey was Canaan Academy in Canaan, New Hampshire, a coeducational school founded by abolitionists that accepted Black and white students. It was here that he met his future wife, Julia Ward Williams. Born in Charleston, South Carolina, she lived in Boston from an early age, attending the Prudence Crandall[73] School in Canterbury, Connecticut, before it faced racist backlash, as well as Noyes Academy.

Julia became head of the Female Industrial School while the family lived in Jamaica. They had three children, and we know very little about any of them except that one boy, James Crummell (namesake of Henry's beloved friend Alexander Crummell), only lived six or seven years. We do know that in 1850 Henry and Julia adopted a daughter, Stella Weems, a fugitive slave, whose father John, a free man, was determined to reunite his family after they had been separated and sold. Henry aided John and testified in a court proceeding that his beloved stepdaughter was so consumed with grief over the loss of her family that he feared she would become mentally ill. The ensuing appeal resulted in the huge sum of $5,000 being raised ($200,00 in today's dollars). The family was eventually reunited, thanks to the outstanding efforts of Charles Bennett Ray. A prominent African American abolitionist, journalist, and clergyman, Ray, who owned and edited a weekly newspaper called *The Colored American*, kept track of family members sold South to slave-holders in Alabama.

Back in Canaan, Henry continued his studies along with his friends, Alexander Crummell and Thomas S. Sydney. Their lives were far from tranquil. Once they had arrived, they proceeded to deliver "fiery orations" at an abolitionist meeting on the Fourth of July. As a result, some local residents fixated on closing the school and ridding the community of the fourteen Black students attending the Canaan Academy. During the school's first year, a mob arrived with ninety-five oxen, and after two days of intense effort, they moved the academy and set it on fire. Then they surrounded the home of George Kimball, a lawyer with whom Henry was rooming. Shots were fired into the room where Henry was confined, dealing with having to use a crutch due to his leg injury while also suffering from a fever. Nevertheless:

> Neither sickness nor infirmity, nor the howling of the mob could subdue his spirit; he spent most of the day in casting bullets in anticipation of the attack, and when the mob finally came he replied to their fire with a double-barreled shotgun, blazing from his window and soon drove the cowards away.[74]

The three friends soon felt it necessary to leave the school and the town of Canaan far behind. They all landed on their feet at the Oneida Institute in Whitesboro, New York, which proved to be a great boon thanks to the presence of the Rev. Beriah Green, a reformer and scholar who provided a most stimulating and encouraging setting for their studies. Smith had some words of commendation for the education they received at Oneida:

> If they were not so "well up" in Greek, Latin and Mathematics as the graduates of Harvard and Yale, they were more thoroughly the masters of the philosophy of reform and were profoundly taught in these great moral principles, the direct and legitimate outgrowth of the Bible, which stood them in better stead in the path through which they were destined to tread.[75]

Four years later, in May of 1840, Henry delivered his first public speech. He was twenty-five years old and he spoke at the American

Anti-Slavery Society in New York City. In the speech he challenged his audience "to listen to the shrill sound of the plantation horn, that comes leaping from the South, and [finds] an echo even among our northern hills." Henry was equally critical of the North for its racial prejudice. His speech was well-received, and no doubt the reception encouraged him to pursue an orator's life. William Lloyd Garrison, after hearing one of his speeches, commented, "Patrick Henry never spoke better." Henry was well-launched.[76]

Upon graduating with honors from Oneida in September 1880, he made his home in Troy, New York. Although he was not yet ordained, the Liberty Street Presbyterian Church of Troy asked Henry to be its minister. His theology teacher there was the well-known minister and abolitionist Nathaniel S.S. Beman. While studying to become a licensed minister, Henry also taught school. In fact, he created a sabbath school for young Black children in the community. He was committed to the church and its Black congregants, and determined for it to become fully established. By 1842 Henry had received his license to preach, and a year later he was ordained a minister—the first pastor of the Liberty Street Church. He continued in this role until 1848.

Studying, teaching, and ministering somehow still left Henry with time for other pursuits, including assisting in editing the *National Watchman,* an abolitionist paper out of Troy. He also edited the *Clarion,* which combined abolitionist and religious themes. Another endeavor was his efforts on behalf of the Temperance Movement. In 1843, he secured a stipend of $100 per year ($4,300 in today's dollars) from the American Home Missionary Society, combining his abolitionist work with his temperance work. But when the society objected to his engaging in politics from the pulpit, he severed ties with the group, even as he was receiving wide recognition for his temperance work—so much so that, in 1848, one of the Daughters of Temperance Unions in Philadelphia was named for him.

Henry also became involved in state politics via "Colored conventions," which occurred from the 1830 until the 1890s. Black men—free and once enslaved—met before the Civil War to discuss ways to achieve educational, labor and legal justice when these rights were being curtailed at all levels of the government. After the war, with many threats to the safety, labor rights, and land, education and legal rights, even more men participated.

Henry worked tirelessly to extend the franchise to Black men in New York State. This goal was thwarted by the state legislature when a qualification requiring owning property was inaugurated. Despite putting forth several petitions protesting the law to the New York legislature, it remained in effect until the Fifteenth Amendment in 1870. Of course, Henry had some choice words to express his disappointment and outrage:

> Ask a color hating politician when he does not want your vote if he favors emancipation and he would reply, 'Oh, no, that would destroy the country.' But the same politician would be quite another man if he needed a black person's vote.[77]

With the creation of the Liberty Party in 1839, Henry found a political group that strongly advocated for abolition. The national election of 1840 saw few votes cast for the new party, but it was determined to make a splash in 1844. Henry spoke forcefully at the party's 1842 meeting in Boston. His oratory helped convince the revived National Convention of Colored Men to endorse him at its meeting in Albany the next year. His words were impassioned and arousing:

> To accomplish the object in view we must feel for the slaves 'as bound with them,' we must place ourselves, so far as we can, in their position, and go forward with fixed consciousness that we are free or enslaved with them.[78]

He also sought to compel white people to feel what enslavement meant and what Black people were entitled to for having been enslaved: "Give us our freedom, remunerate us for our labors and protect our families for I cannot be free while there are millions of my countrymen who are wailing in the dark prison house of oppression."[79] It was a clear call for reparations!

Few doubted his speech-making ability after he succeeded in turning around a New York City meeting that sought to distance itself from the Liberty Party. The party peaked in 1844, after which time the Free Soil Party started to appeal to voters seeking reform. Free Soilers advocated "free soil, free speech, free labor, and free men," but their motives for advocating against the western spread of enslavement were questionable. William Lloyd Garrison labeled the party "white manism" as much of its motivation stemmed from wanting to protect white workers from the possibility of enslaved labor. The Republicans followed the Free Soilers with the goal of not only opposing the expansion of slavery but condemning the hateful institution on moral grounds as well.

With Henry's active engagement in politics, the stage was set for him to break with Garrison, who "rejected politics in favor of moral reform." At the Buffalo, New York, meeting of the Negro National Convention in 1843, Henry delivered what became known as his Address to the Slaves of the United States. As mentioned, this speech drew some of its inspiration from David Walker's Appeal, written in 1829, which many contend was the most radical anti-slavery document in history. The appeal called for the immediate abolition of slavery and argued for equal rights for Black people. Putting his life on the line, Walker wrote about "the hypocrisy of Christian slaveholders, urged African Americans to violently oppose their oppressors as necessary, and denounced the racism evident in proposed 'reforms' including plans to relocate free Blacks to a new colony in Africa."[80]

Henry, whose address first appeared in print in a preface to the second edition of Walker's Appeal, expanded on Walker's vehement opposition to slavery. He called for a general strike if masters refused to free their enslaved people voluntarily. He spoke unflinchingly: "If they, [the slave masters] then commence the work of death, they and not you, will be responsible for the consequences. It is far better to die than live as a slave and to pass a degraded status on to children." He poignantly challenged the enslaved:

> Brethren, arise, arise! Strike for your lives and liberties. Now is the day and the hour. Let every slave throughout the land do this, and the days of slavery are numbered. You cannot be more oppressed

than you have been—you cannot suffer greater cruelties than you have already. Rather die freemen than live to be slaves. Remember that you are FOUR MILLIONS!

The address is well worth reading in its entirety (see appendix) and assuredly deserves to stand alongside Frederick Douglass's "What to the Slave is the Fourth of July?" Its effect was immediate and dramatic. Nevertheless, it lost by one vote in an election held by the convention organizers to determine whether it should be endorsed.

Douglass, who found the speech overly violent in tone and content, led the opposition and secured additional votes in a second ballot. He got more support by criticizing the violence in the speech and he continued advocating for nonviolent means for at least a little longer to attain abolition. In the opinion of Dr. Carter G. Woodson, an American historian, author, journalist, founder of the Association for the Study of African American Life and History, and one of the first scholars to study African American history, it was with these votes that Douglass's influence went beyond that of Henry.

But that didn't stop the Address and its impact from spreading. Douglass bested Henry at the national level, but Henry played a major role in the state movement, especially among white abolitionists. Included among these supporters was John Brown, who is said to have published the address at his own expense and was significantly influenced by its precepts. But it wasn't until 1849 that Douglass accepted the need for violence to free enslaved people, just before the passage of a national Fugitive Slave Act on September 18, 1850, that required that any enslaved person found to be seeking his or her freedom be apprehended and returned to their enslaver even if they were captured in a free state.

In 1847, at another national meeting of the Negro National Convention held at Henry's church in Troy, the delegates again refused to endorse the Address. Douglass advocated for the role of education and propaganda, which served to soften the power of Henry's words. Nevertheless, a trio of those with more radical views was appointed by the convention to draft an address to the slaves—Garnet, Thomas von Rensselaer, who had escaped enslavement in 1819 from New York's

Mohawk Valley, and Amos G. Beman, whose grandfather, Cesar, earned his right to freedom by fighting in the Revolutionary War in place of his master. With his freedom, he took the name Beman, claiming his right to "be a man." It also passed a resolution that encouraged enslaved people to "instruct their sons in the art of war."[81]

Two years later, at a convention in Ohio, it was resolved that five hundred copies of both David Walker's Appeal and Henry's Address would be printed and distributed.

Another issue dividing the rivals was that Henry was at the epicenter of efforts to redress the ills of enslavement and also at the forefront of the movement advocating for enslaved people to return to Africa. He espoused a position proposed by the American Colonization Society (ACS) that was assuredly contentious. As early as 1817, most Black people fiercely opposed the ACS. They were both suspicious of its aims and of the nation it sought to create, Liberia, which became an independent country in 1847. Given his personal history with the deep and abiding pain of enslavement, it was with a sense of hope that there could be a place where Black people could be treated with respect and dignity that Henry came to favor Black emigration. His own suffering at the hands of racist whites as a free Black man in the summer of 1847, when he was choked, beaten, and thrown off a train in New York State, certainly factored into the evolution of his thinking. Here he describes the incident:

> I was told that colored people cannot be permitted to ride with the whites on this road, for southern ladies and gentlemen will not tolerate it...This was not a sufficient reason to [move my seat] and not being accustomed to yielding my rights without making at least a semblance of lawful resistance, I quietly returned towards my seat, when I was prevented by the conductor, who seized me violently by the throat, and choked me severely.

> I have been for many years a cripple. I made no resistance further than was necessary to save myself from injury; but nonetheless, this conductor and another person, whose name I do not know, continued to choke and to assault me with the first. A part of the time my

legs were under the cars near the wheels, and several persons were crying out—'don't kill him, don't kill him!'[82]

As a result of such mistreatment, and countless other such scenes he had witnessed or heard about, Henry, again breaking with Douglass, saw salvation in oppressed African Americans returning to Africa. He did not feel that four million uneducated and enslaved people could achieve equality in America. Of course, he promoted education, including starting a school for Black children in Geneva, New York. Garnet's pamphlet "The Past and Present Condition and the Destiny of the Colored Race," celebrating African history and achievements and advocating for social and political equality, was so eloquently persuasive that it is still being referenced and admired today.

Nevertheless, Henry's pamphlet and his rhetoric were simultaneously promoting a way out for enslaved African Americans. Voluntary colonization provided the out—the place where his people could lead their own lives free from the racism and oppression that even came with being "free" in America. He was inspired by the spirit of nationalism that was flourishing worldwide by 1848. He greatly admired Kossuth in Hungary, Mazzini in Italy, and O'Connell in Ireland, all of whom advocated for nationhood.

Henry believed that there would never be a path to economic equality for Black people who stayed in America. His immediate goal was the "evangelization, civilization and development of agriculture and commerce in the Yoruba Valley (now in Nigeria), while its larger purpose was the creation of a 'grand center of Negro nationality' that would unite Africans throughout the diaspora."[83] He created the African Civilization Society with the hope to accomplish these goals.

Henry also employed a different tactic. He had already tried political, religious, and moral appeals to gain support for abolition, so he devised an economic approach, promoting a boycott on all products grown by enslaved people in the South. The increasingly industrialized North, with its reliance on cotton for the burgeoning textile industry, was not going to risk losing its supply, so Henry realized the best chance to gain sufficient support to make a difference was in Great Britain. The effort to stop the importation of cotton and other Southern products was dubbed the Free Labor Movement, and the leaders of the movement invited Garnet to come to England in 1850.

His family joined him in 1851 and he remained on the speaking circuit for two and a half grueling years. As mentioned earlier, tragically, Henry and his wife, Julia, had lost their beloved seven-year-old son, James. Their shared grief prompted him to accept a position, offered by the United Presbyterian Church of Scotland, to be a missionary in Kingston, Jamaica. In accepting this role, Henry was the first Black man appointed to this mainly white organization. With this job he could focus on education and church work as well as spend some time with his family.

He did effective work in Jamaica until a severe prolonged illness caused his doctors to order him north. In 1855 he was called to Shiloh Church on Prince Street, where he became the successor of his mentor, Theodore S. Wright.

Henry and Douglass clashed fiercely over the issue of emigration of freed Black people to Liberia. Support for emigration was growing within the Black community. Henry's boyhood friend Alexander Crummell started a new life in Liberia after earning a degree from Cambridge University in London. He endorsed Henry's position as did Edward Wilmot Blyden, an influential West Indian. Nevertheless Henry had to face sharp criticism for his position in favor of colonization. Once again, his main critic was Frederick Douglass.

Henry made a trip to England as president of the ACS in 1861. In doing so, he created yet another cause célèbre—a civil rights breakthrough for the times. He insisted that his passport contain the word "negro." Prior to his efforts, the few passports Black people received avoided the issue of the bearer's race. Instead the bearer received a label like "dark." But thanks to Henry, that was forever changed.

Henry next planned a visit to Africa, but his trip was short-circuited by the start of the Civil War. He was obliged to let go of his dream of a life in what he saw as his mother country, as he joined with other Black leaders including his rival, Douglass, in calling for the creation of Black fighting units in the North. Although it took two years to convince the Lincoln administration of the value of Black soldiers, when the president finally agreed, in 1863, Henry traveled to recruit Black troops and even served as their chaplain in New York State.

He was steadfast in his opposition to the awful conditions the recruits faced on Riker's Island where they trained. Widescale corruption limited everything from access to weapons to fair pay. When new draft laws were enacted on July 13, 1863, to increase recruitment of white men in the military, the widespread anti-Black attitudes of many New Yorkers who resented having to go to war to fight for the freedom of Black people culminated in the horrors of the Draft Riots in New York. The false belief that free Black people took jobs away from white people ignited the riot, which was intensified by the pre-existing prejudice towards Blacks.

In the wake of the destruction caused by the Draft Riots, a group of prominent New York City merchants set up a relief committee for Black people left destitute and appealed to Black leaders for help. During a meeting of the committee, Henry delivered a speech that anticipated a sermon he would deliver just before the war's end that would have even greater significance. In addition, he effectively wed preacher with activist. "Intermingling biblical and secular discourse, he compared the merchants' charity to that of New Testament figures—before reminding them that they had not yet fulfilled their obligation to provide both jobs and protection to Black New Yorkers."[84]

In March 1864, Henry became pastor of the Fifteenth Street Presbyterian Church of Washington, DC. The following year, two months before the war's end and days before the passage of the Thirteenth Amendment freeing the enslaved, Henry was invited to deliver a sermon in the chamber of the House of Representatives. He was one of the first Black people allowed to enter the Capitol building—which had, along with the White House, been constructed by enslaved African Americans—and the first Black person to deliver a sermon there.

He called the speech "Let the Monster Perish," and it deserves to be commemorated and analyzed to understand its significance beyond Henry being the first African American to speak in the hallowed hall. He took the text from Matthew 23:4, in which Jesus enters the temple and chastises the scribes and Pharisees: "Woe to you, teachers of the law and Pharisees, you hypocrites! You shut the kingdom of heaven in men's faces. You yourselves do not enter, nor will you let those enter who are trying to." Here's how Garnet framed this passage: "They [the Pharisees] demanded that others should be just, merciful, pure, peaceable and righteous. But they were unjust, impure, unmerciful—they hated and wronged a portion of their fellowmen, and waged a continual war against the government of God."[85]

Henry placed himself in the role of Jesus and referred to American political leadership as the Pharisees. He focused his attention on what he called "this fearful national sin." He followed the biblical language of Matthew in depicting slaveholders as "those who bind heavy burdens...and lay them on men's shoulders" while experiencing neither compassion nor remorse.

He then expanded his view to include America's founders, whose secular laws as evidenced in the Declaration of Independence and the Constitution were predicated on "the Magna Carta of human rights" and the "lightnings of Sinai." To make his point he asked, "What is slavery?" In his answer he referenced his earliest memories of his childhood under slavery:

> The first sounds that startled my ear and sent a shudder through my soul were the cracking of the whip and the clanking of chains. These sad memories mar the beauties of my native shores and darken all the slaveland, which, but for the reign of despotism, had been a paradise.[86]

He generalized from his own experience to encompass the ways in which America's system of enslavement transformed human beings: "Slavery is snatching man from the high place to which he was lifted by the hand of God, and dragging him down to the level of the brute creation, where he is made to be the companion of the horse and the fellow of the ox." But Henry made it abundantly clear that this was not the fate of his fellow enslaved African Americans when he said:

> The caged lion may cease to roar, and try no longer the strength of the bars of his prison, and lie with his head between his mighty paws and snuff the polluted air as though he heeded not. But is he

contented? Does he not instinctively long for the freedom of the forest and the plain? Yes, he is a lion still. Our poor and forlorn brother whom thou hast labeled "slave," is also a man. He may be unfortunate, weak, helpless and despised and hated; nevertheless he is a man.[87]

Henry provides vivid and horrific detail of the impact of enslavement in robbing Africa of its people, the destruction of marriages, the breakup of families, and the loss of one's culture. He explores the history of those who opposed enslavement and paired religious and secular leaders— Plato and Augustine, Patrick Henry, and Jonathan Edwards, whom he quotes as declaring, "that to hold a man in slavery is to be every day guilty of robbery, or of man stealing." Unbeknownst to Henry, Edwards was actually an enslaver who preached such hypocritical words in the hometown of one of the authors, Northampton, Massachusetts.. He was striving to convey to his audience in the chamber, as well as to those in governing positions across the country, that the sacred and the secular must go hand in hand in their lawmaking.

Henry approached the end of his appeal—yes, it acted as an appeal, similar to the words David Walker used and to his own Address to the slaves—by looking to the future, asking: "When and where will the demands of the reformers of this and coming ages end?" Once again he answered his own question: "emancipate, enfranchise, educate." The difference this time, and his use of the imperative is essential to understanding his intent, was that he was not demanding that the enslaved "arise, arise." No, at this point in time he demanded that white America support Black America in its efforts to become full citizens.

Taken separately, "emancipation" meant that white America would free all enslaved people from bondage. "Enfranchisement" required that black males be granted suffrage "at the dictation of justice," and this would mean "a Constitution that shall be reverenced by all." He did not mean that the "education" he spoke of would be solely that of Black people. He was seeking the broadest vision of education, which would have to include whites. How disturbingly ironic that the same efforts to educate young white people about the true and full history of this country continues to meet with staunch, misguided resistance and fear. His awareness of the importance of representation was evident when he asked for the nation's literature and arts to avoid caricature and instead portray a more "faithful and just light on the character and social habits of our race."[88]

Henry concluded his sermon with a vision of what the country would look like to those watching from abroad:

> Then shall the people of other countries, who are standing tiptoe on the shores of every ocean, earnestly looking to see the end of this amazing conflict, behold a Republic that is sufficiently strong to outlive the ruin and desolations of civil war, having the magnanimity to do justice to the poorest and weakest of her citizens. Thus shall we give to the world the form of a model Republic, founded on the principles of justice and humanity and Christianity, in which the burdens of war and the blessings of peace are equally borne and enjoyed by all.[89]

We believe many readers of this book would join with us in proclaiming that America continues to struggle with "having the magnanimity to do justice to the poorest and weakest of her citizens" and with our capacity to "give the world the form of a Republic, found on the principles of justice and humanity in which the burdens of war and the blessings of peace are equally borne and enjoyed by all."[90]

We hope that many readers will join with us in seeing Henry's sermon as one of the outstanding orations in American history, distinguished both by his eloquent rhetoric and his message. We will do well to heed his call, much as Dr. King's Letter from Birmingham Jail asked all of us to recognize what still needs to happen if Henry's last paragraph is ever to become reality.

Following the end of the Civil War, Henry moved to Washington, DC, and became the editor of the Southern Department of the *Weekly Anglo-African*. One of his tasks was to see first-hand what was taking place in the South at war's end. Prior to his departure, the state of Virginia passed a law preventing Black citizens from voting, even though they had been given full protection of their rights under the military rule of General

Butler. Soon after his departure, the deeply distraught Black citizens of Norfolk commissioned him to write an "Address from the Colored Citizens of Norfolk, VA."

He began the address by accentuating the point that America was not exclusively a white nation and that Black people had fought and labored for the country as well. He then expressed his anguish that, in the two months since the end of the war, eight hundred Blacks had been incarcerated by a secessionist mayor, and all over the state Black people were being beaten for resisting forced labor. His words highlighted the accomplishments of Black people as well as their rights, which he felt they must demand. He expressed these principles in no uncertain terms in the address. He encouraged his listeners to be sure that "contracts made with Black workingmen be enforced." [91]

Henry's conviction, which he did not hesitate to include in this address, was that the surest way for Black people to gain equality was to own their own land. He urged his fellow Black citizens to establish associations through which they could invest in the land via mortgages so that once the mortgage was paid in full the land would be theirs. He concluded his address with the words, "Without economic power, political power has no meaning."[92]

His assignment to travel the South and report on what he saw took him to many places, but his visit to Louisville is the one most worthy of close examination. Delivering another prophetic sermon, this time at the Center St. Methodist Episcopal Church, he told his audience that it was far better "to work for Mr. Cash than Mr. Lash." He predicted the effect of Black men "making it" in a world that was still very much a white world, in the South and throughout America. "A Black man now looks better to whites than he used to. He looks taller, brighter and more like a man," he wrote, but his next words are tragically still the case: "[T]he more money you make, the lighter your skin will be, the more land and houses you get, the straighter your hair will be."[93] If only the approval and the standard of appearance and beauty were no longer defined by white people....

Upon his return from his four-month journey Henry wrote about his disillusionment and fears. He described the situation in the places he traversed as "totally unacceptable" with the "emancipation crumbling" as former slaveholders returned their "madness to the South." He went on to say that, these slaveholders would rather see "Black people blotted out of existence than to see them free." He felt strongly that unless the federal government realized the dire situation and provided a hundred thousand Black soldiers to safeguard the freed Black people, southerners would re-enslave them.[94]

Henry wrote that Johnson's reconstruction plan was a "disaster," but when he showed it to his former teacher, Beria Green, he tore it up and "smashed it into a thousand atoms."[95]

Not surprisingly, as the years progressed, Garnet continued to find himself in the middle of challenges and controversies. One noteworthy example was his effort to bring effective schools to his adopted hometown of Washington, DC. The controversy arose regarding the teachers. The Freedman's Relief Association was a private philanthropic organization that arose out of the need to prevent the federally endorsed and funded Freedman's Bureau from sinking under the weight of the enormous demands for funds. Henry welcomed the support offered by the Relief Association, but, characteristically, he resented the control the group insisted on exerting.

The association took the position that white teachers would do better than Black teachers in the new schools because most of the freed Black people were more comfortable with them. Henry took the opposite view and expressed his conviction that Black teachers would be much more effective because white teachers "did not understand the manhood of Black men." He argued that white teachers did no more than "corrupt the minds of Black people" and that "education can only be meaningful if it exists upon the basis of the equality of race." Henry's position likely alienated the Relief Association and resulted in less money being appropriated for the African Civilization School, with which he was associated.[96]

In 1868, the trustees of Avery College near Pittsburgh persuaded Henry to give up his position as pastor of the Fifteenth St. Baptist Church and become the school's president after the death of its founder. One of the richest cotton merchants in the city and a former Underground Railroad conductor, Charles Avery created the Allegheny Institute and Mission Church in 1849. Avery wanted to offer elementary and advanced education to qualified Black students without regard to sex. Only Black teachers were hired because Avery believed the Black man would show his true potential when "trained in an institution where he feels himself welcomed, at home, and taught by his own kind." It was renamed Avery College after his death in 1868.

The presidency was not Henry's finest hour as he struggled with administrative duties and lacked the expertise needed to make the college more viable. He was gone by 1870 and returned to his old position in NYC at the Shiloh Church. His beloved wife, Julia, died that year, and nine years later he remarried Susan Smith Thompkins, a noted teacher and principal.

While Henry's physical and mental condition had begun to decline, in 1881 he successfully lobbied President James Garfield to appoint him as United States Minister and Counsel General in Liberia, a position analogous to ambassador, fulfilling his lifelong dream to travel to Africa. Henry preached his farewell sermon at Shiloh on November 6, 1881, and landed in Monrovia on December 28. Unfortunately, Garnet died only a few months after his arrival, on February 13, 1882.

We would like to conclude this chapter with words from the 1928 journal article by William Brewer quoted at the beginning of this tribute. The portrait of Garnet was written long enough ago to really impress upon us that this man was once seen for the heroic and important role he played.

> Beginning in the 1830's Garnet truly blazed the way for negro abolitionists and kept the flame of freedom burning while the nation was absorbed with the problems of expansion and the contest over the extension of slavery in the Trans-Mississippi territories. On the platform and through the press Garnet's message was delivered in the defense of his oppressed fellow sufferers in bondage. With them he was able fully to sympathize in that he had escaped from that estate and knew the bitterness of slave life. Such experiences burned into his soul an ambition and determination to lead the way in protest and action for the liberation of his people. Like one crying in the wilderness, Garnet pointed out a way which was modified and finally adopted.[97]

The time has come, as other sources are acknowledging, to give Henry the recognition he so richly deserves. In so many ways he can be seen as the Malcolm X to Frederick Douglass's Dr. King of the nineteenth century. Just as it was Malcolm X who consistently pushed Dr. King to consider a more radical analysis and approach, Henry was a figure of immense power who stirred up tremendous controversy and really challenged Douglass. As is true for Malcolm X, his impact on the times through which he lived is immeasurable. It is our hope that with our tribute and that of others, Henry Highland Garnet's undeniable influence will be fully recognized and appreciated.

Mary Ann Shadd Cary, courtesy
of Library and Archives Canada
C-029977

Abraham Doras Shadd stamp,
courtesy of
Delaware Public Archive

CHAPTER 6

Mary Ann Shadd Cary
So Visible and So Vocal

A word about our decision to include a picture of Mary Ann Shadd Cary's father taken from a commemorative Canadian stamp is in order. This is partly due to the scarcity of images of any of this book's subjects, much less their parents. Beyond that, the stamp also testifies to the significance of Abraham Shadd. By dedicating himself to helping enslaved black people escape bondage and distinguishing himself in service to his adopted country of Canada, he clearly merits the honor the stamp represents. That he is pictured holding a lantern, symbolic of the offer of safety and succor of the Underground Railroad, of which he was a conductor, is yet another reason for his inclusion here.

But this is Mary Ann Shadd Cary's story, and she was a force of nature when being such a force, as a woman and Black person, was exceedingly risky. Here's how her *New York Times* obituary, which took far too long to be written for all the reasons racism provides, titled "Overlooked No More" begins, with Mary Ann's words:

> We should do more and talk less. We have been holding conventions for years. We have been assembling together and whining over our difficulties and afflictions, passing resolutions on resolutions to any extent. But it does really seem that we have made but little progress considering our resolves.

These words appeared in a long letter Mary Ann wrote in 1848, after Frederick Douglass invited readers of his *North Star* newspaper to submit. She was twenty-five years old and she was a woman of action, not just words. She was completely fed up with abolitionists who continued to support segregation in schooling and housing. She sought full equality and would accept nothing less.

There has been some recognition of the vital role Mary Ann played in our nation's history and in the abolition of enslavement. Jane Rhodes, who has written extensively about her, described Mary Ann's letter thus: "It was fearless, and it was fierce."

Her life of risk-taking and devotion to the cause began on October 9, 1823. We know the precise date because she was born in the slave state of Delaware to free parents, Abraham Doras Shadd and Harriet Parnell, both ardent abolitionists. She was the great-granddaughter of Hans Schad (alias John Shadd), originally from Hesse-Cassel in Germany, who served as a soldier with the British Army during the French and Indian War. When he was wounded, two African American women cared for him. They were mother and daughter and both named Elizabeth Jackson. John married the daughter in 1756. Their first son arrived six months later, possibly causing "a marriage of necessity as well as affection." Mary Ann's grandfather, Jeremiah Shadd, their second son, was born in 1758. "Thus a German soldier became the patriarch of a family of people of color."[98]

Mary Ann was blessed with strong female ancestors. Her great grandmother Elizabeth had a stellar reputation as both the proprietor of a popular tea shop in a prime location overlooking the Delaware River, and as a "consummate businesswoman." She was referred to as the "queen of her class" by a local author and the shop was "celebrated for its nice refreshments and everything was the best of its kind." Perhaps most significant, in terms of Mary Ann's ancestry, though: "while people of color seemed to be segregated from their white neighbors in some social circumstances, the Shadds had no difficulty attracting a white clientele."[99]

Another major factor besides Elizabeth's first-class food and drink was her lighter skin color. White people's domination of all facets of life meant that African Americans with the skin color closest to white had significant advantages. Both of Mary Ann's parents had white ancestors and were light-skinned. Though this did not serve to protect them from the racism that was fully institutionalized during Mary Ann's life, it did afford her some personal and economic freedom that her darker sisters and brothers did not possess.

Mary Ann's father, Abraham Shadd, a shoemaker, became a deeply committed abolitionist. His journey to becoming an Underground Railroad conductor was largely inspired by his fierce opposition to the "Back to Africa" movement promoted by the African Colonization Society (ACS). Based on his own family's experience, he believed that Black men and women, through freedom, education, and hard work, would successfully integrate into American society. The ACS believed that African Americans would never experience true freedom and equality in a country where enslavement was written into the Constitution. Its members' efforts to establish an African nation culminated in the creation of Liberia in 1847. When a branch of the ACS was formed in Wilmington two years later, Shadd Cary became an outspoken critic.

Motivated by his ongoing opposition to colonization for African Americans, Abraham became increasingly involved in the abolitionist movement. He began attending anti-slavery meetings both in Delaware and Philadelphia. In 1831 he was elected to the vice-presidency of a national meeting in Philadelphia.

By 1833 Shadd had had enough of Wilmington. Delaware was still very much a slave state. With events in the country deepening the polarization between North and South, being Black in Delaware was increasingly difficult. Even more personally, Abraham and Harriet were the parents of four daughters and one son. The schooling options were poor enough for boys—one school for Black children in Wilmington that met once a week—but the public schools didn't even accept girls. Shadd's decision to move his family to the free state of Pennsylvania was precipitated by the worsening climate in Wilmington. The Quaker influence in West Chester offered far more possibilities. Another factor in the decision to leave Delaware involved Abraham's increasingly prominent role in the abolitionist movement. He was elected president of the Convention for the Improvement of the Free People of Color in Philadelphia, but his involvement went beyond words and conventions. He and Harriet were actively involved in enabling enslaved people to become free. Their homes, first in Wilmington and later in West Chester, were stops on the Underground Railroad.

Upon their arrival in West Chester, Mary Ann and her sisters were enrolled in Price's Boarding School, founded by Quakers. From the age of ten to sixteen, Mary Ann received a Quaker education, yet another source of her abolitionist leanings.

After concluding her education, she was determined to provide similar school experiences for African American children and returned to Delaware, knowing the opportunities, especially for Black girls, were essentially nonexistent. For the next ten years she taught Black children there as well as in Norristown, Pennsylvania, and New York City.

With the passage of the Fugitive Slave Act in 1850, Mary Ann's involvement with the quest for freedom for her people intensified. The new law was condemned by abolitionists in the North because it denied escaping slaves the right to a jury trial and the chance to defend themselves in court. It also imposed heavy fines on anyone who assisted an enslaved person to escape.

In a powerful foreshadowing of the Black Lives Matter movement that began in 2013 to confront America with its systemic injustice toward Black people, Mary Ann felt the Fugitive Slave Act was so unjust that Blacks were better off moving to Canada and elsewhere to enjoy a better quality of life. Joined by her brother, Isaac, and his wife, Amelia Freeman Shadd, she made the move and did not look back. They settled across the border from Detroit in Sandwich (now Windsor), Ontario.

The experience moved her to write a pamphlet called "A Plea for Emigration or Notes of Canada West" in which she argued forcefully that the Fugitive Slave Act put all Black lives throughout the US in jeopardy. She provided details on where African Americans should settle and what their lives would be like. Fanning the fear the act engendered, her words inspired a significant migration, and by the end of the 1850s, fifteen thousand had followed her strong suggestion.

W.E.B. DuBois recognized the contribution that Mary Ann's pamphlet made to both saving and improving the lives of African Americans who, following her guidance, became African Canadians. He wrote about her in an essay called "The Damnation of Women":

> Well-educated, vivacious, with determination shining from her sharp eyes, she threw herself single-handed into the great Canadian pilgrimage when thousands of hunted Black men hurried northward and crept beneath the protection of the Lion's paw.[100]

On September 10, 1851, the first North American Convention of Coloured Freemen took place in St. Lawrence Hall in Toronto. It was the first to occur outside the US. Mary Ann attended. She watched Henry Bibb, Josiah Henson, and J.T. Fisher lead the convention of Black community leaders from all over Canada. Many of the delegates echoed the message of Mary Ann's pamphlet, encouraging enslaved Americans to come to Canada.

It was at this convention that Bibb and his wife, both activists and publishers of the newspaper *Voice of the Fugitive,* succeeded in persuading Shadd to teach at a school near their home in Sandwich, Ontario. She set up a racially integrated school for Black refugees from the US that was open to all children whose families could afford for them to attend, since Canadian education was not funded by the government. The school received considerable support from the American Missionary Association (AMA).[101] Here's what Mary Ann had to say about integrated schools:

> Whatever excuse may be offered in the states for exclusive institutions, I am convinced that…none could be offered with a shadow of reason, and with this conviction, I opened school here with the condition of admission to children of all complexions. [102]

Such a school did not conform to the education that the Bibbses favored—segregated schools. They had agreed on much, but as a result of this divergence, they and Mary Ann conducted a heated debate, much of which took place in *Voice of the Fugitive.* In letters to the newspaper,

Mary Ann "accused both the AMA and the Refugee Home Society (RHS) of catering to the slave mentality developed by those who were owned by white Christians."[103]

Mary Ann had put forth the notion that the new arrivals should be encouraged to become independent quickly rather than have them become dependent on begging (her term for accepting charity), which she accused the RHS of fostering. She believed white Canadians would only accept former slaves if they saw them as independent—not living on charity.

The Bibbs argued that "Black, racially exclusive education in all Black Canadian settlements was the best anti-slavery weapon Blacks could wield." They were convinced that "Black success with no help or interference from whites would provide indisputable evidence of Black self-reliance and achievement for skeptical whites." Mary Ann was vehemently opposed, convinced that Black people "could only overcome the arguments of white racists through self-help and rapid assimilation into white Canadian society." She saw that both races would benefit from being educated together, "because only exposure would guarantee each race's appreciation and respect of the other."[104] Thus she incurred the criticism and judgment of segregationists in the White community and Black nationalist views from some of those in her own community.

The Bibbs reacted with hostility and saw Mary Ann as a "public disgrace and a nuisance." She was definitely challenging the Black male establishment by entering a male-dominated public sphere. Men and women alike denounced her for what was considered improper conduct for a Black woman. In 1853, the public dispute caused her to lose the funding from the AMA that her school depended upon.

Not to be undone by this setback, Mary Ann moved on to yet another arena that same year. Recognizing the power of owning a newspaper, she founded one of her own, along with the Reverend Samuel Ringgold Ward. *The Provincial Freeman* was the first publication edited and published by a Black woman in North America. At the outset, the paper was produced in Windsor, but Toronto and Chatham, Ontario, eventually became the headquarters. The paper's slogan was "Devoted to anti-slavery, temperance and general literature," and its motto was "Self-Reliance Is the True Road to Independence." Its prospectus stated:

> It will open its columns to the views of men of different political opinions reserving the right, as an independent Journal, of full expression on all questions or projects affecting the people in a political way; and reserving, also, the right to express emphatic condemnation of all projects, having for their object in a great or remote degree, the subversion of the principles of the British Constitution, or of British rule in the Provinces.[105]

From the first issue, Mary Ann alienated some readers with her progressive and unorthodox views. She voiced strong disapproval for abolitionists who supported what she saw as half measures like segregated schools and communities. Another cause she took up was confronting refugee associations that gave financial support to fugitive slaves but refused to acknowledge the plight of free Black people in Canada who were living in poverty due to racism.

Shadd was not only seeking racial equality, but gender equity as well:

> The newspaper also implicitly championed women's rights, documenting the lectures of prominent American activists like feminist Lucy Stone and abolitionist Lucretia Mott. Moreover, it provided a forum for Black women, showcasing their talent and accomplishments. The paper sang the praises of such African American women as opera singer Eliza T. Greenfield and poet and orator Frances Ellen Watkins (later Harper). It also printed letters to the editor authored by Canadian Black women.[106]

Considering the powerful influence of her outspoken father, her private Quaker schooling, her engagement in the world of ideas, strong moral convictions, and cosmopolitan view of society, it is no surprise that Mary Ann's assertiveness found expression in her own newspaper. The paper's opposition to Harriet Beecher Stowe's *Uncle Tom's Cabin* was particularly scathing. She had this to say about a character in Stowe's book:

> One of the most manly specimens of oppressed human nature, in "Uncle Tom's Cabin," is George Harris. The manner in which Mrs. Stowe disposes of him, and the words she puts into his mouth, as reasons for his going to Liberia, always struck us as a piece of needless and hurtful encouragement of the vile spirit of Yankee colonizationism.

Of course, Mary Ann's incendiary views drew criticism. A writer for a rival paper opined that "Miss Shadd has said and written many things which we think will add nothing to her credit as a lady."

Such a remark would not have affected Mary Ann in the least. She encountered much criticism, especially from Black men in leadership roles. Women also took issue with her views, since she consistently put herself out there. Her actions challenged the prevailing attitude regarding women remaining in the home.

Having a Canadian readership for the *Provincial Freeman* was not enough for Mary Ann. Even though returning to the US entailed tremendous risk, she, the paper, and its message crossed the border. During these trips, she traveled on horseback and by stagecoach with the dual purpose of telling Black audiences about what life in Canada offered them and of getting folks to subscribe to the paper to keep it afloat. In her speeches, as in her writing, she was a strong advocate for self-sufficiency, consistently voicing opposition to segregation in schools and churches, and Black people receiving charity of any kind.

In 1856 Mary Ann married Thomas F. Cary, a barber who lived and worked in Toronto. Unfortunately, this meant she had to raise their daughter, Sarah Elizabeth, on her own, three hundred miles away in Chatham. Sadly, Thomas died while Mary Ann was pregnant with their second child, Linton.

The *Provincial Freeman* remained in publication until 1859, when financial struggles led to its demise. Shadd Cary never became discouraged and continued being a spokeswoman for equality and integration. She went back to teaching and taught at an integrated school in Chatham. As for the *Provincial Freeman*, historian Jason Silverman has argued that "The black press...engendered a sense of racial pride that was crucial to the well-being of the refugees in Canada West." Perhaps this was the newspaper's greatest achievement.[107]

With the start of the Civil War, Mary Ann returned to the US with her children. She saw a role for herself in encouraging Black men to enlist in the Union Army. After the war she chose to live in Washington, DC, and kept her commitment to children, founding a school for the children of former slaves. She maintained her conviction that education was the key to self-sufficiency for her people.

Not only did Mary Ann teach school while raising her children, she also enrolled at the newly created Howard University Law School. Breaking down another barrier, she attended evening classes where she was the only woman, and during the day she continued teaching. Despite the enormous rigors of this life, she graduated from Howard with a law degree in 1883 at the age of sixty—making her the second Black woman lawyer in the country.

Whatever else Mary Ann was engaged in—parenting, teaching, studying, writing—she never let it interfere with her work as a political activist. Her writing appeared in the African American newspaper the *New National Era*, and she continued to lecture Black people about the crucial importance of solidarity in the effort to leave enslavement behind.

Mary Ann next threw herself into the suffrage movement and addressed the House Judiciary Committee in January of 1874. She was a member of the National Woman Suffrage Association, working alongside Susan B. Anthony and Elizabeth Cady Stanton in demanding that Congress grant women the right to vote. She also became the first African American woman to vote in a national election.

When she addressed the House, Mary Ann began with these words: "I am not vain enough to suppose for a moment that words of mine could add one iota of weight to the arguments from these learned and earnest women," but then detailed how, as "a colored woman" and yet as "a resident of this district, a taxpayer," she was allotted only a portion of the rights of her male counterparts.[108]

For reasons having to do with who writes our history and how little valued have been the lives of Black women, Shadd Cary's legacy largely faded from view after her death from stomach cancer in 1893.

Despite all of the ways in which her devotion and tenacity to the abolitionist movement and the suffrage movement were extraordinary, she was both a woman of influence and a woman on the fringe.

> This seeming contradiction - that Shadd Cary would be viewed simultaneously as an object of respect and leadership and as an object of derision - is central to the story of the African-American woman.[109]

Thankfully, in the years since the civil rights movement and the women's movement legitimized the contributions of Black women such as Mary Ann Shadd Cary, her accomplishments, her strong will, and her undying dedication to the cause of freedom are finally appreciated. This is an affirmation of the degree to which she is fully recognized and appreciated in Canada:

> Perhaps her greatest contribution was the role she carved out for herself as a Black woman in the public sphere, whether as a teacher and community activist, writer, newspaper editor, public speaker, recruiting agent for the Union Army or lawyer. By pushing the boundaries and limitations normally ascribed to her race and sex, she blazed a trail not only for Black people but also for generations of women.

That numerous subjects of this book have not yet received their much deserved recognition for acting in defiance of the culture in which they lived is evidence of the systemic nature of racism. Thankfully Mary Ann Shadd Cary emerges from the shadows, in the sources we've cited and in this account of her extraordinary life, to take her rightful place in history and in the quest for justice and equality.

CHAPTER 7

Robert Morris
Crusader for School Integration, circa 1849, Boston

Courtesy of Boston Social Law Library

"He who knows the law is the more guilty if he willfully violates it, or incites others to do so," US Commissioner Benjamin Hallet said, as quoted in the March 10, 1851, edition of the *Boston Post*.

Hallett addressed this pronouncement to Robert Morris who, a month earlier, had joined a mob to free a fugitive slave. Hallet placed even greater blame on the man to whom he spoke because Morris was a lawyer, in fact, the first black lawyer to ever file a lawsuit in the United States. Moments later, Hallet ordered that Robert be charged with treason. Hallett continued:

> It is the defendant's own act which has brought him into the peril in which he now stands, and which, if committed by the most distinguished member of the bar, or the bench, would produce the same result and the same judgment that are now to follow as the consequences of that act.[110]

How did such a turn of events come to pass? When the full story is told, it will not appear to be such a contradiction that the first Black attorney in America to argue a case in front of a jury was subsequently charged with treason.

As with many of the subjects of this book, a precise date for Robert's birth is not known. The closest we can come is June 8, 1823. Little is known of his family other than that his grandfather was enslaved in Massachusetts and freed after the Quock Walker decision in 1783. The story of Quock Walker played out over a series of court cases, each of which had some influence on the ultimate result. The decision didn't end chattel slavery, but the acknowledgment of Walker's right to be free meant that enslavement would never again be upheld by the state courts of Massachusetts. It marked one of the earliest instances of a state's constitution being applied to a legal decision.

Since this decision had such far-reaching consequences, we have chosen to provide the actual charge to the jury in full. Many attribute the decision in *Commonwealth v. Jennison* to the abolition of enslavement in the state. Others at the time saw the weight of public opinion as an even more significant contributor to abolition. One prominent

American, John Adams, ascribed the abolition to "a measure of economy." Regardless, even though the constitution was never amended to specifically prohibit enslavement, Chief Justice Cushing's words had a deep and lasting impact, which was what provided the basis for Robert Morris's grandfather becoming a free man:

> As to the doctrine of slavery and the right of Christians to hold Africans in perpetual servitude, and sell and treat them as we do our horses and cattle, that (it is true) has been heretofore countenanced by the Province Laws formerly, but nowhere is it expressly enacted or established. It has been a usage—a usage which took its origin from the practice of some of the European nations, and the regulations of British government respecting the then Colonies, for the benefit of trade and wealth. But whatever sentiments have formerly prevailed in this particular or slid in upon us by the example of others, a different idea has taken place with the people of America, more favorable to the natural rights of mankind, and to that natural, innate desire of Liberty, with which Heaven (without regard to color, complexion, or shape of noses—features) has inspired all the human race. *And upon this ground our Constitution of Government, by which the people of this Commonwealth have solemnly bound themselves, sets out with declaring that all men are born free and equal—and that every subject is entitled to liberty, and to have it guarded by the laws, as well as life and property—and in short is totally repugnant to the idea of being born slaves.* [Emphasis added]. This being the case, I think the idea of slavery is inconsistent with our own conduct and Constitution; and there can be no such thing as perpetual servitude of a rational creature, unless his liberty is forfeited by some criminal conduct or given up by personal consent or contract.

Robert Morris's father, York Morris, was born free in 1786, three years after the Supreme Judicial Court supported Quock Walker's freedom. York was a well-regarded waiter in the homes of the wealthy white residents of Salem. Robert's mother, Mercy, as is too often the case with Black women, does not appear in the historical record, though we know that she gave birth to ten children in addition to Robert.

Robert experienced racial discrimination in Salem at an early age. There were no separate churches for Black people in Massachusetts, so they were obligated to sit in the balcony, or what the local whites referred to as "nigger heaven."[111] He also had to deal with segregation in school. There had been a school for Black students in Salem, but it was closed the year Robert was born, which meant Black parents were forced to enroll their children in white schools. That resulted in a protest by Salem's white citizens not unlike the fierce opposition that met the court-ordered busing of Black and white children in Boston 160 years later.

Salem's Black school, now called the African Writing School, reopened in 1827 but lasted only a year, with the school's lone teacher having to instruct seventy students of all ages in a single room. Another school opened in Salem in 1837, but it was too late for Robert. With next to no formal schooling, he followed in his father's footsteps. He went to work as a waiter and learned a great deal. His father inspired him to take equality of the races seriously. One such action was teaming up with Charles Redmond, (see Chapter 9) to dress up Black women as men to increase the Black vote for the Federalist Party, which was more favorable toward Black people's rights, including enabling them to vote. He also encouraged Robert to find ways to support the family, and waiting on tables was what his son came to do best.

It was while working as a waiter in the home of the lawyer John King that thirteen-year-old Robert caught the notice of Ellis Gray Loring. During one of the Loring family dinners at the King's home, Loring was favorably impressed by Robert's cleverness and demeanor. By the evening's conclusion Loring had decided to ask Robert to come to Boston with him to become his housekeeper. He asked Robert's mother, Mercy, for permission, which she granted, and Robert was soon headed to Boston with the Lorings.

We need to press the pause button before proceeding with Robert's saga. Tom's friend and collaborator on the play of his first book (*Called to Serve: Stories of the Men and Women Confronted by the Vietnam War Draft*, Peter Snoad, whose masterful work in creating "The Draft" gets a nod here), read this chapter. He had suggested that we include Robert after reading the book he lent Tom, upon which much of this chapter is based, *Sarah's Long Walk*. Peter is an anti-racism activist from Jamaica Plain, Massachusetts, and in an email after reading the Morris chapter he had this to say about Boston:

> Morris was a prominent activist in the free Black community on the North Slope of Beacon Hill, which itself played a defining leadership role in both the burgeoning abolitionist movement and early civil rights struggles (e.g. for equal education, desegregation of public spaces.) I think it's important to recognize and affirm this social movement context because, as we know, in our culture, crusading lawyers—indeed most unsung heroes—are often tagged as courageous independent actors. Stories like Morris's provide us with an opportunity to talk about social movements as the driving force for social change. Boston was a center of such a movement when the events you've depicted took place.[112]

Because he was a young Black person, Robert rode the thirty miles from Salem to Boston on the outside of the coach. He was quite frozen by the time they reached the city—an experience, along with many others he endured, that would surely contribute to the fervor he brought to his law practice and his efforts to promote equality.

Robert worked for the Lorings and lived within their household for the next ten years. It was a "warm, liberal environment where he was encouraged to learn and to closely observe and absorb the richness of the city called the Athens of America."[113] Robert impressed Loring with his devotion to books and his learning habits. At one point Loring commented, "Robert, you are capable of making something of yourself. Now I want you to tell me what you want to do and I will secure for you the opportunity to make the trail. Do you wish to learn a trade or do you wish to study law?" The choice Robert made transformed his life. Later on he expressed his gratitude:

> At a time when it was dangerous for a white man to utter a word of sympathy for a brother with a skin not colored like his own,

this good man showed his firm adhesion to principle by placing a colored boy in his office to fit him for those pursuits from which public opinion had proscribed him.[114]

The two men had similar values, but they differed in style and temperament. Their differences became more visible as Robert moved through his law studies. Loring gradually receded in his public role. His abolitionist friends noticed him becoming less confident in himself as a public speaker and removing himself from performing roles he had once enjoyed. In contrast, Robert gained a national reputation by his late twenties. He was seen as forthright and even aggressive. One could surmise that Loring was passing the torch to Robert from these descriptors of their respective behaviors and roles. Robert passed the bar on February 2, 1847, was admitted to the Court of Common Pleas, won his first court case, and "never looked back." Though there is no record of his first case, here's how Robert responded:

There was something in the courtroom that made me feel like a giant. The courtroom was filled with colored people, and I could see, expressed on the faces of every one of them, a wish that I might win the first case that had ever been tried before a jury by a colored attorney in this county...[115]

Looking forward, the case that was to become one of his three major involvements can also be seen to look backward to the past when he confronted the segregation of Boston's public schools as a child. The circumstances surrounding the case, *Roberts v. City of Boston*, mirrored some of the same impossible conditions that Robert faced when he was unable to further his own education.

In the early 1840s, Boston's free Black community leaders sought to have their children attend any public school in the city. Their efforts were consistently thwarted by a Boston School Committee that in 1846 declared, "The less the colored and white people become intermingled the better it will be for both races."

Alexis de Tocqueville could not comprehend the depth of racism he encountered in America, and when touring Boston he observed, "In Massachusetts the blacks have the rights of citizenship, they may vote in elections, but the prejudice is so strong that it is impossible to receive their children in the schools."[116]

Starting all the way back in 1787, Boston's Black parents were determined that their children have schools separate from their white counterparts. Teachers and students in the white schools were exceptionally prejudiced, subjecting Black children to constant mistreatment, denigration, and worse. With some meager financial help from the Boston School Committee, the all-Black Smith School was eventually set up, but the committee essentially took over its governance, providing an inferior building, grounds, and curriculum, paying the teachers so little that turnover was frequent, and burdening the staff with extra tasks beyond their teaching responsibilities, including appearing in police court on behalf of indigent children.

Enter Benjamin Roberts. As the father of the child who would be front and center in the first school desegregation case in American history, Benjamin would access his personal experiences with segregation:

> Traveling from the residences of our parents, there, we passed the doors of several schools, and while we witnessed the boys and the girls of our neighbors enjoying the blessings of the nearest schools to their homes, and we were not only compelled to go by them, but several others, as we passed, took particular notice of our situation; and we were looked upon, by them, as unworthy to be instructed in common with others.[117]

Benjamin was thus particularly sensitive to the unfairness of having his five-year-old daughter, Sarah, obliged to walk past fine all-white schools in order to attend the Smith School, which was not only mightily struggling due to the conditions imposed upon it by the all-white school committee, but was also a very demanding walk from their home, especially for a four-year-old. Benjamin sought relief for his child and petitioned the district committee for Sarah to attend the nearest school. His plea was denied—by the General School Committee. Monumentally frustrated, but undaunted, Benjamin tried enrolling his daughter in not one, but two different white schools, the first of which turned him down immediately and the second of which somehow enabled Sarah to be the first Black child in over fifty years to learn with white children.

This did not last, of course. Several months later, a police officer called by the school showed up to remove her. This traumatic event surely could have ended the quest for Sarah to attend a white school, but Benjamin had heard about a young Black lawyer who had managed, despite the odds against him, to defeat a white lawyer in court and by so doing become an instant celebrity.

Roberts believed that denying his daughter the right to an education at a neighborhood school was in violation of both the US Constitution and Massachusetts laws pertaining to the rights of *all* residents. With this assertion as the strategy to be employed, Roberts was convinced that a favorable decision was possible.

Meanwhile, Robert Morris was looking for distraction. His wife of a year had converted to Roman Catholicism, much to his chagrin, and he was available to take Roberts's case. That he would be mightily challenged to come up with convincing legal arguments was not a deterrent. Of course, the Fourteenth Amendment, unfortunately still almost twenty years away, was not available What he did have was the 1780 Massachusetts Declaration of Rights that stated, "All men are born free and equal."

The suit Morris brought rested on the 1845 statute that provided monetary compensation for any child prevented from attending Boston's schools. The basis for using this statute was that segregation denied school privileges, uncannily similar to the arguments used in *Brown v Board of Education* over 100 years later. Coincidentally, Morris's wife, Catherine, gave birth to their first child the year before the suit was filed, no doubt adding to his determination to win this case so his son, Mason, could attend a neighborhood school regardless of his race.

Morris focused his arguments on the notion of children attending the school nearest to their residence, which was expressly stated in the School Committee rule concerning assigning students. In addition, what was emerging from the case was the moral principle that segregation created inferior schools. Despite such powerful arguments, not surprisingly, the court found in favor of the school committee.

But it turns out this was never a simple case that pitted Black integrationists and their white allies against white segregationists. Numerous free Black men and women opposed integration and wanted to maintain the Smith School, largely because of their experience of racism. They were deeply concerned that, without any schools exclusively for Black children, they would inevitably suffer mistreatment at the hands of white schoolchildren, teachers and parents. They strongly opposed Morris's lawsuit and expressed their opinions vehemently at many meetings between the two sides. Eventually those supporting integration began a boycott of the Smith School in 1844 that lasted over 5 years. During this period, tensions simmered.

On September 17, 1849, Black integrationists blocked the entrance to the Smith School. Having pulled their own children out of the school, they had chosen to keep *all* of the Black children out of the segregated institution. The police were eventually called, and it requires a leap of the imagination to picture, "unlike the late 1950s scene in Little Rock, the police then escorted children *into* a segregated black school to avoid the threat of militant integrationists."[118]

The attempted blockade caused a major backlash. Some of the angrier segregationists started heaving cobblestones into the church where both sides had gathered for an attempt to come up with a plan. The police were called for a second time, and efforts to get both sides talking in subsequent days failed. Instead, as the date for an appeal of the original case approached, an article in the *Boston Post* projected a negative outcome should the effort to integrate the school be successful:

> If this desegregation became a reality, these [Black] students would again encounter the kind of harassment that made them demand separate schools in the 18th century. Otherwise whites would leave the Boston schools.[119]

Women deserve much credit for maintaining hope and confidence even in the darkest moments when the men became dispirited. Robert sought to inspire both sexes at a meeting of integrationists when he said, "Let us war upon the whole scheme of wickedness, and let the measures for our success become the great thought of our lives." He was most definitely ready for round two.

Charles Sumner was a staunch abolitionist. In 1849, when Robert asked him to argue the *Roberts* case on appeal, he was so enthusiastic about the cause of integration that he accepted without payment. Sumner was considered a strong supporter of equal rights for Black people, about whom Frederick Douglass said, "None have uttered the feelings of the Black man so well."

Robert presented the facts with which he was more familiar than Sumner and his comrade, again not able to reference the future Fourteenth Amendment's Equal Protection clause, was obliged to make an argument predicated on moral and philosophical grounds. Sumner felt most comfortable with such arguments and enthusiastically sought compelling points to present. He argued that Massachusetts was founded, based on its constitution, on the eradicating of all forms of inequality. He continued with his most impassioned plea, "They [the committee] cannot in any way violate that fundamental right of all citizens, equality before the law. To suppose that they can do this would place the Committee above the Constitution." Sumner even went so far as to assert that "the whites themselves are injured by the separation. Who can doubt this?" In doing so, he made one of the core arguments in defense of affirmative action that would be made in the 1960s.

Arguing for the city, Peleg Chandler cited the "separate but equal" argument along with the substantiation of the school committee's legal right to create the schools that it saw fit. He believed the justices of the state's Supreme Court would be sympathetic to such appeals.

Optimism was widespread in the Black community following the powerful and persuasive seeming arguments of Robert and Sumner, so it was particularly devastating when the court issued a unanimous judgment in favor of the school committee.

What followed, though insufficient to douse the feelings of despair and anger triggered by the verdict, was an effort to bring political pressure to bear upon the state legislature. The result of this effort was a law passed in 1855 by the House that mandated that, "In determining the qualifications of scholars to be admitted into any public school, or any district school in this Commonwealth, no distinction shall be made on account of race, color, or religious opinions of the applicant or scholar."[120]

It must be sadly pointed out that forty-six years after the decision in *Roberts v. City of Boston*, the US Supreme Court cited the case's ultimate acceptance of the notion that separate could be equal in its verdict in *Plessy v. Ferguson*. The court completely ignored the 1855 law passed by the Massachusetts legislature and instead issued a verdict that lasted until it was undone in 1954 in *Brown v. Board of Education*. The NAACP legal team's brief in that case, very likely the most important decision in civil rights history, drew upon the arguments Robert and Sumner had made in *Roberts v. City of Boston*. They quoted extensively from *Roberts* and referred to the lawyers' argument as "one of the landmarks in the crystallization of the egalitarian concept."[121]

Now to return to the events that began this chapter. With the passage of the Fugitive Slave Act, virtually concurrent with the loss on appeal of the school integration case, an enormous impediment was put in the path of those escaping enslavement. Nowhere was the impact of this dreadful law more profound than in Boston. Slave catchers descended upon the city driven by the profit motive and now empowered with the full force of the law behind them to bring those who had succeeded in escaping back to their owners.

Shadrach Minkins was working as a waiter in a Boston hotel when he was captured. The abolitionist community was outraged, and a group of between one hundred and two hundred Black and white abolitionists stormed the courthouse, enabling him to escape. Of course, this was against the Fugitive Slave Act. Robert wanted to defend Minkins in court but was unable to do so, since the new law denied legal recourse. But he was crucial in helping Minkins make his escape. Robert had prepared a habeas corpus request that enabled him to go in and out of the courtroom. When he saw the opportunity, he flung open the doors, and twenty armed Black men stormed in and left with Minkins. Minkins briefly hid in the attic of a Black woman sympathetic to his cause and left Boston that night, headed for Canada and freedom. But Robert and one of his key co-conspirators, Lewis Hayden (see Chapter 18), were in serious jeopardy. Hundreds had witnessed their federal crime, but they chose to return to their jobs as if there was no reason to be concerned.

The story exploded in the newspapers and eventually made its way to the desk of President Millard Fillmore. He was enraged and held a special session of his cabinet where he issued a proclamation calling for the apprehension of Minkins with the assistance of civil and military personnel and the serious prosecution of the abettors.

It took about two weeks before Robert and nine other Bostonians were arrested, facing $2,000 bail ($70,000 in today's dollars). Josiah Quincy, former mayor of Boston, donated the necessary funds to free Robert from jail. Prior to his trial, there were some encouraging developments. John Hale, a senator from New Hampshire and a staunch abolitionist, had agreed to defend him. He also learned that his friend Lewis Hayden had been acquitted of similar charges in a separate trial and that the grand jury had reduced the charge against him from treason, for which a conviction could have resulted in the death penalty, to a misdemeanor. Still the possibility of six months apart from his family and a $1,000 fine ($35,000 in today's dollars) was cause for great anxiety.

The trial began on November 4, and the prosecution's case essentially consisted of two young men's testimony that they'd seen Robert committing the crime, one asserting that he'd seen him with his arm "laid across Minkins's hip, as I have seen friends walk together," as Minkins was escaping. Their testimony was intended to prove that the rescue was premeditated and thus treasonous.[122]

The defense was predicated both on Robert being swept up by the mob supporting Minkins and on the unconstitutionality of the Fugitive Slave Act. Hale went further to assert that there was no plan to free Minkins—that it was spontaneous and therefore unpremeditated. He even sought to demonstrate that Minkins's enslaver could not prove that Minkins was a slave under Virginia law.

Numerous witnesses including Josiah Quincy testified to the fine character of Robert. Quite remarkably, the judge who had ruled against him in the *Roberts v. City of Boston* case, Chief Justice Lemuel Shaw, took the stand and spoke on Robert's behalf, saying "[a] better witness for a Boston jury could not be found." Hale ended his defense with these words:

> You have got to swear he was a SLAVE! That a man whom God made and whom Christ redeemed was a SLAVE, a thing, and not a MAN! And you have got to find that there was a conspiracy, because parties have intimated to officers of this Court that there was a God in Heaven who would judge them for their works.[123]

Thus did Hale make it abundantly clear that if the jury found the Fugitive Slave Act defied the Massachusetts constitution, it must acquit his client. The judge's charge acknowledged this, but he told the jury they were not to consider the legality of the federal law, but rather to rule on the "facts as found" He posed the jury's role this way: "If he was present and did nothing to prevent it, this would render him guilty."[124]

The jury began its deliberations at 2:30 PM and returned its verdict about seven hours later. Here is the editorial from William Lloyd Garrison's *The Liberator's* November 14 edition announcing that Robert had been acquitted of all charges:

> The rescue of Shadrach was so noble and praiseworthy an affair, that we hardly know whether to congratulate Mr. Morris on the return of a verdict, which, while it saves him from fine and imprisonment, cuts him off from the historical renown which would have attached to his name, in case he had been convicted. But we are glad that the malice of wicked men has been frustrated. It is some honor to have been tried on such an accusation.[125]

Robert had one more arena in which to demonstrate his complete devotion to equality for African Americans. He had begun his quest in the mid-1850s by helping to form a Black military company, the Massasoit Guards (named after a revered Wampanoag tribal leader), which defied laws that stated only white men could take up arms. His efforts encountered resistance in the North as well as the South, since the majority of white people were raised to see Black men as threats to, not defenders of, law and order.

Robert fought long and hard to have the "whites only" designation removed, but it was not to be. The company dissolved without receiving federal or state recognition, only to be replaced by a group of Black soldiers known as the Liberty Guard, who did not seek such acknowledgment.

As the Civil War approached and many Black men saw the opportunity to fight for freedom with the Union Army, numerous issues arose. The leaders of the Black community incorrectly assumed that equal pay would not be an issue, but Robert in particular, saw that who commanded the Black units was of particular importance insofar as a manifestation of equality...or not. The governor put forth his plea to Charles Sumner, Robert's former co-defense attorney in the Roberts case, but the War Department refused to accede to the demand for Black non-commissioned officers to head up the Black company. A colleague of Robert's summed up the situation: "Equality first, guns afterward."[126]

Resorting to a technique that had proved effective in the school desegregation case, Robert urged potential enlistees and recruits to boycott the call to arms. Many Black men did ultimately enlist in the Massachusetts 54th Regiment under the leadership of Robert Gould Shaw, a white man who condemned the boycott. But it is of note that there were far fewer from Boston who chose to fight for the Union thanks to the Robert-initiated boycott.

Abraham Lincoln eventually came to see the essential role Black soldiers were playing, and with their success and his praise, more volunteered, but it is well worth recognizing that the dot connection between military service and equality was not solely a result of the exemplary service performed by Black soldiers. It was also forged in the struggles over recruitment, equal pay, and Black commissioned officers.

These struggles challenged white Americans to understand Black enlistment in the Union military not as an unthinking or inevitable response to Lincoln's invitation, but as a self-conscious moral and political act. By insisting on complete equality as a bedrock principle, these rebels and dissenters helped policymakers and citizens throughout the Union see African Americans in the terms Robert had long dreamed of: not just as men willing to don a uniform, but as fellow citizens, cognizant of their rights and determined to secure them.

In conclusion, we want to recognize formally a source we have relied on for considerable parts of Robert's story, a book that at long last pays homage to his contributions, titled *Sarah's Long Walk*, by Stephen and Paul Kendrick. Notwithstanding this book's existence and its merits, once again as with several of the personages in this book, their fame is localized and needs to be nationalized. Once a brighter light is shined upon the justice Robert and the others sought in their communities, we will be much better able to see the significance of their work for our culture.

Courtesy of Library of Congress, LC-USZ62-110530

CHAPTER 8

John Stewart Rock
First Black Supreme Court Lawyer and Always Supreme Spokesman for His People

"Black is beautiful" is a phrase we associate with the rise of the Black Power movement of the sixties, but it had a significantly earlier start. Indeed, a version of these words entered the rhetoric of the civil rights movement as a result of a fashion show in 1962, but the eminent jurist John Stewart Rock coined a close facsimile of this phrase—in 1858!

That might have been enough to enable him to be included in this project, but there was so much more to distinguish him in his far too brief life. He seemed to know his life would be short, because he succeeded in opening up a dental practice, and becoming a doctor aiding injured escaping slaves. And then, when it appeared that there just couldn't be enough hours in the day unless he gave up sleep, he became a lawyer and the first Black man to be admitted to the US Supreme Court. Living the lives of at least three people, John Rock richly merits inclusion here, despite the speed at which his candle burned.

John Stewart Rock was born free in Salem County, New Jersey, on October 13, 1825. His parents could have followed the common practice of having him work rather than getting an education, but they saw his potential and evidently believed he could accomplish more by going to school than adding to the family income. John repaid their commitment to his learning by demonstrating his pleasure in acquiring knowledge and his brilliance as a student. His education continued until he reached the age of eighteen, and a year later he became a Greek and Latin teacher at a Black public school in Salem, Massachusetts.

Teaching was not to be John's only career. Instead, while still working at the school from 1844–1848, eventually becoming its director, he apprenticed with two white doctors, Quinton Gibbon and Jacob Sharpe. His teaching day over, he would head to the doctors' libraries to glean all the knowledge he could from their books. Despite being "exceptionally well versed in medicine," he was denied admission to medical school in 1848 because of the color of his skin, (as happened to James McCune Smith, discussed in Chapter 5).[127]

Undaunted—a characteristic that comprehensively describes his life—instead of leaving the country to study as Smith had done, John turned to dentistry, pursuing a similar path of apprenticing with a white dentist, Dr. Harbert, and studying intensely on his own. Having obtained a dentistry certificate, in 1850 he opened a private practice in Philadelphia. A year later he received a silver medal for creating a unique set of silver dentures that went on display.

But John had not given up on becoming a physician. He gained admission to Philadelphia's American Medical College and received his medical degree at the age of twenty-six in 1852, becoming the second African American to achieve a degree in medicine. Thus, by the age of twenty-seven, John had overcome prejudice that would have denied him a career as a doctor or a dentist and added both to his teaching skills.

While still in Philadelphia, he not only gained recognition as an exceptional doctor, but also for his passionate support for his fellow Black Americans. He had married Catherine Bowers in 1852, and the following year they moved farther north to Boston's Beacon Hill, with its vibrant African American community. Considered the most liberal city in the country at the time, Boston is where John set up a medical and dental practice and provided care to many fugitive slaves seeking freedom via the Underground Railroad, especially after the passage of the Fugitive Slave Act in 1850. He also treated members of an integrated abolitionist organization, the Boston Vigilance Committee, which assisted escaping Black people targeted by the new law. As a member of this group, he participated as a delegate in the Colored National Convention in Philadelphia in 1855. The following year he requested the Massachusetts legislature to delete the word "colored" from voting and tax lists.

Not content to simply have three occupations, John became an acclaimed orator in the cause of the emancipation of his people. At the age of twenty-five, he delivered his "Address to the Citizens of New Jersey," demanding that the disenfranchised Black citizens of New Jersey be given the right to vote. The powerful speech was published by Frederick Douglass in the February 8, 1850, edition of the *North Star*. Here is an illustrative excerpt:

> Although the above Declaration declares that "all men are created free and equal," those noble words, in their common acceptation, do not and cannot apply to the disfranchised people I am now speaking of, because, indirectly, you deny the disfranchised are men. You say that all men are created free and equal and at the same time, you deny that equality, which is nothing more nor less than denying our manhood. If we are not free and equal, (according to the Declaration of Independence), we are not men, because "all men are created free and equal."

> There are many reasons why colored men should be enfranchised. We have been reared in this State, and are acquainted with her institutions. Our fidelity to this country has never been questioned. We have done nothing to cause our disfranchisement; on the contrary, we have done all a people could do to entitle them to be enfranchised. [128]

In 1856 John received an invitation to speak on "Unity of Human Races" before the state legislature. The following year he returned to Philadelphia and delivered a lecture titled "The Light and Shadows of Ancient and Modern Tribes of Africa." In an issue of the *Liberator*, William Lloyd Garrison noted how the speech was so well-received that he hoped John would agree to present a similar version of the speech if he returned.

It was in the midst of a speech in Faneuil Hall on Crispus Attucks Day (honoring the man of African and Indigenous descent believed to be the first American to die in the Revolutionary War) that John, who was tall and dark-skinned, asserted the idea that Black is beautiful. His words proclaiming the "inherent beauty" of African people and their culture repudiated the prevalent view in white America that African Americans were unattractive.

As it turns out, John did not say "Black is beautiful." Not exactly, but he spoke so eloquently and forcefully of the beauty of Black people, praising "the beautiful, rich color of the negro," that his words marked a turning point in how Black people were encouraged to feel about their physical appearance:

> I will not deny that I admire the talents and noble characters of many white men. But I cannot say that I am particularly pleased with their physical appearance. If old mother nature had held out as well as she commenced, we should, probably, have had fewer varieties in the races. When I contrast the fine tough muscular system, the beautiful, rich color, the full broad features, and the gracefully frizzled hair of the negro, with the delicate physical organization, wan color, sharp features and lank hair of the Caucasian, I am inclined to believe that when the white man was created, nature was pretty well exhausted-but determined to keep up appearances, she pinched up his features, and did the best she could under the circumstances. (Great laughter.)
>
> I would have you understand, that I not only love my race, but am pleased with my color; and while many colored persons may feel degraded by being called negroes, and wish to be classed among other races more favored, I shall feel it my duty, my pleasure and my pride, to concentrate my feeble efforts in elevating to a fair position a race to which I am especially identified by feelings and by blood.[129]

It took a hundred years or so for the enormous significance of John's words to be recognized. In early 1962, New York's African Jazz-Art Society & Studios (AJASS) staged a fashion show at a Harlem nightclub called

Courtesy of the Philip Martin Gallery, Los Angeles

the Purple Manor. The event, called "Naturally 62," aimed to promote African culture and fashion. The models were what made the show revolutionary. They had "unabashedly dark skin and natural, unprocessed, curly hair," none of which, theretofore, was considered "fashionable" by the mainstream white fashion industry. Robert Gumbs, an AJASS member, put it this way: "It was a pioneering concept, women coming on stage wearing their hair in a natural way. We didn't know how the community would respond. I think a number of people came to laugh."[130]

By evening's end not only was no one laughing, but the models were receiving cheers. The show's slogan—"BLACK IS BEAUTIFUL"—which was printed on promotional flyers, became a "rallying cry and movement celebrating natural hair, darker skin and African heritage."

The photographer, Kwame Brathwaite, AJASS and Grandassa Models co-founder, deserves much of the credit for popularizing the phrase and its meaning. His photographs would soon appear in influential magazines such as *Ebony* and *Harper's Bazaar* and the images of naturally coiffed black women resulted in the hiring of darker-skinned models. Given his advocacy of Black beauty, Mr. Rock would surely be gratified by these manifestations of his efforts to celebrate Blackness.

It was not until February 2018 when Brathwaite, his son, and the Ghana-born designer Mimi Plange gave a talk at the Metropolitan College of New York that his pioneering "Black is Beautiful" work received the recognition it deserved. Not only did the phrase launch numerous modeling careers, but it also started fashion trends, TV shows and "changed the landscape of American pop culture making it far more open and colorful."[131]

Here's how the concept for the fashion show evolved. In the late 50's Brathwaite and his elder brother, Elombe, were motivated to start AJASS to promote African inspired jazz musicians and to foster Black pride. Seeing the African Nationalist Pioneer Movement's Miss Natural Standard of Beauty Contest in 1961 widened their vision. Their goal was to show Black women, "that they didn't need to spend so much time and money trying to tame their natural tresses." They were troubled when the winner picked up her prize in a processed hairdo. "We have to do something to have these women feel good about themselves. To have pride in their natural beauty," Kwame told his brother.[132]

At this point Africa was considered a primitive continent and the white world did not see it as a source of either culture or beauty. "That wariness of appearing too conspicuously 'African' was why, in the late 1950s and '60s, most Black women had their hair chemically processed or straightened with a hot comb." Even Black oriented magazines like Ebony presented models with light skin, Caucasian features and straightened hair. Those women who didn't process their hair were often the victims of discrimination and taunting. "Women could get fired from their jobs (for wearing their hair natural) because it was interpreted as being militant," said the sister of Jean, a former Grandassa model. "Even within the Black community, people would laugh at my sister."[133]

Fast forward to the present day, and there are still many states that do not protect Black women's fundamental right to wear their hair as they choose. The House of Representatives passed the CROWN Act ("Creating a Respectful and Open World for Natural Hair Act of 2022"), affirming this right nationally, in September 2020. As of July 2023, twenty-four states have passed a version of the bill. The Senate has yet to act. Here are some of the findings contained in the House bill that accentuate the need for federal protection of the right to wear one's hair how one chooses:

> Racial and national origin discrimination can and do occur because of longstanding racial and national origin biases and stereotypes associated with hair texture and style.

> For example, routinely, people of African descent are deprived of educational and employment opportunities because they are adorned with natural or protective hairstyles in which hair is tightly coiled or tightly curled, or worn in locs, cornrows, twists, braids, Bantu knots, or Afros.

> Racial and national origin discrimination is reflected in school and workplace policies and practices that bar natural or protective hairstyles commonly worn by people of African descent.[134]

Former Grandassa model Eunice Townsend, who went on to study speech and language pathology after her fashion stint, said, "Blacks had tried to emulate and assimilate into society because we had been outcasts for so long. So for one to step out and do something different, you were sort of ostracized." Townsend, who is now 71 and lives in Harlem, told The Post that she had never thought about wearing "Afro-centric" clothes or "being natural" before joining Grandassa, but once she did, the ridicule she faced only made her more defiant. Defiance thus continues to be a necessary response to systemic racism.[135]

Over time the "Naturally" shows became "a reminder of how even when faced with intense social violence, Black people continue to find ways to express themselves with style," according to historian Tanisha C. Ford, author of Liberated Threads about Black style. "They show that

Black people have long been having our own conversation around beauty and style, and have influenced the most popular fashion and beauty trends around the world."[136]

John Rock used his oratorical gifts to enhance the self-esteem of Black men and women as well as to advocate for direct action in his speeches. He practiced what he urged others to do by helping to organize the new, anti-slavery Republican Party. In an 1858 speech, he expressed his view that African Americans should use violence and self-improvement to end enslavement. Strongly criticizing the Dred Scott decision of 1857, John said, "No man shall cause me to turn my back upon my race. With it I will sink or swim." He was a staunch supporter of John Brown's raid on Harpers Ferry and on Crispus Attucks Day in 1860 he repeated his views on Black empowerment.[137]

Unfortunately, in 1858 John developed a chronic illness with unknown diagnosis that represented a serious threat to his health. Because he had direct knowledge of the latest medical developments, he reached out to a well-known group of French doctors and they agreed to have him as one of their patients. Sadly, an ugly example of racism threatened his treatment. Due to the Dred Scott decision and its denial of rights of citizenship to Black people, Secretary of State Lewis Cass refused to allow John to obtain a passport. Chief Justice Roger B. Taney, in his opinion, wrote that a Black man "had no rights which the white man was bound to respect."[138]

To its credit, the state of Massachusetts overrode this decision and issued John a passport of its own, describing him as a citizen of the commonwealth. John was able to visit France, during which time he had the opportunity to tour the country and study its language, but his prognosis was not encouraging. He was strongly advised to give up his dental and medical practices.

In Europe, undaunted by his health crisis, he took up the study of both French and German. In 1860, he gave a lecture that showed both his command of the two languages and his deep admiration for Madame de Staël, whom he described to his audience as an "active opponent" of Napoleon. He also made remarks to the effect that "women were the intellectual equals of men."[139]

Upon his return to America, John continued to try to regain his health, no doubt overruling his physicians. In place of his dental and medical work, which he had been forced to give up due to his health issues, he chose another demanding career as...a lawyer. On September 14, 1861, just months after the start of the Civil War, J. K. Lothrop, a white lawyer, asked Judge Russell to arrange for John to be examined. He passed the exam and gained admission to the Massachusetts Bar Association.

Months earlier, in April, John had become president of the "colored citizens of Boston" (each month a different president was elected) and endorsed the measure introduced by Robert Morris (Chapter 7) calling for the federal government to permit Black men to enlist in the Union Army. At a meeting called to discuss the measure, he aimed to create a Home Guard of Black Men, charged with defending the lives and the property of all Boston's citizens. Rock had much success as a lawyer, but he was never able to enjoy his achievements while his fellow Black people continued to be enslaved. "An educated negro," he said, "feels the oppression much more than does an uneducated one."[140]

After a brief improvement in his health, he began another slow, steady decline. Nevertheless he remained outspoken against injustice. At a meeting of Boston's Anti-Slavery Society in early 1862, he expressed his staunch opposition to Lincoln's plan known as "negro colonization"— sending freed Black people to Haiti. In so doing, he echoed Frederick Douglass in the belief that the US was the home of African Americans. John's eloquence was on full display in the speech as he spoke of his country in the midst of the Civil War. The entire speech is brilliant, but here are the last two paragraphs:

> I believe the conduct of both the bond and the free has been exceed-ingly judicious. It is times like these that try men. It is storms and tempests that give reputation to pilots. If we have a foreign war, the black man's services will be needed. Seventy-five thousand freemen capable of bearing arms, and three-quarters of a million of slaves wild with the enthusiasm caused by the dawn of the glorious opportunity of being able to strike a genuine blow for freedom, will be a power that "white men will be bound to respect." [Applause.] Let the people

of the United States do their duty, and treat us as the people of all other nations treat us—as men; if they will do this, our last drop of blood is ready to be sacrificed in defense of the liberty of this country. [Loud applause.] But if you continue to deny us our rights, and spurn our offers except as menials, colored men will be worse than fools to take up arms at all. [Hear, hear.] We will stand by you, however, and wish you that success which you will not deserve. [Applause.]

This rebellion for slavery means something! Out of it emancipation must spring. I do not agree with those men who see no hope in this war. There is nothing in it but hope. Our cause is onward. As it is with the sun, the clouds often obstruct his vision, but in the end we find there has been no standing still. It is true the government is but little more antislavery now than it was at the commencement of the war; but while fighting for its own existence, it has been obliged to take slavery by the throat, and sooner or later must choke her to death. [Loud applause.] Jeff Davis is to the slaveholders what Pharaoh was to the Egyptians, and Abraham Lincoln and his successor, John C. Fremont [Applause.], will be to us what Moses was to the Israelites. [Continued applause.] I may be mistaken, but I think the sequel will prove that I am correct. I have faith in God and gun-powder and lead, [Loud applause.] and believe we ought not to be discouraged. [Applause.] We have withstood the sixth trial, and in the seventh our courage must not falter. I thank God I have lived to see this great day, when the nation is to be weighed on the balances, and I hope not found wanting. [Applause.] This State and the National Government have treated us most shamefully, but as this is not the first time, I suppose we shall live through it. In the hour of danger, we have not been found wanting. As the Government has not had the courage to receive the help that has been standing ready and waiting to assist her, we will now stand still, and see the salvation of our people.[141]

In a subsequent speech, delivered on August 1, 1862, in Boston, John shared his searing criticism of the "ambiguities of Black life in Boston." Whereas the city was advertised as "the most liberal place for Negroes" with open schools, open colleges, and the vote, Rock saw only frustration for those who received an education. Those free Black people could not find decent employment or housing. He said that Blacks were essentially "colonized" in the city of Boston.

When John learned through a telegram that Lincoln had signed the Emancipation Proclamation, even though it didn't free all of the enslaved people in the US, he was jubilant and joined Frederick Douglass in song. On January 1, 1863, along with a celebratory gathering, they sang "Blow Ye the Trumpet, Blow" at the Tremont Temple Baptist church in Boston. Afterward, John continued to push for Black men to serve in the Union Army and was instrumental in the formation of the Massachusetts 54th Regiment, which was vividly depicted in the film *Glory*.

John next pursued the goal of being admitted to the bar of the Supreme Court of the United States. In this endeavor to become the first Black man to achieve this position, he sought out the assistance of Charles Sumner whose support for Black equality was well- known. The obstacle to this appointment was none other than Chief Justice Roger Taney, whose opinion in the Dred Scott decision denied the rights of citizenship to Black people whether they were free or not. Taney had veto power, and Sumner told John that he would never be admitted to the bar of the court while Taney was the chief justice. Taney was in his eighties at this point, and Rock wrote to a friend that, "I suppose the old man lives on out of spite."[142]

Fortunately for John, Taney died on October 12, 1864. President Lincoln appointed Salmon Chase to replace him. Chase had a history of supporting anti-slavery efforts, so John was encouraged by this development. Sumner once again took up the cause of promoting Rock. In a letter to Chase, he wrote:

> I know not how far the Dred Scott decision may stand in the way. Of course, the admission of a colored lawyer to the bar of the Supreme Court would make it difficult for any restriction on account of color to be maintained anywhere...Streetcars would be opened afterwards.[143]

Following several delays, on January 28, 1865, Sumner was asked to make a motion for John's admission to the bar. On February 1, 1865, four of the justices who had supported Taney's Dred Scott opinion were still on the court, but Chase nodded and John took the oath.

The timing could not have been more auspicious in terms of other major developments in the struggle for equality. Three days earlier, the House of Representatives voted to support the Senate's effort to pass the Thirteenth Amendment, which officially abolished slavery throughout the US. Lincoln signed it, making it the first and only amendment signed by a president.

This moment of enormous significance,—the first time a Black person had ever addressed the Supreme Court—made it into the press. An article in the *New York Daily Tribune* on February 7, 1865, included this description:

> This inky hued African stood, in the monarchical power of recognized American Manhood and American Citizenship, within the Bar of the Court which had solemnly pronounced that black men had no rights which white men were bound to respect; stood there a recognized member of it, professionally the brother of the distinguished counselors on its long rolls, in rights their equal, in the standing which rank gives their peer. By Jupiter, the sight was grand.[144]

The editorial continued with reference to the very brief motion of Sumner:

> The grave to bury the *Dred Scott* decision was in that one sentence dug; and it yawned there, wide open, under the very eyes of some of the Judges who had participated in the judicial crime against Democracy and humanity. The assenting nod of the great head of the Chief Justice tumbled in the corpse and filled up the pit, and the Black counselor of the Supreme Court got on to it and stamped it down, and smoothed the earth to his walk to the rolls of the Court.[145]

Almost immediately after this triumph, ironic misfortune befell John. On the return train journey to Boston after his swearing-in ceremony, he was arrested by a white Washington police officer as he boarded the train, because he didn't have the travel pass free Black people were obliged to carry in the nation's capital. Then, insult was added to injury as he developed a respiratory infection from which he never recovered. He died of tuberculosis on December 3, 1866, without ever having tried a case before the court to which he so valiantly and ultimately successfully sought admission. His gravestone includes the inscription, "The first colored lawyer admitted to the Bar of the U.S. Supreme Court at Washington. On Motion made by Hon. Charles Sumner. Feb. 1, 1865."

The gravestone would have done well to also commemorate his medical, dental, and oratory achievements, all in support of the full freedom and equality of his people and all in his too short life of thirty-nine years, the same age at which we lost Dr. Martin Luther King Jr. and Malcolm X.

CHAPTER 9

Sarah Parker Remond
Firebrand Defying Limits of Age and Sex

In 2018, a young Black blogger named Eric L. Martin asked, "Do the voices of teenagers really matter?" He was responding to the hostile reactions of some local adults to the movement created by his fellow students in Parkland, Florida, after the mass shooting at the local high school there. He followed his question by pointing to the life story of Sarah Remond. Who was she?

Born into a prominent Black family in Salem, Massachusetts, on June 6, 1826, Sarah Remond had many siblings—somewhere between seven and ten. Sarah's mother, Nancy, was born in Newton, the daughter of Susann Perry and Cornelius Lenox, a Continental Army veteran. Her father, John Remond, a free person of color, was born on Curaçao. He arrived in Massachusetts in 1798 at age ten and married Nancy nine years later in the African Baptist Church in Boston.

Working together, they built a successful catering, provisioning, and hairdressing business in Salem and were active in their community promoting equality for free Black people. They were determined to offer their children the finest education available in Salem. However, the fact that they were free citizens of Massachusetts, prosperous and protective of their children, did not prevent them from facing discrimination. When the children tried to attend a private school, they were rejected because of their race. In response, Sarah and one of her sisters passed the entrance examination to the public Salem High School, but the town's school committee would not stand for it and demanded their departure. Remond later said the incident was engraved in her heart, "like the scarlet letter of Hester."[146]

Despite their business and social interests in Salem, their children's education came first, so they relocated to Newport, Rhode Island, where they hoped to find a more welcoming environment. Unfortunately, the public schools there also refused to accept Black children, but some influential African Americans founded a private school, and there Sarah received the education for which she was so eager. At the same time, John and other Black citizens started a campaign to end segregation in the Salem schools, which took several years. By 1841 the schools were open to Black children, and the Remond family returned to Salem.

At fifteen, Sarah was too old to return to the classroom, but her intellectual curiosity found stimulation in the world of books, pamphlets, and newspapers, which she borrowed from friends or purchased inexpensively from the anti-slavery society in Salem.

Salem became a hotbed of anti-slavery activity in the 1840s, and the Remonds were at the center of it. They hosted such major abolitionist figures as William Lloyd Garrison and Wendell Phillips, and provided sanctuary for many fugitive slaves heading north to freedom. John was a lifetime member of the Massachusetts Anti-Slavery Society, and Nancy was a founder of the Salem Female Anti-Slavery Society. She taught her daughters the necessary skills to run their households, and she also inspired them with the desire to seek freedom and equality for all Black people. Nancy and her daughters all became members of the state and county female anti-slavery societies and attended anti-slavery lectures in Salem and Boston.

Sarah found her own powerful voice early on. With her family providing the requisite emotional and financial support for her to become an anti-slavery lecturer, she delivered her first anti-slavery lecture in Groton, Massachusetts, in July 1842—one month after her sixteenth birthday. Also on the podium that day was her brother Charles, sixteen years her senior, who offered his reflections as well.

Well-launched, Sarah was determined to take every opportunity to speak out and to put her words into action. Her next big moment of defiance came in May of 1853. Sarah had purchased tickets by mail for a performance at the Howard Atheneum, one of the most popular opera venues in Boston at the time, for Donizetti's *Don Pasquale*. She had planned to bring along two friends, one of whom was William C. Nell, journalist, publisher, author, and civil servant who worked for the integration of schools and public facilities in Massachusetts.

Upon their arrival they were shown to segregated seats, not the ones for which they had tickets. Sarah refused to accept this mistreatment. As a result she was escorted out of the theater, and because of her defiance, was pushed down a flight of stairs.

Undaunted, Sarah followed her mother's teaching to fight for equality through legal means and sued the theater for damages. She won the case and received $500 in damages (almost $20,000 in today's dollars). The theater management was obliged to acknowledge that it had wronged Sarah. Most importantly, the theater was forced to integrate its seating. Judge Thomas Russell chose to accept Sarah's testimony that she had planned to test the segregation policy's legality. She asserted that she simply wanted to occupy the seat she had paid for. This legal victory brought Sarah considerable fame.

In 1856, when Sarah was thirty years old, she and her brother Charles became agents of the American Anti-Slavery Society and traveled together all over the eastern US. Not surprisingly, they encountered many obstacles, inconveniences, and worse. There was no *Green Book*, as there would be starting in the 1930s, listing safe places for Black travelers to eat and to stay. Sarah and Charles had to make prior arrangements with families in the cities and towns where they delivered their lectures. Once, when Charles was staying with a white abolitionist friend in Washington County, New York, a visiting neighbor told them of a nearby family suffering from smallpox that was being neglected and shunned. Charles asked for his sympathy to be conveyed and stated, "To the colored people, it is the same as having the smallpox all the time."[147]

During her lecture tour, Sarah encountered women's rights activists including Susan B. Anthony and Abby Kelley Foster, a noted white abolitionist. Sarah was one of the speakers at the annual Women's Rights Convention of 1858 in New York City. She gained confidence in her public speaking and was well received by leaders in the abolitionist movement. William Lloyd Garrison praised her "calm, dignified manner, her winning personal appearance and her earnest appeals to the conscience and the heart." An article by Sarah L. Clay, a white abolitionist, in the November 5, 1858, edition of the *Liberator* offered praise for Sarah's lectures:

> She certainly processes a mind of no ordinary culture, and a heart deeply imbued with every high and noble sentiment, seems perfectly familiar with history, especially that relating to human rights, and some of the very best authors of the age are occasionally quoted by her, in most beautiful and illustrative appropriateness. It seemed to me, as I sat and heard her, especially in the evening, that her every sentence must have thrilled each human with an almost envious admiration, and have waked up dormant aspirations which would vibrate through the ages.[148]

Over time, Sarah became one of the society's most persuasive and powerful lecturers. In late 1858, Sarah's reputation as an effective speaker and fundraiser earned her an invitation to take her message across the ocean to Great Britain. Weeks later, following a dreadful crossing during which Sarah became quite ill, she gave her first lecture at the Tuckerman Institute and delivered her next lecture, "Slave Life in America," three days later. Sarah spoke eloquently about the inhumane treatment of the enslaved, and her descriptions of the widespread discrimination faced by free Black people in the US shocked her listeners.

Among her stated goals in touring Britain was to gain sympathy for the abolitionist cause throughout England. She solicited money subscriptions to aid the work of the American anti-slavery societies. In addition, she hoped her appearances would encourage the English churches to support their American counterparts. On December 28, 1858, Sarah wrote Abby Kelley Foster, with whom she had toured the previous year:

> I feel almost sure I never should have made the attempt but for the words of encouragement I received from you. Although my heart was in the work, I felt that I was in need of a good English education

... When I consider that the only reason why I did not obtain what I so much desired was because I was the possessor of an unpopular complexion, it adds to my discomfort.[149]

In another letter to Foster during this time period, she wrote that she feared not "the wind nor the waves, but I know that no matter how I go, the spirit of prejudice will meet me." During the next two years, Sarah gave forty-five lectures throughout the British Isles, including several appearances with Frederick Douglass. She had expected to encounter the same racial intolerance in England that she had faced in the United States, but to her surprise and pleasure, Sarah found herself "received here as a sister by white women for the first time in my life...I have received a sympathy I never was offered before."[150]

In her speeches, she emphasized the sexual exploitation of enslaved Black women along with such common themes as family, womanhood and marriage. She sought an emotional response from her audiences. She achieved her goal.

Her British lectures of 1859 were well-received. One paper described them as "broad, comprehensive and impressive," featuring "a clear elucidation of just principles, not clap-trap." She did not "play on the sympathies of her audiences by a long recital of the horrors of slavery." Rather, she made no exceptions for any individual or group when it came to being forthright. This broad view led her to ruffle some feathers among her middle-class and elite sponsors when she compared the horrors of African enslavement to the misery of the working-class laborers to whom she spoke.[151]

In early December, Sarah planned a visit to France and sought a visa from the American Embassy. She was refused by an official at the embassy, simply because "a colored person is not a citizen of the United States." When she protested this edict, she was threatened with forcible removal, akin to her mistreatment in the Boston theater. Her subsequent written requests were rebuffed with the following words: It is a "manifest impossibility by law" and that in her case, "the indispensable qualification for an American passport was that of a U.S. citizenship." Fortunately she obtained a passport from the sympathetic British foreign secretary.[152]

With the outbreak of the Civil War, Sarah encouraged Britain to support the Union blockade of the Confederacy as well as the Union cause. This Northern strategy of blockading Southern ports seriously affected British manufacturing because it required cotton grown in the South. In an effort to reach the soul of the citizens of Great Britain, as well as the leadership, she gave an 1862 speech in London: "Let no diplomacy of statesmen, no intimidation of slaveholders, no scarcity of cotton, no fear of slave insurrections, prevent the people of Great Britain from maintaining their position as the friend of the oppressed negro."[53]

Sarah's words and the sympathy of British cotton workers for the enslaved African Americans whose labor supplied their industry resulted in a meeting in Manchester on December 31, 1862. The workers threw their support behind the opponents of slavery, despite their own impoverishment from the loss of work. The decision to side with Lincoln, of which they were suitably proud, was deeply connected with their resentment and anger toward the factory owners, who were felt to be akin to slave masters. Workers were also bitter toward the government for supplying them minimal relief. What they did receive came from wealthy donors who lived outside of Lancashire, not from the wealthy owners of the shutdown factories where they'd been employed. The result was several riots that finally pushed the government to provide employment in rebuilding urban environments.[154]

With the end of the Civil War, Sarah became an advocate for the plight of the millions of her freed black countrymen, seeking clothing and funds for their welfare. She lectured on behalf of the millions of freedmen, soliciting funds and clothing for them. She was an active member of the London Emancipation Society and the Freedman's Aid Association in London. Her lecture "The Freeman or the Emancipated Negro of the Southern States of the United States," delivered in London, was published in the *Freedman* in 1867.

Not content to pursue her own studies, which she did at first at Bedford College for Women (founded in London in 1849 as the first higher education college for women in the United Kingdom) and later at London University College from which she graduated as a nurse, Sarah continued her involvement in racial and gender equality struggles in London. She joined the London Emancipation Committee and then helped found and served on the executive committee of the Ladies London Emancipation Society. Sarah is thought to be the only Black woman among the 1500 signatories to a women-only, 1866 petition for the right of British women to vote. Returning briefly to the US in 1866, she joined with the American Equal Rights Association, her brother, and Frederick Douglass in working for equal suffrage for women and African Americans.

Upon her return to London, Sarah was hosted by Clementia Taylor, philanthropist, suffragist, women's health advocate and campaigner for married women's property rights, and introduced to several luminaries including author George Eliot, the abolitionist and social theorist Harriet Martineau, and the Italian revolutionary Giuseppe Mazzini. The latter so impressed Sarah as he crusaded for Italian unification that she became a speaker and fundraiser for the cause.

At the conclusion of the Civil War, Sarah left London for Italy. An undated newspaper clipping from 1871 states that Sarah, the insatiable seeker of knowledge, received the degree of Doctor of Medicine from a medical school in Florence, Italy. The scholar and historian Dorothy Porter, who put together the pieces of Sarah's later years, suggested that Sarah was weary of combating racism in her home country and sought a new field such as medicine in a new country where she would not be obliged to navigate the limitations to expressing herself and her beliefs, nor would she face denials of her desire to be of service.

In Florence, she was visited by Mrs. Elizabeth Buffum Chace (explored further in Chapter 15), a Quaker and former abolitionist. Ms. Buffum remarked upon Sarah's, "indomitable energy and perseverance" as a result of which, "she had won a fine position in Florence as a physician and also socially." She quoted Sarah as saying that white Americans had sought to prevent her success by "bringing their hateful prejudices to Italy." [155]

Sarah continued to practice medicine in Florence into the 1880s. One of her close friends was the African American sculptor Edmonia Lewis, and she was visited by Frederick Douglass and his second wife, Helen Pitts Douglass. She never returned to the States, and it is likely that she elected to remain abroad due to the failure of Reconstruction. Several of her eight siblings came to visit for various lengths of stay, but Sarah was to spend her last days outside the country she worked so valiantly to transform. She expressed her great disillusionment in what may be seen as a farewell letter to America:

> [T]he hatred of race...is now a ruling element. No one who really comprehended the terrible influence which for so many generations has corrupted the moral sense of the people, ever supposed that the contaminating influence of the system would be readily effaced... What a record could the victims of this terrible hatred present against the dominant race...It never will be written. It never can be written.[156]

At age fifty, Sarah married a Sardinian named Lazzaro Pintor in Florence, Italy, but the union did not last. Within three years, she was on her own and living in Rome. Coincidentally, his given name and his surname are traditionally Jewish. Sarah's father, John, was described as having African, Dutch, and Jewish heritage, which was common among natives of Curaçao, where he was born.

Sarah died in Florence in 1894 and was buried in the Non-Catholic Cemetery, also known as the Protestant Cemetery, under her married name, Sarah Remond Pintor. Thanks to the efforts of Marilyn Richardson, a writer about art and history, funds were raised in 2013 to provide for a plaque in honor of Sarah in the cemetery.

In 1999, Sarah was among six outstanding women—including Dorothea Dix, Florence Luscomb, Marry Kenney O'Sullivan, Josephine St. Pierre Ruffin, and Lucy Stone—honored by the Massachusetts State House with a series of tall marble panels featuring a bronze bust of each woman. Her tireless efforts to speak her truth inspired those of her era as well as Eric Martin, with whom this chapter began. A more recent honor occurred in 2020, when University College London renamed its Centre for the Study of Racism and Racialization the Sarah Parker Remond Centre. The words Sarah chose to end one of her letters speak no less powerfully to us today:

May the colored race receive a fresh increase of the power to endure and bear, with such patience as they can command, fresh insults and injustice. May God and their integrity keep them in this new conflict.[157]

HON. ABRAM GALLOWAY.

(Secreted in a vessel loaded with turpentine.)

CHAPTER 10

The Anguish of
Abraham Galloway

What follows is neither an ambush nor a crime, but the final offer in a stalled negotiation: "By the light of a single candle, he sees a formidable black man with a pistol in his belt. Beside the stranger, he recognizes a tall, well-built black man of light complexion: 26-year-old Abraham H. Galloway. Behind them are numerous other black men and women—expectant, curious, defiant, anxious, suspicious." So defiant is the youngblood named Galloway, he slides out of his belt a long, dull revolver, cocks it, and places the muzzle to Edward W. Kinsley's ear. Silence inhabits the attic room. Kinsley will always remember this as the most thrilling moment of his life. He does not hate Galloway for threatening him. On the contrary, from this Kinsley developed a deep admiration for Galloway's uncompromising zeal, forever counting him a friend and a "man of more than ordinary ability."

This is how an article about the life and times of Abraham begins, but there is much to know about what led up to this scene. We begin with Abraham's birth on February 8, 1837, in Smithville, North Carolina, a small fishing village at the bottom of the Cape Fear River known today as Southport in Brunswick County. He was born the enslaved son of a Black woman, Hester Hankins, and a white boatman, John Wesley Galloway, who was "protective of his son, despite the circumstances."[158] His mother was enslaved to Marsden Milton Hankins, who let Abraham become apprenticed to a brick mason at the rental price of $15 a month when he was ten or eleven years old. Once Abraham mastered the craft of masonry, he moved with his owner to Wilmington, North Carolina's largest city and busiest seaport, and worked as an unpaid child bricklayer for the next ten years.

Sick and tired of slavery by the age of twenty, he became a stowaway in the cargo hold of a boat carrying naval stores, pine tar, and turpentine. Unable to read or write, Abraham left no record of himself, but thanks to William Still, an abolitionist and the corresponding secretary for the Philadelphia Vigilance Committee, we have an account of the escape. Abraham and his friend Richard Eden followed the North Star from Wilmington to Philadelphia. Still highlighted the perils of their escape and classified them both as "among the bravest of the brave." Abraham ultimately made it to Canada via the Underground Railroad, and eventually succeeded in freeing his mother from bondage in a heavily guarded Wilmington in 1863.[159]

Abraham never hid his mixed-race origin. Instead, he openly expressed his "outrage at a social system that can declare one human being to be the property of another based on such fine distinctions of racial mixing." His rage led him to Haiti in 1860, where he sought to recruit men for a John Brown-style military invasion of the American South. He was preparing for a war to end enslavement.[160]

As the Civil War spread across the Disunited States of North America, in April 1861, Abraham returned from Haiti and began working as a spy for Major General Benjamin F. Butler. His missions took him to North Carolina, Louisiana, and Mississippi. On a mission to Beaufort, North Carolina, he learned about the possible marine landings in preparation for General Ambrose Burnside's efforts to secure the North Carolina coast during the winter of 1861 and into the new year. Having grown up in North Carolina, Abraham was invaluable to Butler because of his many friendships with enslaved people in the area. In February 1862, Butler was ordered to Louisiana to mount an attack in New Orleans. African intelligence was known to the generals as an effective military weapon in taking enemy territory, and now they gave Abraham the chance to build upon his successes in North Carolina down in New Orleans. He and several other enslaved men were immediately sent to Vicksburg, Mississippi.

The strategy was to have the Union army split the Confederacy in half by taking Vicksburg, but the resistance they encountered prevented them from achieving this goal. The city was abandoned, but the Black men whom the army had used to try to pave the way for an invasion were left behind, including Abraham, who was captured.

Abraham either escaped or was released, but he took on one last assignment for Butler and ended up in New Bern, North Carolina. It was the spring of 1862, and the US Army desperately needed reinforcements as the war was taking an enormous toll, far greater than had been anticipated. Many Union officers were against the recruitment of black soldiers "and few politicians risked their careers to champion, (but) the wheel of history has turned. General Order Number 143 of the U.S. War Department, dated May 22, 1863, authorized the creation of a Bureau of Colored Troops "to recruit and train freedmen and emancipated slaves to fight."

William Henry Singleton was one such recruit. He was born a slave on a plantation on the Neuse River in North Carolina. Because he was his owner's "nephew" (a euphemism for being born out of wedlock to an enslaver and an enslaved women), he was sold further south to Atlanta in order to hide the family's shame. At age nine, he was able to escape back to North Carolina and found his way back to his mother's cabin. The pattern of escaping, being recaptured, being sold off, and running back to his home was recursive. Finally he was able to stay home.

With the Civil War looming, William desperately wanted to get as close to the battlefield as possible. He begged to be a manservant to a commander. Here is his account of joining the army:

> I was very anxious to go with him as his servant and my master, at his request, let me do so. The reason why I was anxious to go…was because I wanted to learn how to drill. I did learn to drill. In fact I learned how to drill so well that after a while when he was busy with other matters he would tell me to drill the company for him.[161]

Abraham single-handedly brought in hundreds of other men and drilled them using cornstalks for muskets. They were eager to fight, and waited desperately for the day when their service would be accepted.

But acceptance did not translate into equal treatment by any stretch of the imagination. Racism was rampant in the Union Army as well as with political leaders like Edward Stanly, the provisional governor of North Carolina. He believed the war was to be "a war of restoration and not of abolition," and went so far as to outlaw the recently established schools for the children of escaped slaves. He quit the post to which he'd been appointed by President Lincoln over a dispute regarding the Emancipation Proclamation. Stanly felt the law "would do infinite mischief and crush any hope of realizing peace by conciliatory measures."

Written records reveal that white Union soldiers didn't consider the Black troops intelligent enough "to master the manual of arms and complicated battlefield maneuvering—let alone to handle artillery and command decisions."[162] Then there were the Black soldiers' attitudes towards one another:

> Black volunteers come to the army inherently divided by their experience. Slave or free man, they bring all sorts of complicated attitudes about class, color, and talent toward one another. There are no automatic loyalties to kin, neighbors, old friends, the flag, or—especially—white officers. Alliances must be formed from scratch, trust earned through deeds.[163]

Adding insult to injury the Black soldiers had to not only fight the military enemy, but also the US government and army for equal pay, serviceable uniforms, and weapons that actually worked when their lives were at stake.

To make matters much worse, there were the racial codes of the Confederacy. To attempt to discourage enlistment in the Union Army, the codes provided that if a Black soldier were captured, he would be subject to the laws in force in the place of his capture—"summary execution as slaves in insurrection or a return to bondage." The *Wilmington Journal* let it be known that those white commissioned officers captured in command of Black troops would be put to death. Naturally some of the commanding officers who had been specially chosen to be in charge of Black troops did not respond well to this threat, and their reaction had a deleterious effect on their treatment of those under their command.

Abraham knew full well all of these vicissitudes of serving in the Union Army. By the time of his encounter with Kinsley he had already been one of fifty Black men who guarded Union camps from raiders as "night pickets." These men knew the region well and were crucial guides for the Union to conduct raids. Whether in the swamps, river fords, or hidden trails, their role was essential in enabling these raids to be successful. Needless to say, another role became recruiting other Black men to fulfill this function.

In New Bern, where Abraham was stationed, ten thousand white troops were headed south to attack Charleston, South Carolina. There were no replacement troops that could be called upon, so the opportunity for freed slaves to fight for their own freedom and that of their brothers and sisters presented itself. Abraham rose to the occasion. From the beginning of the war, knowing that Black men might be recruited, he had held fast to four conditions that he insisted had to be met before any of those who had escaped enslavement in North Carolina would enlist:

1. They must receive pay equal to that of the Massachusetts regiments that were already serving.
2. While they are serving, the Army must provide for their families, who are nearly all refugees.
3. The Freedmen's Bureau must set up schools to teach their children to read and write, so they have a chance of advancing their prospects after the war.
4. Most crucial of all, the US government must guarantee that, in the event they are captured, they will have all the rights of legitimate military prisoners of war.[164]

It was in pursuit of these demands and with the fervent belief that they were fair and just that Abraham held the gun to Kinsley's head and ordered him to promise to satisfy each condition. He was convinced that Black men needed to fight for their own freedom.

> If Blacks stand on the sidelines and allow others to give them their
> freedom, that freedom will never be complete; it will always be

counted a gift, not a right. Their own blood must be part of the bargain, their investment in the cause, but they must be treated as equal partners. His goal is not mere grudging freedom from physical bondage but full political equality. "And if this should be refused them at the ballot box," he exhorts in public speeches, "they would have it at the cartridge box!"[165]

Kinsley was unable to offer such reassurances in prior meetings given the limits of his authority, but this time, with the gun pointed at his head, Kinsley granted the four demands. It was far from clear that he had the authority to guarantee that they would be carried out, but two of the promises—for schools and the support of families the soldiers were leaving behind—were kept. The other two—equal pay and the honorable treatment of POWs—remained unfulfilled. The former was the source of much contention throughout the war, and the latter was out of the hands of Kinsley or any Union officer. White prisoners of war were often treated horribly by the Confederate government, and Black prisoners suffered even worse forms of punishment and mistreatment.

Given how desperately men of African descent wanted to fight for their freedom, despite the failure to secure assurances about pay and POW treatment, Galloway managed to quickly mobilize hundreds of enlistees to present themselves in front of the Christ Episcopal Church in New Bern. He was able to follow through on his commitment to have soldiers ready because many had for months been training in secret in Black militia companies. Abraham knew full well of the hardships associated with serving in the Union Army. Abraham and his fellow Black troops lived in a space where "rules are never quite clear, laws are slanted toward white people, and the same action is deemed either a heroic use of initiative or gross insubordination." Skillful at crossing back and forth over enemy lines, Abraham, between his roles as scout, spy, recruiter, and night picket, married Martha Ann Dixon in the summer of 1863.[166]

As a spy, especially on his missions to the Deep South, Abraham witnessed horrible mistreatment and atrocities against enslaved people. These firsthand experiences drove his tireless commitment to achieve freedom, end enslavement, and guarantee equal rights under the law. It was by slipping into Wilmington in 1863 that Abraham freed his mother, Hester Hankins, from bondage. General Edward Augustus Wild championed his efforts to obtain safe passage for her. Wild was an admirer of Abraham throughout the war years. The general was a fighting surgeon who had been grievously wounded at the Battle of South Mountain. An exploding bullet shattered his left arm and he ended up supervising the amputation of his arm at the shoulder – an indication of the "sand in his character."[167]

The following year, on April 29, 1864, Abraham headed a delegation of five Black southerners who met with President Abraham Lincoln. Their purpose was to advocate for citizenship, suffrage, and political equality. Later that year he was one of the 144 Black leaders to attend the National Convention of Colored Citizens of the United States in Syracuse, New York, one of the most important gatherings of African leaders during the Civil War. From it came the founding of the National Equal Rights League, for which Galloway co-organized a state chapter as well as five local chapters.

Through the efforts of Kinsley, Wild, and Abraham, three regiments of Black troops were created. A fourth was raised by General William T. Sherman as he marched through the Carolinas, and by war's end five thousand North Carolina Black men—most of them former slaves—joined with 174,000 other Black soldiers in 175 regiments. Sixty-eight thousand died in their quest for freedom. Sergeant Singleton's words ring true to the cause for which these men were willing to sacrifice their lives: "I wore the uniform of those men in Blue, who through four years of suffering wiped away with their blood the stain of slavery and purged the Republic of its sin." Then there's this truth: "Beyond their labor and bondage, they have now paid a new price in blood for their homeland."[168]

The end of the Civil War was not the end of Abraham's war. His undying commitment to equality and justice for his people was expressed when he mounted the market house, previously an auction block for the enslaved. He spoke these words to a torchlight procession of fellow Black citizens: "My people stand here tonight fettered, bound hand and foot by a constitution that recognizes them as chattel."

Abraham and his wife, Martha Ann, moved to Wilmington in the fall of 1865, and their first child, John, was born in December of that year. While in Wilmington, Abraham saw that whites who had reasserted their political power were not protecting the rights of the new African Americans. White reaction checked the efforts of Abraham and others to ensure the right to vote, and they pushed instead for free education.

It was the quest for equality and universal suffrage that drove Abraham to seek election to the Constitutional Convention. He thus helped to pass the Reconstruction Acts in 1867. This forced the former confederacy to pass universal male suffrage. Abraham advocated strongly for the Republican Party and on October 17, 1867, he was elected as a delegate to the Constitutional Convention of 1868. Soon after this honor, he had the distinction of being the first Black delegate from North Carolina to a presidential convention. Meanwhile he contributed to the creation of an accord that included Black and white citizens. With these guarantees supposedly in place, he was elected to the state senate in 1868. It was the first election in which Black citizens were eligible to hold state office, despite threats from the recently formed Ku Klux Klan.

For the next two years Abraham continued his efforts to promote civil rights for Black men and women. He was one of three Black senators and eighteen Black representatives in the North Carolina General Assembly of 1868–1869. One of his acts as a senator was to amend a proposal to segregate the senate galleries. He offered a compromise—an optional middle section that could be occupied by both races. He was also able to vote to ratify the Fourteenth and Fifteenth amendments to the Constitution during his time in office.

Abraham pushed for women's suffrage through his exceptional oratory skills and his political acumen—despite his inability to read or write. He went up against the Klan "with fists and clubs and walks the streets with a horse pistol tucked in his belt, always wary of assassins."[169]

We are left to contemplate what other contributions Galloway would have made had he not died a mere two years later, on September 1, 1870, at the tragically young age of thirty-three, having just been re-elected to the Senate. He was suddenly stricken with fever and jaundice and passed away at the home of his mother, whose freedom he had secured. His quest for justice for all African people left him penniless.

His death shocked his community. Two days later, six thousand mourners attended funeral services at St. Paul's Episcopal Church to pay their last respects. The enormous crowd escorted this courageous seeker of freedom and equality to his final resting place that is today unmarked. On October 3, 2014, a North Carolina Highway Historical Marker dedicated to Abraham Galloway was installed at Third Street and Brunswick in Wilmington, North Carolina, in New Hanover County.

What might Abraham have accomplished with even just another decade of life? He surely would have been disturbed by the undoing of Reconstruction and the rights he had fought for in war and peace. Regardless of the obstacles, there is no doubt that he would have been in the thick of the fight for justice and reparations.

Courtesy of Library of Congress, LC-USZ62-96916

CHAPTER 11

Francis Pastorius
and the Germantown Petition of 1688

What could cause a group of four men to take a stand against enslavement—in 1688? How might their religion feature into their actions? What would enable them to go up against William Penn, founder of the community they had joined? Could the answer be as simple as the Golden Rule? Should we be surprised that the Germantown Quaker Petition Against Slavery, the first such document ever written by a group of white people in the British colonies, was rejected? By Quakers, no less! Or that it was then lost for almost 156 years? Yet Germantown is cited as the birthplace of the anti-slavery movement—because of the petition.

What follows is a chronicling of the origin, creation, and significance of a document that needs to come out of the shadows of history. Alongside its story is that of a man immortalized in "The Pennsylvania Pilgrim," a poem by John Greenleaf Whittier. That man is Francis Daniel Pastorius.

The roots of the Germantown Petition lie in the history of the Quakers. George Fox, the group's founder, was disillusioned with the religion he encountered in England and in the 1640s set off on a spiritual quest. England itself was also in a period of religious upheaval. The Church of England was under siege as many of its constituents tried to reform unsatisfying practices or start their own churches.

Fox found kindred spirits searching for a more direct experience of God's presence. He ended up believing that it was within people that the presence of God resides rather than in churches or the clergy. He felt God was speaking directly to him in what he called "openings" and the word quickly spread. Along with a shared belief in these openings, Quakers—the derisive nickname given by opponents because Fox believed in the biblical passage that said people should "tremble at the Word of the Lord"—opposed elaborate religious ceremonies, eschewed clergy, and believed men and women were spiritually equal. These were radical notions and landed Fox and numerous others in jail, but by 1650 there were fifty thousand members of Fox's Society of Friends.

That is the origin of the religion, but to get to the Germantown Petition the question that must be answered has several parts, the first of which is, where were Quakers on the issue of enslavement in 1688? As will be affirmed in subsequent chapters, many English Quakers in the seventeenth century took pride in the slave trade. The enslavement of African people was seen as both a symbol of prosperity and an economic necessity. To the Quakers who made their living as merchants, Black people were a mere commodity.

Fox gets credit for moving some Quakers towards an anti-slavery stance, but he did not go far enough and refrained from condemning enslavement. In 1671, on a trip to Barbados, he went so far as to encourage Quaker slave masters to limit the length of enslavement and to provide an education for the enslaved. Fox expressed two concerns about enslavement. The first was a strange application of the Golden Rule that was to be the centerpiece of the petition. He urged Friends to treat Black people as they would want to be treated—were they themselves enslaved! He wanted Quakers to train the enslaved in Quakerism, though that this did not mean that they could worship together. Fox's second fear was entirely self-serving. He worried that the presence of non-Christian strangers—free Black people—would dilute the family, which he saw as a sacred institution. While the concerns were starting to be voiced by abolition-leaning Quakers, many of his flock feared that Pennsylvania might see its own rebellion by the enslaved, like the ones that had occurred in the Caribbean.

In 1681 William Penn, a devout Quaker, invited Quakers from several European countries to form a new colony, which became Philadelphia in 1682. Penn's goal was to provide a safe place for Quakers and other persecuted people to create an ideal Christian community, one he felt was not possible in England. Before he left in 1682, he held numerous gatherings along with other Quakers in the Netherlands and in the Rhine Valley.

With this background, we return to Francis Daniel Pastorius. He was born in Summerhausen in Bavaria, Germany, in 1651 to a Lutheran family of upper-class community leaders. He was an only child who studied the classics in Latin. He had a facility for languages and learned to speak German, Latin, Italian, French, Dutch, English, Spanish, and Greek. Francis felt the effects of the words he heard Penn speak. He was increasingly dissatisfied with his lucrative law practice and he "turned inward looking for philosophical purity in his life." Penn's words appealed to the disillusioned Pastorius

Friends believe that a person's spiritual life and character are more important than the quantity of goods he possesses or his monetary worth. Francis saw these precepts as an opportunity to start a fresh life apart from the libertinism from which he felt alienated. In the Netherlands, Quakers often found themselves imprisoned, since only the Reformed Church, Catholicism and Lutheranism were permitted by the government.

When Francis finished law school, he practiced law for two years in Windsheim (1676–1678) after which he left his home and joined the Lutheran Pietists in Frankfurt for whom he felt an affinity. The Pietist movement had strong connections to Quakerism. Its founder, Philipp Spener, was a Lutheran theologian in the late seventeenth century. In the spirit of evangelism, he emphasized that individuals could be personally transformed through a spiritual rebirth, personal devotion, and piety, all of which he saw in small supply in the Lutheran church of the time. The Frankfurt pietists formed the Frankfort Land Company for purposes of both purchasing land in Pennsylvania and moving there. Francis felt a "desire in his (soul) to continue in their (Pietists) Society and with them to lead a quiet, godly and honest life." With the Pietists support and the still echoing words of William Penn, Pastorius emigrated in 1683 to Pennsylvania.[170]

There is some controversy over whether Francis made the move to become a Quaker or remained a lifelong Lutheran with Pietism as his foundation. For him the most important element of his Pietist leanings was the adherence to the Golden Rule. But there was a sizable rift between the English and the Dutch-Germans in Pennsylvania, and this rift played a major role in how the petition ended up being received.

Some of the settlers from England were wealthy landowners who depended on enslaved Africans to do the farm work. The contradiction between having themselves immigrated to escape religious persecution and then preventing others from being free was not evident to these individuals. By 1500, serfs in northwestern Europe were no longer property, but servitude remained widespread in Europe. Indentured servants secured passage to the new colony by committing to work for several years.

Enslavement was rampant throughout the colonies, with local slave markets making the purchase of African people accessible and affordable to many. The British crown protected the owners, and many argued that slavery was essential for economic prosperity and growth. Many in Britain justified their actions by convincing themselves that African people were part of inferior and uncivilized cultures. "Penn, though a pacifist Quaker, kept several Black enslaved people during his time overseeing his colony—even as the practice grew increasingly unpopular among Pennsylvanians."[171]

Francis entered this culture on August 20, 1683, with a group of Mennonites, Pietists, and Quakers. Among them was Abraham op den Graeff, a cousin of Penn, the proprietor of the colony, who asked him to act as their agent in obtaining land. He visited Penn the day after he arrived in Philadelphia and was met with great warmth. Penn inspired him with "preaching courage for a new beginning for himself that would use his talents and intellect and call upon his faith."[172]

Francis and Penn negotiated the purchase of fifteen thousand acres within which the settlement of Germantown was created. Significantly, the ethnic Germans who came to populate this place were outsiders, and this enabled them to see plainly and subsequently question what the English were so inured to—enslavement. The Dutch-German settlers did not enslave people. They understood enslavement as a consequence of the shortage of labor, but they refused to purchase enslaved people and recognized the contradiction in seeking freedom while denying it to others. In seeing a basic equivalence between their right to be free of persecution and the right to be free from forced labor, these citizens of Germantown made a revolutionary leap, one that had not yet occurred in Europe or the colonies.

Francis is credited as the founder of Germantown, but the name is a bit misleading since almost all of the thirteen Quaker and Mennonite families who settled there were Dutch. It was so named because of the fifty-four German families living very close by to the settlement.

Francis went on to become something of a Renaissance man of his day. He married Anneke Klosterman on November 26, 1688. He taught at the Friends School in Philadelphia and later founded his own school in Germantown. As mentioned, he spoke several languages, was an avid gardener, and kept an extensive library of 250 books, most impressive for the time. His intellect spanned many fields of knowledge, and he wrote numerous books in German and English, including *A New Primmer or Methodical Directions to Attain the True Spelling, Reading, and Writing of English,* first sold in 1698. Pastorius was also active in the life of the community he created. He was the first mayor of Germantown and simultaneously served as town clerk. From 1687–1691 he was a member of Pennsylvania's assembly.

Notwithstanding all of these involvements, it could well be argued that his work on the petition is his most noteworthy accomplishment. In 1688, Francis and three others met at the home of Thones Kunders. Having cultivated an awareness of the immorality of slavery and its prevalence among English Quakers, they wrote a petition based on the Golden Rule, urging their fellow congregants to abolish slavery.

The petition does not begin with the traditional salutation to fellow Quakers that English Quakers were familiar with and would have expected, nor does it make any reference to God or Jesus, again the habit of English Quaker petitions. Its central tenet is that every human being, regardless of race, ethnicity, or religion, has rights that should not be obstructed. The petitioners challenged their readers to imagine themselves as enslaved people and to reflect long and hard about the values of equality they espoused. What was expressed had not been proposed in any previous document in Europe or the Americas and was thus a landmark

Photo of table in Germantown Courtesy of Germantown
Mennonite Historic Trust

in the struggle for human rights. Not only is it the first anti-slavery document in the colonies, but it also bears a striking resemblance to the UN's future Universal Human Rights Declaration, which stated that the rights asserted in the petition should be guaranteed to all people.

But herein lies the greatest divergence between English and Dutch-German Quakers, and the reason for the ultimate demise of the petition. English Quakers did not consider Blacks to be the social equals of whites—period. In fact, just getting to the point of considering Black people the spiritual equals of whites—the notion that Blacks were capable of salvation through belief in God and Jesus—was radical.

The petitioners and other Dutch-German Quakers did see Black and white people as social and spiritual equals. In their reading of the Golden Rule, there was no difference among people based on "generation, descent, or color." The divide proved unbridgeable—for almost a hundred years.

The petition draws upon the Golden Rule to argue against slavery. Yes, it is that basic. The argument employed seems indirect since the meeting members were not being asked to condemn the practice of enslavement. The petitioners instead ask why Christians are allowed to buy and own enslaved people. The question is asked, in what appears to be mock sarcasm, to encourage the enslavers among them to understand its underlying reasoning. The petitioners argue that the capture and sale of enslaved people and the separation of families would never be tolerated by their community of believers.

They go on to express their conviction that enslaved people have the right to revolt, once again using the Golden Rule to reinforce their position. They assert that having additional people come to settle and colonize the land would be very difficult if the readers of their petition could see the contradiction inherent in enslavement. By acknowledging that enslaved people were entitled to revolt, as had been happening for decades in the Caribbean, they were indicating, especially to the English colonists who participated in enslaving African people, that slavery would discourage potential settlers from coming to the colonies. The goal of such arguments was to convince the enslavers that continued enslavement would have a negative impact on their colony. The following passage from the petition confirms this purpose:

> If once these slaves (wch they say are so wicked and stubborn men) should joint themselves,—fight for their freedom,—and handel their masters and mastrisses as they did handel them before; will these masters and mastrisses take the sword at hand and warr against these poor slaves, licke, we are able to believe, some will not refuse to doe; or have these negers not as much right to fight for their freedom, as you have to keep them slaves? [173]

In addition to the central importance of the Golden Rule, the Petition of Rights that England had codified in 1628 was another key facet of the Germantown petition. The major contribution of the earlier declaration was that the universal rights laid out applied not just to the "civilized" but rather to all human beings, as was implicit in the Germantown Petition. Written shortly after the Germantown petition, the British Declaration of Rights of 1689 was similarly inclusive.

Three aspects of the Germantown petition are especially worthy of clarification. The first is grammatical. The authors of the petition were not fluent in English, so they often used nontraditional spellings that might have confused readers. The second aspect is the petition's mention of Turkey as an example of a nation that took people from ships and enslaved them. The reference is to the Barbary pirates who operated off the coast of North Africa and had been plundering ships for centuries. The pirates were initially aligned with the Byzantine Empire in Constantinople, but later on they became more independent and made their living through plundering. The motivation was economic, with as many as twenty thousand Christians captured and enslaved. They came from Italy and Spain as well as England, France, and Germany, and were allowed to buy their way to freedom. Upon returning to their homelands they recounted stories of the marauding pirates enslaving their captives. Even the captain of the ship that had brought Francis to Pennsylvania five years earlier had been captured.[174]

Bringing up Europeans enslaved by pirates was a most clever way for the petitioners to appeal to their audience. They knew that the widely spread stories of the pirates enslaving people were true. In fact, in the very year that the petition was written, several Quakers were captured and enslaved in Morocco. With an awareness of the injustice, the first paragraph of the petition highlighted the immorality of capturing and enslaving Africans by the English. This was part of the case the authors made that slaves—European and all others—had the same social and political rights and entitlement to fair and just treatment as any ordinary citizen.

The final aspect of the document that requires mention involves how enslaved Black people were referred to. A German and Dutch word, "negers" was used. It meant black or negro and was in no way intended to be derogatory. To the contrary, throughout the petition the authors took a respectful attitude towards enslaved people of every race and culture and declared them equals, which was ultimately what sunk their efforts.[175]

The petition was presented at a local monthly meeting in Abington. The four creators knew what they were up against. The Quaker community accepted their views, but as outsiders who struggled with English, trying to get the entire colony to rid itself of enslavement was indeed a daunting task. In what can only be described as a blatant runaround, various Quaker communities literally passed the buck (the petition) on and on, to little avail. The initial response from members of the meeting at Abington was that, while the petition was essentially accurate, it was too challenging and too important for them to make a recommendation. Further consideration was needed, so, following standard operating procedure for Quakers, the petition was sent to the Philadelphia Quarterly Meeting. It was then passed along to the Philadelphia Yearly Meeting in Burlington, New Jersey. At each stage in the process, it was realized that banning enslavement would have profound consequences for the colony, both economically and socially. None of the meetings chose to pass judgment on such a weighty matter. The London Meeting minutes make no mention of the petition. Thus they could readily avoid its demand as had all others.

While the petition's authors continued their anti-slavery efforts, nothing changed. The colony prospered with enslavement systematized and firmly entrenched, and as a result several of the petitioners chose to depart to avoid appearing to support the dreadful practice.

In the next few decades, several other petitions surfaced, but these were predicated on racist arguments of the inferiority of Black people and intolerance for their race. Some protests got mixed up with politics and religion and were readily dismissed by the Philadelphia Yearly Meeting. It took thirty years before another petition as spot-on as the one written in 1688 arrived, but it too fell on deaf ears. Nevertheless, the moral leadership of the four authors of the Germantown petition most assuredly influenced future Quaker abolitionists and Philadelphia society.

Other dedicated Quakers continued working to expose the horrors of slavery, but there was sufficient resistance and backlash that many who were determined to get their words into print had them published anonymously in Benjamin Franklin's newspaper. In 1776, ninety years after the Germantown petition, the Philadelphia Yearly Meeting produced a proclamation banning the ownership of enslaved people. By then, monthly meetings took place with the aim of helping freed Black people start businesses, attend Quaker meetings, and educate their children.

As for Francis, he lived another thirty-one or so years, to the age of about sixty-eight. There is no official record of his passing. A book of his writings, *The Francis Daniel Pastorius Reader: Writings by an Early American Polymath* (Max Kade Research Institute) 2019, is now available and here are the comments of Marianne S. Wokeck, (author of *Trade in*

Strangers: The Beginnings of Mass Migration to North America) that highlight his uniqueness as a true polymath as well as the value he has for today's audience:

> The editors' careful selection of Francis Daniel Pastorius's writings, showcasing his thought, experience, and hope for settlement in early America, invites twenty-first century students and scholars to explore Pastorius's work and engage with it more fully in all of its range and complexity. Readers will reap the rewards of adding to their knowledge of Pastorius as an extraordinary thinker, author, and doer in the North Atlantic world of the seventeenth and eighteenth centuries.

The 1688 petition (see appendix for full text) was rediscovered in 1844 and soon became a focus of the abolitionist movement. Somehow, following a century of exposure, it was misplaced once more and only rediscovered in 2005, in the vault of the Arch Street Meetinghouse in Philadelphia. It now resides in Haverford College's Quaker and Special Collections, the joint repository (with Friends Historical Library and Swarthmore College) for the records of the Philadelphia Yearly Meeting. It serves as a reminder of the work of four men who made a plea for human rights—freedom and equality—for all. It also reminds us that there is still much work to be done to finally and fully establish equality and justice.

CHAPTER 12

Benjamin Lay
A Small Man with An Outsize
Passion for Justice

Courtesy of National Portrait Gallery

Virtually every reference to the life and times of Benjamin Lay mentions his diminutive stature and contrasts it with his enormous influence and impact on the culture. Perhaps his small size inspired him to ensure that his voice be heard, helping to propel one of the most dramatic moments in the history of abolitionism. But his values and his dedication to his principles are what led him to the efforts that first shocked and then inspired his fellow Quakers.

The incident took place in Burlington, New Jersey, in 1738. Lay entered the Philadelphia Quaker Yearly Meeting dressed as a soldier. Carrying a sword and a Bible concealed beneath his overcoat, he delivered a long and impassioned speech describing the horrors of enslavement:

> Oh, all you negro masters, who are contentedly holding your fellow-creatures in a state of slavery during life, well knowing the cruel sufferings those innocent captives undergo...especially you, who profess to do unto all men as ye would they should do unto you...you might as well throw off the plain coat as I do—

Just as he arrived at the climax of his oration, he took off his coat, held the Bible in one hand, and pierced it with his sword. Inside the Bible he had placed a rubber bag filled with bright red pokeberry juice. The juice splattered those sitting close by, and he continued to speak:

> It would be as justifiable in the sight of the Almighty, who beholds and respects all nations and colors of men with an equal regard, if you should thrust a sword through their hearts, as I do through this—[176]

His intention, that the liquid would symbolize the blood on the hands of his fellow Quakers for not opposing enslavement, was made with dramatic flair. As will become increasingly clear, Benjamin did not hesitate to employ drama to shine a light on the evils of enslavement.

Benjamin's life got off to a rocky start. He was born in Copford, Essex, England, in 1682. His father was a Quaker, though hardly devout. He was married twice, first outside the faith and then to Mary, a Quaker. Worshipping outside the Church of England resulted in considerable discrimination. Benjamin had health struggles as a child. He did not experience the growth spurt of adolescence, which confirmed that he had a congenital disorder. The consensus is that he was born with spondyloepiphyseal dysplasia congenita, a common form of dwarfism often accompanied by curvature of the spine. When he was fully grown, Benjamin was just four feet tall with a humped back. Thankfully, he possessed both considerable strength and agility, both of which would be beneficial in adulthood. These attributes also surprised those who knew him....[177]

Benjamin greatly enjoyed being a shepherd, but when offered the opportunity to become one by his elder half-brother, William, his father decided he was to become a glover in Colchester. This was not what Benjamin wanted for himself. At the age of twenty-one, he decided to take matters into his own hands and ran away to London to become a sailor.

He spent the next twelve years sailing around the world, and his wide array of experiences in dozens of countries contributed to his life-long openness to other cultures, a rare quality in his era. But while his stature was not a problem at sea, his physical struggles caused him to identify more with the oppressed than with the oppressors. The stories of enslavement that he heard horrified him, and he refused to work on a slave ship or to befriend anyone who had performed such detestable labor. One last grand advantage of his life aboard ship: despite minimal schooling, he became a voracious reader.

Between voyages, Benjamin met the love of his life. Sarah Smith, who also had small stature, was born in 1677 in Colchester, but her family relocated to Deptford when she was young. Her family were not Quakers, but the faith drew her as a youth. She was so devoted that she gained the respect of many and became the minister of the congregation in Deptford. This is where she likely met Benjamin, since the meeting house was located on the Thames close to where the sailors lodged. Their courtship lasted five years. During this period, Benjamin decided to abandon sailing in favor of becoming the glover his father had wanted him to be. In 1717, at the age of forty, Sarah agreed to marry Benjamin, who was five years her junior.

Marriage proved to be a complicated affair, not least because of

Benjamin's "opinionated mind, and his willingness to speak those opinions, which had made him enemies of ministers in the meeting house that he had argued with."[178] He was denied permission to marry. Not to be undone by this rather small-minded response, Benjamin returned to the sea, sailing to the British colony of Massachusetts in order to ask the local meeting house for the certificate he was refused by the Devonshire House Monthly Meeting. Here is the response of the Devonshire meeting to the request by the Massachusetts meeting to determine if he was a member in good standing. It describes characteristics he would continue to demonstrate throughout his life, both as a Quaker and as a human being:

> The reply noted that he was "clear from Debts and from women in relation to marriage," but added: "We believe he is Convinced of the Truth but for want of keeping low and humble in his mind, hath by an Indiscreet Zeal been too forward to appear in our publick Meetings." Lay was disturbing the Quaker meetings' peace by calling out those he believed were "covetous"—corrupted by worldly wealth.[179]

The certificate was granted, but with a passage "exhorting him to 'lowliness of mind' and to behave himself peaceably in church." Benjamin being Benjamin refused to comply, so he was refused the official copy.

Returning to England and no less determined to make Sarah his wife, he appealed this time to the London Quarterly Meeting, which oversaw all of the city's Quakers. They condemned his behavior but did not support the withholding of the certificate by the folks in Devonshire. Finally, in July 1718, he and Sarah were wed. By September, with lingering tensions from the marriage conundrum, the couple left for Barbados.

Here's where Benjamin saw the horrors of enslavement up close. He and Sarah succeeded in establishing a profitable general goods business, but their growing awareness of the life of the enslaved took a major toll on their peace of mind. Sugar cane was the source of the island's wealth, but working on sugar farms was both backbreaking and deadly. The plantation owners used the labor of those kidnapped in Africa and those captured in the wars against indigenous people. Their life expectancy was short, but the owners didn't care. An enslaved person who worked for a year on the plantation labored enough to compensate the owner for his purchase, and all that mattered was making profits. The sugar shipped over to the table of Europe was created from a rich wellspring of human misery, with workplace fatalities from injuries or fatal scalding a daily occurrence. As Benjamin put it, "sugar was made with blood."

When these woebegone people came to Benjamin and Sarah's store, he would encourage them to share their experiences. Virtually all their accounts were about being beaten for minor infractions or for no reason at all, the goal being to teach them "their place." Sarah was appalled when she discovered a slave hanging in chains outside the home of a fellow Quaker. When the man commenced a tirade about the ungrateful enslaved man, she was even more horrified.

Benjamin and Sarah soon realized they needed to do more than just bear witness to such atrocities. They began conducting prayer meetings in the homes of enslaved people. They served meals to starving workers. When the masters learned that they were preaching against enslavement, they forbade their enslaved people to attend, but that did not stop hundreds from going to the meetings. As the enslavers were making plans to expel the couple for "fraternization," the Lays returned to London after only eighteen months in Barbados—but it was long enough to change them and drive them for the remainder of their lives.

They lived in London for the next twelve years, during which time Benjamin continued to ruffle Quaker feathers. The Devonshire meeting expelled him, but the Colchester Monthly Meeting worked out far better since its membership was almost as radical as he was. One aspect of this particular meeting that suited both him and Sarah was its adherence to the old tradition of having a single meeting for men and women. His conviction that this was both right and proper led to numerous arguments. Despite Benjamin's checkered Quaker record due to his outspokenness, Sarah maintained her standing as a deeply respected minister. She chose to travel around the country and was well-received wherever she journeyed.

In 1730 they made the decision to emigrate to America. They needed a letter from the English Quakers that would enable them to join an American meeting house. Given the troubles that accompanied

Benjamin's involvement with the British meeting houses he frequented, it took over a year to obtain the necessary papers. They set sail in March of 1732 for Philadelphia.

It was with considerable enthusiasm that Benjamin and Sarah began their new life in Philadelphia. In time their optimism was replaced by disillusionment. They encountered "men of renown," as Anthony Morris Jr., Robert Jordan Jr., Israel Pemberton Sr., and John Kinsey Jr. were then known. They epitomized the notion that Friends came to Pennsylvania to "do good" and in turn "did well." They had become powerful and wealthy men—and three of the four were enslavers as were the majority of Philadelphia Quakers.

No, what they saw in Philadelphia was not the utter inhumanity of Barbados, but having rarely encountered enslavement in London, what they saw shocked them. The scale in Philadelphia was also far smaller than in Barbados—one in ten persons in the city was enslaved compared with nine out of ten on the island. There was less violence, too, but the mistreatment—violence, bondage, and repression—of the enslaved was a daily occurrence in the so-called City of Brotherly Love.

Here are some of Lay's observations:

> Enslaved men would plow, sow, thresh, winnow, split rails, cut wood, clear land, make ditches and fences, fodder cattle, run and fetch up the horses. Enslaved women were busy with all the Drudgery in dairy and kitchen, within doors and without.[180]

For Benjamin what made matters even worse was the contrast between these endless labors and the idleness of the slave owners:

> ...the growling, empty bellies of the enslaved and the "lazy Ungodly bellies" of their masters. Worse, he explained with rising anger, slave keepers would perpetuate this inequality by leaving these workers as property to "proud, Dainty, Lazy, Scornful, Tyrannical and often beggarly Children for them to Domineer."[181]

Benjamin found inspiration in the life and dedicated anti-slavery efforts of a fellow Quaker, Ralph Sandiford. In Sandiford's essay "A Brief Examination of the Times," he sought to deliver a death blow to enslavement starting with his condemnation of the slave trade. He was in very poor health when he and Benjamin met, which Benjamin interpreted as a sign of his mistreatment by the slave-owning Quakers his own words so offended. Interestingly, Benjamin Franklin printed two editions of Sandiford's work, but not wanting to possibly offend future clients by announcing his role in the publication of the vehemently anti-slavery document, the two editions went out minus his imprint.[182] When Benjamin next visited his friend, he found Sandiford on his deathbed in a delirious state. He later wrote that when he died, in May 1733 at the age forty, Sandiford was "in great perplexity of mind." Lay's conclusion was that "oppression makes a wise man mad."[183]

Nevertheless, Benjamin took up the cause to which Sandiford had devoted his life: ending enslavement permanently and throughout the land. As testament to their shared cause, an 1815 book by Robert Vaux bore the title *The Memoir of Benjamin Lay and Ralph Sandiford – Two of the Earliest Advocates for the Emancipation of the Enslaved Africans.* As a result, they were joined together in memory as they were in life.

Lay, a pioneer of guerrilla theater, (used by protesters to dramatize political and social issues) captured the attention of his fellow Quakers. His goal was to wake them up to the injustice in which they were participating. On one occasion, Lay arrived at a yearly Quaker meeting carrying three tobacco pipes. He sat between the divided galleries of men and women and, as the meeting ended, took decisive action to protest the exploitation of the workers who produced these items:

> Benjamin rose in indignant silence and "dashed one pipe among the men ministers, one among the women ministers, and the third among the congregation assembled." With each smashing blow he protested slave labor, luxury and the poor health caused by smoking the stinking sotweed. He sought to awaken his brothers and sisters to the politics of the seemingly most insignificant choices.[184]

Seeking to draw attention to the awful conditions suffered by the enslaved, he once again took performative action, this time in the dead of winter following a deep snowfall. He stood outside the meetinghouse where all would see him on the way in and left his right leg and foot bare, thrust into the snow.

> Like the ancient philosopher Diogenes, who also trod barefoot in snow, he again sought to shock his contemporaries into awareness. One Quaker after another took notice and urged him not to expose himself to the freezing cold lest he get sick. He replied, "Ah, you pretend compassion for me but you do not feel for the poor slaves in your fields, who go all winter half clad."[185]

Benjamin was not above calling people out during meetings as well. Isaac Hopper, the nineteenth-century Quaker abolitionist and Underground Railroad co-founder, remembered what he had heard about Benjamin as a child:

> Benjamin gave no peace to slaveowners. As sure as any character attempted to speak to the business of the meeting, he would start to his feet and cry out, "There's another negro-master!"[186]

Due to these provocations, Benjamin found himself unwelcome at one meeting after another, to the point where a "constabulary"—a military force—was appointed to prevent him from crashing the meetings around Philadelphia. Undaunted, he returned to the main door of a meetinghouse after being thrown out in a rainstorm and lay on the wet ground in the mud, forcing every Friend leaving the meeting to step over him. When a Friend expressed concern for his well-being, he urged them to have the same concern for the enslaved, who were forced to work outdoors throughout the winter in wholly inadequate clothing. For good measure, he would reinforce his point by quoting from the Book of Matthew.[187]

Sarah and Benjamin chose to leave Philadelphia for the nearby village of Abingdon when the reactions of slave-owning Quakers became too much to withstand. Sarah's dear friend, a fellow Quaker missionary, Susanna

Morris, lived in Abingdon. Their friendship began as young missionaries but was cemented when they survived a shipwreck en route to Amsterdam in the 1720s. Benjamin relied on the support of the Morris family, especially when Sarah died suddenly in 1735, at a mere fifty-eight years old.

Sarah had been an exceptional advocate for justice for enslaved African Americans, and for Benjamin she had been a calming influence. Her less confrontational manner and wellspring of compassion had served as important checks to Benjamin's angry outbursts. "She was fiercely intelligent and charismatic, and spent her life teaching people about what she thought was right and wrong." Her death took an enormous toll on Benjamin. He had been convinced that since she was in better general health, she would outlive him. Six months after her death, Benjamin began work on the book that would be his major life's work. One possibility is that he missed her so much—their shared mission, their conversations—that he began a "conversation with the world."

With Sarah no longer there to temper his responses, Benjamin became even more confrontational. One of his targets was Ralph Morris, one of the authors of the infamous "An Act for the Better Regulating of Negroes in this Province." Numerous provisions of the act restricted slaves and free Black people, and every one outraged Benjamin. It is worth seeing what he found so objectionable.

- (Section I) if a slave was sentenced to death, the owner would be paid full value for the slave.
- (Sec II) Duties on slaves transported from other colonies for a crime are doubled.
- (Sec III) If a slave is freed, the owner must have a sureties bond of £30 to indemnify the local government in case he/she becomes incapable of supporting himself.
- (Sec IV) A freed slave fit but unwilling to work shall be bound out [as an indentured servant] on a year-to-year basis as the magistrates see fit. And their male children may be bound out until 24 and women children until 21.
- (Sec V) Free negroes and mulattoes cannot entertain, barter or trade with slaves or bound servants in their homes without leave and consent of their master under penalty of fines and whipping.

- (Sec VI) If fines cannot be paid, the freeman can be bound out.
- (Sec VII) A minister, pastor, or magistrate who marries a negro to a white is fined £100.
- (Sec VIII) If a white cohabits under pretense of being married with a negro, the white will be fined 30 shillings or bound out for seven years, and the white person's children will be bound out until 31. If a free negro marries a white, they become slaves during life. If a free negro commits fornication or adultery with a white, they are bound out for 7 years. The white person shall be punished for fornication or adultery under existing law.
- (Sec IX) Slaves tippling or drinking at or near a liquor shop or out after nine, 10 lashes.
- (Sec X) If more than 10 miles from their master's home, 10 lashes.
- (Sec XI) Masters not allowed to have their slaves to find and or go to work at their own will receive a 20 shilling fine.
- (Sec XII) Harboring or concealing a slave: a 30 shillings a day fine.
- (Sec XIII) Fine to be used to pay the owners of slaves sentenced to death.[188]

Such codes were, of course, not unique to Pennsylvania, but that a Quaker had helped to write them was more than Benjamin could bear. To the Friends' credit, Morris was officially denied membership in the Pennsylvania Monthly Meeting and later on in the Abington Monthly Meeting as well. Such actions did little to deter Benjamin from continuing to condemn those members of the congregation who owned enslaved people as unfit to preach or to speak at meetings. Here is one of his chastisements:

> For Friends, all you that are Ministers of Anti-Christ, whether in Pulpits or in Galleries, you that are of the Royal Offspring, of the King of the Locusts, and are creeping out of the Bottomless Pit a little, to see what Mischief you can do to Mankind, & Service for your King Lucifer, who was (and is now to you) as the Son of the Morning, and to see what good you can get for your God, your Bellies.[189]

All the while, Benjamin was hard at work on what would become one of the first anti-slavery books to be published in North America: *All Slave-Keepers That Keep the Innocent in Bondage* (1738). The publisher was none other than an even more well-known Benjamin—Franklin. Lay's undeniably deep commitment to the abolitionist cause had a profound impact on Franklin, who was unsure about what position to take. Ultimately the two Benjamins became lifelong friends and Franklin, once he had taken the side of the abolitionist, was very proud of having published Lay's book.[190]

Franklin's editing greatly improved the quality of Lay's writing, and the contents were explosive. Lay began the book with a statement of devotion to his Quaker beliefs and his desire to serve the community with the book. His goal in writing the treatise was to expose the great and grave contradiction between the beliefs and actions of too many of his fellow Quakers and to undo "the great hypocrisy at the heart of the American self-image."[191] One could easily argue that the same hypocrisy remains alive and well in contemporary America, but Benjamin was embarked on a course to eliminate it from the Quaker tradition.

The book helped get the word out. Benjamin chronicled the many abuses he had witnessed and honored those he knew who had opposed slavery. He provided biblical justification for calling enslavement a great sin. He sought to engage those who opposed the hateful institution but who needed significant nudging to speak out. He had written off the "great men" of the Quaker community as irredeemable, and it was the younger generation in which he saw hope for abolitionism.

Many of the most influential abolitionists of the eighteenth century were personally gifted with a copy of the book. Benjamin knew that to build a movement within the Quaker faith he needed to network, so he made sure to connect those he met with others who shared their values. He was wise in the way of movements and knew that the change that needed to happen would have to come from the bottom up.

Six months after the book's publication, Benjamin performed the act that begins this chapter. He would not be limited in the ways in which he forced those attending meetings to confront their racism. Such actions invariably had consequences, and in his case, the consequence was banishment from the faith.

One of the "eminent men" who had witnessed Benjamin's performance with the sword, Bible, and "blood" was John Kinsey, speaker of the Pennsylvania House of Representatives, attorney-general of Pennsylvania, and de facto head of the Quaker faith in the colonies—the most powerful Quaker leader in America—and an owner of enslaved people. Benjamin, in naming names in his book, had called out Kinsey, and he retaliated. Kinsey was also head of the Board of Overseers, and this group's purpose was to judge whether books written by Quakers conformed to the faith. Given the great divide between them, it is no surprise to discover that the overseers declared that not only did Benjamin's book not conform, but they also declared that "the Author is not of their religious community." Benjamin was ousted and he would never return.[192]

Two more of Benjamin's values are worthy of mention. Today he would no doubt be a considered a vegan because he believed that no creature should be kept in bondage, including animals. He did not use or consume animal products. In addition, he did not purchase commercially made clothing since he believed that the connection between capitalism as practiced in the Colonies and enslavement was fundamental to both. He chose to build his own house within a cave, for which he was mocked by his enemies, but the home was quite comfortable. The painting that introduces Benjamin at the outset of the chapter depicts him standing in front of his cave home. He did not know the painting was being done since it was commissioned by Benjamin Franklin's wife as a gift to her husband to honor Benjamin's passionate commitment to abolition.

Benjamin was not above inflicting discomfort on the comfortable. One of his most powerful actions (though possibly apocryphal) involved a Quaker family who had a young enslaved Black girl. They also had a young son, and Benjamin managed to persuade him to come to his cave to play. The child thoroughly enjoyed romping around the cave while Benjamin waited at the door. When he saw the boy's parents frantically running down the road, he asked what was wrong. They told him their son had been missing all day and they feared for his safety. Benjamin replied:

Your child is safe in my house, and you may now conceive of the sorrow you inflict upon the parents of the negro girl you hold in slavery, for she was torn from them by avarice.[193]

Much to his own surprise, having had a most challenging life, Benjamin lived well into his seventies. He was still traversing the colonies, meeting with abolitionists, and protesting enslavement until the age of seventy-five. He spent his last two years at home, receiving occasional visitors. It was in 1758 that one of his many visitors brought him the news he had been anticipating for so long—the Philadelphia Yearly Meeting had finally voted against its leadership, "that any Quaker who traded in slaves would be disciplined and eventually disowned." It was an ongoing bitter pill to have to accept that ownership of the enslaved would have to wait until 1776 to be declared unacceptable, but this vote against the trading of slaves was the first official Quaker ruling to recognize what Benjamin had spent his entire adulthood fighting against. "Now, I can die in peace," said Benjamin. The following February, he passed away.

Benjamin was denied his wish to be cremated and was buried beside his beloved Sarah in an unmarked grave in the Abington Quaker cemetery. An engraving of him, based on the portrait Franklin's wife had commissioned William Williams Sr. to paint, was commissioned by his friends and it proved both popular and profitable. It was often hung in homes as a means of showing subtle support for abolitionism. It was unobtrusive only at first, because the original engraving gave no indication of Benjamin's views on the evils of enslavement. But when a copy of the engraving was made in 1815 for Roberts Vaux's *Memoirs of the Lives of Benjamin Lay and Ralph Sandiford,* the title of the book he is holding is changed from *Trion On Happiness* to *African Emancipation,* finally openly acknowledging Benjamin's once controversial views.

Despite the Vaux memoir and his friendship with the eminent Franklin, Lay remained confined to obscurity for many years, a mere footnote in the history of American abolitionists. He didn't lend himself to the sainthood of many abolitionist heroes upon whom historians showered praise. He was too brazen, too confrontational. He didn't make his opinions easy for his opponents to take in. Another huge factor working against the recognition of his accomplishments was his physical differences, which made him unworthy of serious consideration in the eyes of many historians. Perhaps the biggest factor preventing Benjamin from becoming famous and remembered was his lower-class status as a sailor and merchant, because "it suited the authorities to push a narrative of enlightened elders leading the Quaker faith into its abolitionist viewpoint."[194]

In recent decades, historians have begun to acknowledge the major role Benjamin Lay's efforts played in getting Quaker elders to make changes to the faith as it was practiced in the 1750s and 1760s. It took until 2018 for the Abington Monthly Meeting to officially recognize that Benjamin and Sarah had been right all along—that he never should have been expelled from their church.

There is no better way to appreciate Benjamin than the ending to the article frequently cited in telling this story:

> Nowadays, Benjamin Lay still remains an obscure figure, but he should be remembered as one of the few Americans of his generation that recognized and refused to compromise with the evil that lay at the heart of their society. Benjamin made his own life into a parable. He knew that people would tell stories of the apparently crazy things he did, and he knew that through this the moral lesson he was teaching would spread. And while he preached a love for all mankind, he recognized that there was no contradiction between that and refusing to compromise with those who drew their wealth from human suffering. He was, in many ways, a man ahead of his time. But in many other ways he was exactly the man his time needed, and the world today would be a worse place if he had not been in it. For that, we should be grateful.[195]

CHAPTER 13

Anthony Bénézet
Celebrant of African Culture and Educator
of African American Youth

Never one to accept the beliefs and attitudes towards Black people that his fellow Quakers attempted to foist upon him, Anthony Bénézet saw for himself the importance of Africa and its many cultures and the intellectual power of Black people. That he did so before it was either fashionable or even acceptable makes it possible to understand how the following words describe his funeral:

> When Anthony Bénézet died in 1784 at the age of seventy-one, 400 of Philadelphia's Black citizens turned out to mourn his passing. Known for his humility and tireless devotion to the education and uplift of the black population, this gentle Quaker was known as "the single most prolific antislavery writer and the most influential advocate of the Negro's rights on either side of the Atlantic."[196]

Such a man, whose death inspired the devotional response of so many African Americans, must have lived a life worth commemorating and the reasons for such a turnout for a white man felt worthy of exploration. He not only advanced the cause of Black people, he also founded the first secondary school for girls in North America. But his 1817 biographer, Robert Vaux, (yes, Benjamin Lay's biographer two years earlier) acknowledges in the introduction to his *Memoirs of the Life of Anthony Bénézet,* there are many questions that cannot be answered about his life's trajectory.

Vaux tells us that even though just thirty-three years had passed since the death of his subject, and he would have expected to have available many of the documents and memorabilia of Anthony's life, "No traces are discernible of the mass of important and interesting documents, which must have accumulated during more than fifty years of the last years of his life, devoted as it was to the most benevolent of labors." On the cover of the book, Vaux included these words: "He was the offspring of humanity, and every child of sorrow was his brother." Vaux pushed on to create his biography despite the challenges and we shall do the same. Ultimately what emerges enables one to see how apropos his tribute was.[197]

Anthony Bénézet was the second of thirteen children born into a family of Huguenots in San Quentin, France, on January 31, 1713. With the Catholic Church's revocation of the Edict of Nantes in 1685, which had provided for religious tolerance, the Bénézet family, being Protestant, suffered mistreatment including the confiscation of their estate. Eventually they moved to Rotterdam, Netherlands, and subsequently to London. However, even though there were many Huguenots in England at the time, Anthony rejected his family's religion and joined the Religious Society of Friends, the Quakers, in 1727, at the age of fourteen.

The Bénézet family immigrated to the colonies in 1731 and set up their home in Philadelphia, which was founded by Quakers, and Anthony began attending Quaker meetings. He married Joyce Marriott, a Quaker, in 1736. Joyce was from Burlington, New Jersey. They were married for 48 years. At first they moved frequently as Anthony sought a career in business, but he came to realize that such an endeavor was not at all what he wanted for his life's work. He became a schoolmaster at the Germantown Academy, taking over from Daniel Francis Pastorius (see Chapter 11) in 1739. Three years later, he moved to the Friends English School in Philadelphia, where he was offered a yearly salary of £50 ($15,000 in today's dollars) to teach students from impoverished backgrounds, eight hours a day for six days a week. He accepted the offer and taught there for twelve years.[198]

After years of fulfilling his grueling daily schedule, in 1750 Anthony started tutoring enslaved and free Black students in the evenings, teaching them the same subjects he taught his white students during the day. He was one of the few white men of his era who did not subscribe to the theory of Black inferiority, nor to the idea that Africa was a barbaric continent. Citing a variety of sources to document the notable cultures that it had produced, he pointed to the achievements of the scholars he tutored as his final proof.

A word is in order about Anthony's teaching philosophy. Perhaps it is already apparent from his dedication to his students, but underpinning his approach was a steadfast conviction that basic human kindness was not only essential to good relations among people but to a productive learning environment He firmly believed that:

> What is learned willingly, and at the proper season, makes the
> deepest impression, and that much depends on the manner of

conveying lessons of instruction to the juvenile understanding...He investigated the natural dispositions of his pupils, and adapted his management of them, to their various tempers. Persuasion would secure attention and obedience in some, whilst proper excitement to emulation, would animate and encourage others.[199]

Anthony's deep and abiding appreciation for Black people and the land of their origin drove him to become more of an active abolitionist over time. Vaux captures his deepening commitment to the cause:

About the year 1750 it began to be observed that his feelings were deeply affected with the iniquity of the slave trade, the unlawfulness of carrying negroes into captivity, and the cruelty which was exercised by those who purchased and employed them.[200]

With his commitment to honoring all of his students and his firm Quaker beliefs, he came to condemn enslavement as sinful, but unlike many abolitionists, Anthony spent time among Philadelphia's Black population. In fact, he knew and was known by most of the Black population. In 1767 he wrote:

[A]s teacher of a school ... for many years, [I] had [the] opportunity of knowing the temper and genius of the Africans so with truth and sincerity declare amongst them as great a variety of talents, equally capable of improvement, as amongst a like number of whites. And I so bold to assert, that the notion entertained by some, that the blacks are inferior in their capacities, is a vulgar prejudice, founded on the pride or ignorance of their lordly masters; who have kept their slaves at such a distance, as to be unable to form a right judgment of them.[201]

Black children were not the only ones who benefited from Anthony's dedication. In 1754, he left the Friends' English School to set up the first public girls' school in America. His students included daughters from prominent families. Further proof of his commitment to all of his

students is shown in what Anthony did for those with special needs. In an era marked by great intolerance for people with disabilities, he devised a program for a hearing- and speech-impaired girl at the school that enabled her to be part of the community.

Quakers were still very much divided with respect to enslavement. Together with John Woolman, a close friend and a fellow Quaker from his early years in Philadelphia, Anthony sought to convince other Quakers that owning slaves went against Christian doctrine. He and Woolman led the Philadelphia Quaker Yearly Meeting in 1776, which produced a resolution requiring other local meetings to expel Quakers who owned enslaved people—ninety years after the authors of the Germantown Petition had tried and failed to do so.

To further his abolitionist quest, Anthony had an active correspondence with European anti-slavery activists. These included William Wilberforce and Granville Sharp in England and Benjamin Franklin when he was residing in France. In a letter to Sharp, Anthony wrote:

> I am glad to understand from my friend Benjamin Franklin, that you
> have commenced an acquaintance, and that he expects in future, to

act in concert with thee in the affair of slavery. I herewith send thee some pamphlets and in a confidence in thy goodness of heart, which by looking to the intention, will construe the freedom I have taken in the best light.[202]

This man of enormous compassion had great regard and respect for Native Americans. Vaux's memoir contains a ten-page letter Anthony wrote to Lord Jeffrey Amherst laying out the mistreatment the tribe he was confronting had suffered at the hands of white settlers. As a pacifist and as someone who truly understood the injustices heaped upon Indian people, he implored Amherst not to take up arms and instead to negotiate an agreement that would be upheld. His words sadly fell on deaf ears, and the town of Amherst, where one of the authors of this book lives, retains his name despite such cruelty as selling smallpox-infected blankets to Native people of which he was guilty.

When America gained its independence, Anthony continued his quest to ban enslavement in the new country. The Pennsylvania General Assembly finally passed a law calling for the "gradual abolition" of enslavement on March 1, 1780, and his influence was profound.

Anthony continued to teach Black children out of his home until he was able to set up a school of his own. With the support of the Society of Friends, the Negro School of Philadelphia opened in 1770 to serve Black students along with local poor boys and girls. The free Black community in the city increased significantly after the abolition of enslavement in 1780. Over the next six years, the school served about 250 Black students, accepting enslaved children when there were not enough free children to fill the classes. On April 14, 1775, Anthony founded the Society for the Relief of Free Negroes Unlawfully Held in Bondage. It was the first American abolitionist society.

For twenty-five years, Anthony wrote and published letters and pamphlets in opposition to slavery, and persuaded others to do likewise. His publications include *An Account of that Part of Africa Inhabited by the Negroes* (1762), *A Caution and Warning to Great Britain and Her Colonies, in a Short Representation of the Calamitous State of the Enslaved Negroes in the British Dominions* (1767) and *Some Historical Account of Guinea, with an Inquiry into the Rise and Progress of the Slave-Trade* (1772). Here is an oft-referenced excerpt from *A Caution and Warning to Great Britain*:

> Much might be justly said of temporal evils which attend this practice, as it is destructive of the welfare of human society, and of the peace and prosperity of every country, in proportion as it prevails. It might also be shown, that it destroys the bonds of natural affection and interest, whereby mankind in general are united; that it introduces idleness, discourages marriage, corrupts the youth, ruins and debauches morals, excites continual apprehensions of dangers, and frequent alarms. But as these and more reflections of the same kind, may occur to a considerate mind, I shall endeavour to show, from the nature of the Trade, the plenty which Guinea affords to its inhabitants, the barbarous Treatment of the Negroes, and the observations made thereon by Authors of note, that it is inconsistent with the plainest Precepts of the Gospel, the dictates of reason, and every common sentiment of humanity.[203]

His works were read widely in England and the colonies. His book about Guinea made a deep impression on the English abolitionist Thomas Clarkson:

> The influence of his account of Guinea, in giving an impulse to the mind of the indefatigable and benevolent Thomas Clarkson, whose exertions contributed so much toward bringing about the abolition of the slave trade by the British Parliament, is certainly remarkable.[204]

Anthony sent copies of his work along with impassioned letters to the queens of England, France, and Portugal imploring them to both read his work and join him in seeking the demise of enslavement.

In 1782 the schoolmaster John Houghton resigned from the Negro School, and no one could be found to replace him. At sixty-nine, this was a daunting task for Anthony, but he chose to take the position and spent the final two years of his life doing what he loved most.

Although his estate was small, he left it to endow the Negro School, which became a Quaker school with the Overseers of the Friends' Public Schools as trustees. The school, which became the Raspberry Street School, lasted for over a hundred years.

Anthony died on May 3, 1784, at the age of seventy-one and was buried in the Friends' Burial Ground in Philadelphia. As a testimony to his humility and tireless devotion to the education and uplift of the black population, four hundred of Philadelphia's beleaguered Black citizens turned out to mourn a white man. Robert Vaux wrote about his funeral:

> At the interment of Anthony Bénezét's remains, which took place two days after his death, the greatest concourse of people that had ever been witnessed on such an occasion in Philadelphia, was present; being a collection of all ranks and professions among the inhabitants; thus manifesting the universal esteem in which he was held. Among others who paid that last tribute of respect, were many hundred Black people, testifying by their attendance, and by their tears, the grateful sense they entertained of his pious efforts in their behalf.[205]

Even after his death, Anthony continued to influence his contemporaries. The appearance of his ghost in a dream prompted slaveowner Benjamin Rush to devote himself to the cause of abolition. The year of this "conversion" is unknown, but Rush's dream inspired him to join the Pennsylvania Abolition Society in 1787. Rush was not only a forceful spokesperson for abolition, he also authored its new constitution and served as its secretary and president. He was instrumental in the establishment of the city's first Black church, completely free from white control in 1792.[206]

A much more recent biography, *Let This Voice Be Heard: Anthony Bénézet, Father of Atlantic Abolitionism,* by Maurice Jackson (2010), highlights Anthony's global impact. Jackson captures the ways in which his subject created what can be called a "new anti-slavery critique" by combining Enlightenment political and social thought, stories of African life that he obtained from slave traders, and the words of ordinary people.

The influence of this work in challenging pro-slavery views about the "primitive" nature of African society is incalculable. He changed the way people thought about the enslaved. His words, though unattributed, were read into the record of the French National Assembly by the abolitionist Pierre Brissot and the British Parliament by William Wilberforce. As such, they are a worthy tribute to his enduring work.

Finally, at his funeral, a soldier who had served in the American military during the Revolutionary War delivered a brief but stirring eulogy. Summing up his feelings about this extraordinary man, the soldier said, "I would rather be Anthony Bénézet, in that coffin, than the great Washington with all his honor."[207]

We couldn't agree more with this sentiment. It also connects to the white senator who fought long and hard for the Thirteenth, Fourteenth and Fifteenth amendments following the conclusion of the Civil War, Thaddeus Stevens, who chose to be buried in a Black cemetery. Bénézet would no doubt have had great respect for a fellow abolitionist and crusader for equality and justice for *all* people. Here's the epitaph on Steven's tombstone, eighty-four years after Bénézet's funeral, all of which fits Bénézet as well.

> I repose in this quiet and secluded spot, not for any natural preference for solitude. But, finding other cemeteries limited as to race by charter rules, I have chosen this that I might illustrate in my death, the principles which I advocated through a long life. Equality of man before his creator.

Courtesy of the Moses Brown School, Providence, RI

CHAPTER 14

Moses Brown
Defying Family and Convention to Honor Those He Had Once Enslaved

What did it take to change a person's mind—and even more significantly, their heart—about enslavement? What was the catalyst that caused a person to journey from either ignorance of the horrors, or somehow closing down one's sensibilities if one knew, to seeing the imperative need to abolish the hateful institution? We have two examples of men whose change of mind and heart resulted from witnessing the true and undeniable effects of their involvement in the slave trade. The first, John Newton, we know most poignantly from the song he wrote, "Amazing Grace." When the ship he captained carrying African men, women, and children bound for enslavement, confronted a terrible storm on the Atlantic, he vowed, if he lived, to no longer participate in the slave trade. He wrote that it was "amazing grace...that saved a wretch like me."

The other man, Moses Brown, also had an interest in the slave trade. In 1764, he and his brothers, Nicholas, John, and Joseph, sailed their ship, the *Sally*, from Providence, Rhode Island, to West Africa, where 196 Africans were acquired by the ship's master, Esek Hopkins. Of that group, 109 died during the Middle Passage: by suicide, starvation, disease, and a failed rebellion. Witnessing this devastation changed Moses Brown. His conscience could no longer tolerate the knowledge that he was contributing to such atrocities. By 1774 he had become a Quaker and expressed his revelation thus: "I saw my slaves with my spiritual eyes as plainly as I see you now and it was given to me as clearly to understand that the sacrifice that was called for of my hand was to give them liberty."[208]

But he was only one of four Brown brothers, and John was dedicated to the slave trade, believing that enslavement was "right, just and lawful, and consequently practiced every day." America, he argued, was doing Africans a favor by removing them from what he described as their "barbaric homeland." Needless to say this conflict between brothers had a major impact on their lives and their relationship, as well as on the history of Rhode Island. John spoke of abolitionism as "wicked and abominable," words Moses could have readily invoked in condemning his brother's views on enslavement as well as his actions.

It is neither an accident nor a surprise that it took a Black woman, Ruth Simmons, serving as Brown University's first Black president in 2006, to inaugurate a study of the school's past involvement in the slave trade. The study revealed the role Moses and his brothers played, and forms the basis of what follows.

Moses Brown was the youngest of six children born to James and Hope (Power). Born on September 23, 1738, he spent his entire life in Providence and was a Baptist by birth. His was a most privileged childhood. He was descended from Rhode Island luminaries including his great-great grandfather, Chad Brown, an early English settler of the colony and a signatory of the Providence Compact in 1637, and his grandfather Elder James Brown, pastor of the First Baptist Church. His father's generation accumulated their wealth as merchants, trafficking in molasses, rum, and enslaved Africans in the triangle trade between America, Europe, and Africa. His son, James II's ship, *Mary*, may have been the first to journey from Providence to Africa for purposes of enslaving people around 1735. Though little money was made as a result of the expedition, the Browns were more than willing to make the effort.

Four years later, misfortune struck the Brown family. Moses was just six months old when his father was lost at sea. His Uncle Obadiah stepped in to take care of Moses. Like his father, Obadiah was a successful merchant, and by the time Moses reached thirteen years of age, he started working for his uncle as an apprentice in Obadiah Brown and Co. Five years later he became a partner, joining his four brothers. Obadiah traded directly with England instead of going through Newport or Boston, and much of his wealth was derived from investing in the whaling industry. By 1751 he had opened a factory that produced candles out of spermaceti, a substance produced by sperm whales, but he also distilled rum and produced iron in his factories. It was his decision to attempt to capture and enslave Africans, which he began in 1759 when he organized an expedition for the ship named *Wheel of Fortune*. It fell victim to French privateers, living up to its name.

After Obadiah's death in 1762, the company was divided among the four Brown brothers, but the new name, Nicholas Brown and Co., was not accompanied by new endeavors. Instead Moses and his brothers became slave owners, and he participated willingly in a high-risk, high-reward endeavor that was the triangle trade.

Rhode Island was a bustling marketplace where many grew rich. Rhode Island merchants controlled 60 to 90 percent of the American slave trade in the eighteenth century. During a period of seventy-five years, more than 900 ships left Rhode Island for Africa. They returned with over one hundred thousand slaves.

Of course, this was only a fraction of what the European slave captains transported, but Rhode Island merchants outdistanced Massachusetts merchants by the 1730s, and by 1800 they led all states in the importation of enslaved people. Newport had the monopoly. Of the 513 ships that were sent to Africa, all but twenty-one left from its port. Providence sent out nine and the Brown brothers sent one, Sally.

The pages of a 1764 accounting book for the *Sally* provide rich details of the fateful voyage financed by the Brown brothers. The spine of the book is ripped and the back cover has gone missing, but specifics of the journey are still visible, including the number of Africans captured each day. Thirty-seven were taken on June 10, 1764—the same day the captain traded fifty-five gallons of rum and a gun "for a slave girl." The ledger tells of an attempted slave rebellion that was put down by the crew, who killed some of those involved while others died from injuries. When the ship arrived in Antigua over a year after leaving Providence, most of the surviving Africans were then sold.

Moses, along with all of his brothers but John, never again played an active part in the slave trade, and John's ongoing enthusiasm for dealing in the sale of human beings led to the dissolution of the family partnership in 1769. Yet even after the business failed over this issue, the brothers continued to trade in goods produced by enslaved people as well as to do business with slave owners and slave traders. It would take another calamitous event to fully turn Moses away from such practices.

In 1764 Moses married his cousin, Anna Brown, daughter of Obadiah and no doubt someone he knew well, having been raised in the same household. He was already a wealthy man, and he and Anna went on to raise three sons and a daughter together. The same year as his wedding, he was chosen to be a deputy of the Rhode Island General Assembly. During his four-year tenure, he experienced the growing tensions between the British colony and the mother country. He chose to join those beginning to consider revolution.

Moses was far from the most radical of his brothers. In 1772, John set fire to the British schooner *Gaspee* when it ran aground seeking smugglers. This event, along with similar incidents around the same time, were the first violent acts against the crown, occurring a full year before the Boston Tea Party and bringing the colonies that much closer to armed rebellion.

In 1769, Moses played a significant role closer to home. He was instrumental in moving Rhode Island College from its campus in coastal Warren to the city of Providence. The Brown brothers donated the land where the new college was built. Moses was not content to remain exclusively a merchant and sought greater learning. He participated in observations of the astronomical phenomenon known as the Transit of Venus, of lightning bugs, and of the progress of cowpox, a disease that afflicted his own children following their inoculation in 1808.[209]

It was another tragedy—an even more personal one—that added to the momentum driving him to become a fully committed abolitionist. After only nine years of marriage, in 1773, Anna died. Moses, who was already seriously questioning his life and involvement in the slave trade, was bereft. He saw Anna's passing as a punishment for his owning and trading slaves.

The writings of Quakers like Anthony Bénézet (see Chapter 13) served to shake him further, but it was Anna's untimely death that caused Moses to enter a period of self-examination with regard to his political and social attitudes. This taking stock of his life resulted in his withdrawal from his business endeavors and his becoming a member of the Society of Friends the following year, in 1774. Around this time, Moses demonstrated his newfound commitments by not only freeing those he had kept in bondage, but, in an early example of reparative justice, also compensating them monetarily for their servitude and helping them find jobs. He petitioned his fellow Quakers to do the same.

From this point on, Moses's opposition to enslavement became his passionate cause. It lead to a bitter, long-lasting feud with his brother John over the immorality of enslaving African people that no doubt deepened each time he acted to undo the institution. Moses sought to persuade his former merchant colleagues to leave the slave trade behind. He did the same with legislatures in New England that dragged their feet on passing laws to make such trade illegal. He arranged for anti-slavery literature to be printed and distributed. His dedication saw him carry on important correspondences with both American and British abolitionists. None of these actions sat well with John who continued to argue for the perpetuation of enslavement in the Americas.

Perhaps Moses's most important contribution to the cause of freedom for the enslaved was his work in founding the Providence Society for Abolishing the Slave Trade in 1786. A year later, with a strong push to do so from Moses, Rhode Island finally banned the slave trade. The society then focused its efforts on enforcing the legislature's act, though they had next to no support from those in power.

Such endeavors to have Rhode Island become a state supporting freedom and equality were not enough for Moses. He pursued his anti-slavery agenda to the federal level and is credited with helping to get the Slave Trade Act of 1794 passed by Congress. With the goal of limiting US involvement in the international slave trade, the act forbade foreign ships from benefiting from services at American ports. When President George Washington signed it into law on March 22, 1794, it was the first of several anti-slavery trade acts by Congress. The next was the banning of the importation of enslaved people to the US in 1807, but it took the Thirteenth Amendment to finally outlaw the trading and owning of human beings in America, long past the very long lifetime of Moses Brown.

Moses's pursuit of freedom for enslaved people and John's pursuit of profits from the slave trade put them in conflict, but not for the reasons most historians claim. Yes, John sent out two slaving ships in 1785 and 1786, and three years later he railed against Moses's abolition society in a published screed, calling it a Quaker organization determined to ruin honest merchants. This led to an angry debate involving John and officers of the Society of Friends, including Moses, that played out in the *Providence Gazette*. It turns out that John's anger was not from his own position. He had already told his brother he was not going to return to the Guinea trade, but he felt compelled to defend his friends, whom the Quakers were planning on suing.

Another reason for John's wrath against the society was his passionate belief in the need for Rhode Island to sign the constitution. Two years after its creation, it was the only state not to have ratified the document, and much of the opposition came from the Friends. They objected to the slavery compromises that have haunted the nation since its inception. By 1789, the local argument had turned into a full-blown national crisis, and Congress was prepared to cut off all trade with Rhode Island. In the end, it required Congress taking steps that would have forced Rhode Island to become a foreign country to turn the tide, and the constitution passed by two votes. But even then, Providence threatened to secede from the state.[210]

Given all of this intrigue, it is not entirely surprising that John ended up being the first American to face the consequences of violating the Slave Trade Act. Still believing in the viability of enslavement and unaffected by his brother's efforts at moral suasion or the passage of the act, John conspired with Captain Peleq Wood to use the ship (ironically named *Hope*) to remain engaged in the slave trade. The penalties for disobeying the law were clear—the forfeiture of any ill-gotten profits, the possibility of a $2,000 fine (roughly $70,000 today), the forfeiture of any enslaved people on the ship, and a fine of $200 per person. Notwithstanding these punishments, John's ship brought 229 slaves to Havana, Cuba, in 1796, which led to his being arrested and tried for violating the statute. He lost his case and was obliged to forfeit *Hope*.

Somehow, through all of their conflicts about enslavement, the brothers never experienced a total breakdown and estrangement. They were actually involved in many more endeavors that united them than the one, an albeit significant one, that divided them. Their ventures brought them both great wealth, and at times they would join forces. In 1791, they founded a bank, only the fifth private bank in the US at the time. They went on to work together on Providence's infrastructure, building the roads, bridges, and wharves the growing town needed. Even when John was in Congress representing their state, they exchanged warm letters.

Meanwhile, not only was Moses determined to have the US government work to end enslavement, he also supported enslaved people and free Blacks on an individual basis, offering financial and legal assistance that enabled many to actively pursue freedom.

Remarkably, another of Moses's endeavors actually figures into the start of the Industrial Revolution. In 1788, he became partners with his cousin Smith Brown and an associate, William Almy. These men had learned about innovations that were transforming the textiles industry in England. Samuel Slater joined their enterprise in 1790, and he oversaw the construction of the first water powered textile mill in the new nation, in Pawtucket, Rhode Island.

But Moses had another purpose for building such a mill, one that went beyond mere profits. He was seeking a way to encourage those he knew were still invested in the slave trade to invest in domestic manufacturing instead of shipping cotton overseas to have it fabricated. Sadly, it appears he was not yet aware that the mills he was promoting in New England required the king crop of the South and soon, as the mill concept spread, in ever-increasing quantities.

Moses was not content to focus solely on anti-enslavement activism. He became a dedicated supporter of pacifism, the temperance movement, and the rights of Native Americans. He also was very active in the Society of Friends, and was often called upon to assist in the construction of new meeting houses throughout New England. Of particular interest for him were educational causes. Not only was he deeply involved in promoting the university that would become Brown, he also supported the African Union Meeting and Schoolhouse. Prior to the creation of this church, many Black Providence residents attended white churches, but their presence was not fully welcomed. Here's how William Brown described the situation prior to 1819:

> The largest numbers...were Baptists and belonged to the First Baptist Church, but many attended no church at all because they were opposed to going to churches and sitting in pigeon holes, as all the churches at that time had some obscure place for the colored people to sit in.[211]

These observations were supported at the time by Reverend V.R. Osborn, a preacher in a Methodist Church in Providence, who commented: "They were in a deplorable situation. They had no place of worship nor was there a congregation in town which desired their attendance."[212]

Whether from humanitarian impulses or a simple desire to get Black people out of white churches, on March 19, 1819, a group of white philanthropists called a meeting of many leading Black people to discuss establishing a Black church. The men in attendance were asked to solicit funds from their community. However, Moses told them, "Now go and select you out a lot suitable for your purpose and I will pay for it." White churches encouraged these efforts, and the Society of Friends of Providence responded generously. Moses donated a lot worth $200 ($5000 in today's dollars) while the Black community, despite most families living in poverty, raised another $500 ($12,500 in today's dollars).

On the day Moses purchased the property he immediately willed it to the Black community of Providence. He appointed his son Obadiah and his friends, George Benson and Henry Jackson, as lease holders. He had clear ideas on how the new church should run.

There were no Lancastrian[213] teachers available, so that goal could not be fulfilled, but what is more notable is a remark made by Moses: "Providence had done nothing to educate the Negroes before construction of the Meeting House," which showed how the city had comprehensively neglected the community's needs and underscored the dire need for such a school.

Two additional schools benefited from Moses's commitment to increasing educational opportunities. He was a founder of the Yearly Meeting School on Aquidneck Island in 1784 and, following the decision to close the school in 1788 due to a shortage of students and teachers, he set out to restart it. In 1819, it reopened as the New England Yearly Meeting Boarding School in Providence, with Moses donating the land. He did the same for the African Union Meeting and Schoolhouse, which opened the same year and eventually became the Moses Brown School in 1904.

From its inception the school was coeducational, in keeping with Quaker values of gender equality. Spurred on by changing attitudes towards educating girls and boys together, it became an all-boys school in 1926, only to change back to its original coed format in 1976, at least in part due to the resurgent women's movement. The school's reversion to its earliest days would surely have pleased someone with the egalitarian spirit of Moses Brown.

Moses remarried twice following Anna's death, first to Mary Olney and then to Phebe Lockwood. He stayed active in the causes to which he was committed until the end of his life. When he died in 1832, just short of ninety-eight years old, he had paid a steep price for his longevity, having been predeceased by all three of his wives, all of his children, and three of his four stepchildren.

It would take 171 years for Brown University to begin to reckon with its past. Ruth Simmons became the eighteenth president of the renowned institution on November 9, 2000, making her the first Black president of an Ivy League university. In 2003, Ms. Simmons appointed a Steering Committee on Slavery and Justice tasked with exploring Brown's historical relationship to slavery and the transatlantic slave trade. Despite warnings that it was dangerous to examine the school's past, she was not dissuaded. Instead she persisted. "It seemed like the right thing to do," she said, noting America's "long history of forgetting."[214]

In an op-ed in response to some of the criticism her plan received, she wrote:

The Committee's work is not about whether or how reparations should be paid. Rather, it will do the difficult work of scholarship, debate and civil discourse, demonstrating how difficult, uncomfortable and valuable this process can be...This review, though important in its own right, is especially important for an institution like Brown that was founded in 1764, a period in our nation's history when nearly all commerce and wealth was in some manner entangled with the slave trade.

For example, construction of the University's first building involved the labor of Providence area slaves...In addition, in view of the often confusing and contentious discussion of reparations, we wanted to move the examination away from a focus on reparations to learn more about the many ways in which societies past and present have dealt with retrospective justice following human rights violations such as genocide, internment, and certain forms of discrimination. We thought that our students would benefit from an understanding of those histories and experiences.

Finally, we hoped that such an effort, rooted in our particular history, would excite interest among students and help them appreciate and accept meaningful discourse on even the most troubling subjects.[215]

Following the completion of the report, Simmons, who retired as Brown's president in 2012, was invited in 2011 to give a lecture at St. John's College, University of Cambridge. Here is how she expressed her choice of title, "Hidden in Plain Sight: Slavery and Justice in Rhode Island.": "Every day I'm facing the portrait of the first president (James Manning) who was a slaveholder. It is everywhere around and yet invisible to us."

One result of the report was the creation of the Center for the Study of Slavery and Justice, which houses a rotating exhibit of work by Black artists. It is also where the slavery tour, another result of the report, begins and where center staff hold classes and offer programs. One such program takes Providence high school students on a civil rights tour of the South. When there was a suggestion that Simmons should apologize on behalf of the university for its role in the slave trade, she adamantly refused. She said, "That's ridiculous. I can't issue an apology for slavery because of who I am...If the board wants to do it, they are free to do it, but it makes no sense for me to do it. It would be too convenient to have an African American apologizing for slavery."

James Campbell, professor of American civilization and Africana studies, was chair of the committee Simmons appointed. He has made it clear that the report's centerpiece will be the history of the Brown brothers' roles in the enslavement of African people. The focus will be on the debate between Moses and John over the slave trade. Campbell expressed that he was pleased to uncover the debate. He felt that it revealed the moral choices both John and Moses made over time in an historical context and made it unnecessary for the committee to offer its explanation of the moral climate of their time.

Moses Brown was an important historical figure, a major proponent of abolitionism, and a memorable example of someone who refused to profit from the horrors of slavery, long before most people were willing to take such a public stance. Through his words and actions, he made it impossible for his contemporaries to claim ignorance of the inhumanity of enslavement. Moses was also a trailblazer in his home state of Rhode Island, someone who helped pass key legislation that helped bring about the demise of the slave trade, first locally and then nationally. He was most assuredly a powerful influence on the next generation of men and women seeking freedom and equality for African Americans.

Courtesy of Rhode Island Historical Society Collections

CHAPTER 15

Elizabeth Buffum Chace
Memoirist of the Anti-Slavery Movement

I would not have a slave to till my ground,
To carry me, to fan me while I sleep,
And tremble when I wake, for all the wealth
That sinews bought and sold have ever earned.

No; dear as freedom is, and in my heart's
Just estimation prized above all price,
I had much rather be myself the slave,
And wear the bonds, than fasten them on him.

Elizabeth Buffum Chace grew up listening to her father, Arnold Buffum, singing "Abhorrence of Slavery," the William Cowper poem excerpted above, as he went about his daily activities in their Smithfield, Rhode Island, home. How could it not affect a young girl to hear the words of an English poet who inspired Quakers like her father to fight the abhorrent institution of enslavement? The impact was undeniable and propelled her to seek justice as a conductor on the Underground Railroad.

At every opportunity, Elizabeth spoke out and incurred the hostility of her fellow Quakers as well as white women who would deny Black women membership in anti-slavery organizations. She held to her beliefs regardless of such resistance. In her memoir, *Anti-Slavery Reminiscences*, she chronicles the obstacles she confronted and the dogged determination with which she met them. When her beloved father was "disowned" by his fellow Quakers, she chose to resign from the Society of Friends rather than compromise her values, writing:

> Finally, after a long struggle, I was compelled, in order to secure my own peace of mind, to resign my membership in the Society, to which, from my childhood, I had been most devoutly attached... But, with my family cares and labor for the cause of the slave, and the associations it brought me, I had no time or inclination to worry over lost friendships; and the relief from responsibility for the pro-slavery attitude of the Society, was sufficient compensation for all I thus relinquished.[216]

Elizabeth Chace was born on December 9, 1806, to Arnold and Rebecca Gould Buffum. Both parents descended from families with deep New England roots. Her family's origin story was one of coming to America. Her maternal ancestor Daniel Gould arrived from England in 1637, settled in Newport, became a Quaker, and married the daughter of John Coggeshall, the first president of the Aquidneck Colony and a fellow Quaker. The merchants of Newport had long and deep roots in the slave trade. Quakers were speaking out against enslavement as early as 1688, but it wasn't until 1780 that New England Quakers abolished slavery within their community, almost 100 years after the petition of Daniel Pastorius and his fellow Friends.

Much of what we know about Elizabeth comes from her memoir. It began with a brief history of her family followed by a description of her father, Arnold, and his experiences, which were somewhat analogous to her experience of hearing him recite Cowper's poem as a child. In his case, the formative experience she delineates occurred during his childhood when an enslaved family fleeing New York came to Rhode Island and lived on his father's farm. Elizabeth's grandfather was a member of the old Abolition Society of Rhode Island, and it is significant to acknowledge that Arnold's father educated his son in the centrality of immediate emancipation. Seeing firsthand how enslavement impacted this escaping family had a powerful impact on him, which only intensified as he grew up.

As an adult, Arnold visited England and encountered Thomas Clarkson, a leading voice speaking out against the slave trade in the British Empire. He was a founder of the Society for Effecting the Abolition of the Slave Trade and helped achieve passage of the Slave Trade Act of 1807, which ended British trade in slaves. When Arnold met him, he was fighting for the world-wide abolition of enslavement, which was most pernicious in the Americas. In 1840, he was the key speaker at the first conference of the Anti-Slavery Society (now known as Anti-Slavery International) in London, which sought to abolish slavery in other countries. These encounters with anti-slavery men and women of England enabled Arnold to bring to his role as the first president of the New England Anti-Slavery Society in 1832 faith, earnestness, and dedication to liberty for all.

Many Quakers, despite opposing enslavement, were suspicious of the Buffums. This arose from her grandfather's firm belief in immediate abolition, an idea that was too radical for some to swallow. Many favored gradual abolition, and many of these saw the ultimate solution as the emigration of freed Black people to African colonies. Elizabeth attended the Friends School at the age of sixteen in 1822, and no doubt she heard arguments on both sides of this issue.

By the time Elizabeth was a young adult, she was deeply committed to the same cause as her father and grandfather. She was strongly cautioned by several Quaker ministers not to give voice to her position, and faced similar opposition from within her own family. Her Quaker brother-in-law, in flagrant defiance of the official Quaker stance, told her that enslaved Black people should not be free because, "I shouldn't want to see a Black man sitting on the sofa beside my daughter."

At age twenty-three, Elizabeth married Samuel Chace, a Quaker whose father founded several textile mills. They lived in Valley Falls, Rhode Island, and had ten children. Sadly, only the last five of them survived childhood. Three died of scarlet fever, tragically a common occurrence at the time. Elizabeth gave birth to the last child in 1852, when she was forth-five years old. Remarkably, throughout her grueling twenty years of bearing children, Elizabeth remained active in anti-slavery causes. She and Samuel were similarly opposed to slavery, though she was the outspoken advocate for emancipation. Their Rhode Island home soon became a main stop on the Underground Railroad, much as her grandfather's farm had been. It is depicted here:

Courtesy of New York Public Library Digital Collections

Many of the anti-slavery pitchmen and women visited the Chaces in Valley Falls. Here Elizabeth acknowledges some of them, as well as foreshadowing the need for this book:

> After coming to Rhode Island, our house became the resting place for the advocates of freedom for the slave, when traveling, or lecturing in this region, until the fetters which bound him were broken. William Lloyd Garrison, Wendell Phillips, Parker Pillsbury, Stephen S. Foster, Abby Kelley, Henry C. Wright, Charles Remond, Frederick Douglass, Charles and Cyrus Burleigh, Lucy Stone, William Wells Brown and others of less note, were often our guests; and our children were born and bred in the atmosphere which these lovers of freedom helped to create in our household. *The career of all these men and women should*

> *be written for the perusal of coming generations, as grand examples of*
> *noble, self - sacrificing manhood and womanhood, such as the world has*
> *seldom proved itself capable of producing.* [italics ours])[217]

One story that Elizabeth recounts in her memoir serves to illuminate the level of commitment she and her husband had to the cause of justice and equality. Traveling to Boston for the annual meeting of the Anti-Slavery Society, they were to take a train with only one car from Fall River to Boston when they were joined by a fellow white compatriot in the anti-slavery cause along with a Black man and woman. When the conductor saw the Black couple, he demanded that they leave the car. Elizabeth and Samuel requested that the superintendent intervene, but he only echoed the conductor's response. They were then told that a second railroad car would be added to the train for the express purpose of enabling the Black couple to have separate accommodations and to prevent the races from sharing a car. Here is how Elizabeth described what happened next in her memoir:

> We held a little conference among ourselves, and then every one of us entered the car with the colored people. The superintendent was very angry, but he did not quite dare to order us out, so he assured us that our conduct would avail nothing, for no negroes would ever be permitted to be mixed up with white people on that road. They were mixed up with us, however, on that day, and we found them intelligent, agreeable companions.[218]

It was William Lloyd Garrison's commitment to immediate emancipation as founder and leader of the American Anti-Slavery Society that most appealed to Elizabeth when she made the commitment to a more public role in the fight against enslavement. His organization had a reputation as a threat to the social order. But as a woman in the movement, Elizabeth went considerably further in what she was calling for. She and her female comrades strongly encouraged their northern compatriots to protest in the streets in support of enslaved mothers and children. They encouraged mothers to train their children to be activists, and they fervently believed in the power of women to accomplish social change.[219]

Elizabeth was instrumental in the founding of the Fall River Female Anti-Slavery Society in 1835. Once again there was controversy within the ranks. Three years into its existence racism almost ended the newly formed Female Anti-Slavery Society of Fall River, Massachusetts. The society was founded by white women from respected families. Its members organized lectures, signed petitions, and raised money. When three Black women sought membership, it precipitated a crisis for the society. They were already attending meetings, but several members objected to their joining. Elizabeth wrote in her diary, "But they did not think it was at all proper to invite them to join the Society, thus putting them on an equality with ourselves." The society survived, but only after Elizabeth and her sister "maintained [their] ground" and the "respectable young colored women" were invited to become full members.[220]

Julie Roy Jeffrey's *The Great Silent Army of Abolitionism* is a recent exploration of the Fall River incident. It shines a light on the disconnect between the claims of historians—then[221] and now—that acknowledge the critical role of women in the movement while focusing almost entirely on men's contributions. She uses unpublished letters from abolitionist women, "often languishing in the well-mined collections of prominent male abolitionists" along with the words of the women themselves in diaries and organizational records to show how the arduous and constant efforts of women kept abolitionism alive. Certainly, Elizabeth Buffum Chace fits the bill.[222]

Elizabeth was very aware of the conflict within Quakerism in the 1840s regarding enslavement. She had this to say in her memoir:

> Several persons, in various parts of the country, were forcibly carried out of the Friends meeting for attempting therein to urge upon Friends the duty to maintain, faithfully their testimony against slavery, as their Discipline required. A few meeting houses in country places had been opened for the Anti-Slavery meetings, whereupon our New England Yearly Meeting adopted a rule that no meeting house under its jurisdiction should be opened except for meetings of our religious Society.[223]

The hypocrisy and subterfuge no doubt deeply troubled Elizabeth. Such an edict flew in the face of her values and her hopes for Quakerism. But she was not empowered to undo the damage. She doesn't tell us if she was among those "forcibly carried out of the Friends meeting," but we do know that she found alternative ways to practice what she believed in.

This is what she wrote about her Underground Railroad activities in her memoir:

> Slaves in Virginia would secure passage, either secretly or with consent of the Captains, in small trading vessels, at Norfolk or Portsmouth, and thus be brought into some port in New England, where their fate depended on the circumstances into which they happened to fall. A few, landing in some town on Cape Cod, would reach New Bedford, and thence be sent by an abolitionist there to Fall River, to be sheltered by Nathaniel B. Borden and his wife, who was my sister Sarah, and sent by them, to Valley Falls, in the darkness of night, and in a closed carriage, with Robert Adams, a most faithful friend, as their conductor.
>
> Here, we received them, and, after preparing them for the journey, my husband would accompany them a short distance, on the Providence and Worcester railroad, acquaint the conductor with the facts, enlist his interest in their behalf, and then leave them in his care, to be transferred at Worcester, to the Vermont road, from which, by a previous general arrangement, they were received by a Unitarian clergyman named Young, and sent by him to Canada, where they uniformly arrived safely.
>
> I used to give them an envelope, directed to us, to be mailed in Toronto, which, when it reached us, was sufficient by its post-mark, to announce their safe arrival, beyond the baleful influence of the Stars and Stripes, and the anti-protection of the Fugitive Slave Act.[224]

Elizabeth and Samuel were once awakened in the middle of the night by a mother and her two boys. She had escaped slavery in Maryland, moved to Fall River and quietly earned a living as a laundress. A notorious slave catcher started snooping around her neighborhood asking about her. Her friends sent her to the Chace's house in Valley Falls, where she and one of her children awaited the arrival of her oldest son, who would bring their belongings. Elizabeth described the scene:

> We kept them three or four days, in hourly fear and expectation of the arrival of the slave-catcher; our doors and windows fastened by day as well as by night, not daring to let our neighbors know who were our guests, lest someone should betray them. We told our children, all, at that time, under fourteen years of age, of the fine of one thousand dollars, and the imprisonment of six months, that awaited us, in case the officer should come, and we should refuse to give these poor people up.[225]

Elizabeth did not take on such responsibilities lightly or without clear awareness that her actions could get her arrested. Here she writes about that awareness:

> Had the slave-catchers come for those young men, we should not have opened our doors to them, and we should have done everything in our power, consistent with our peace principles, to prevent their capture. The consequences would, probably, have been serious to us, but we were prepared for whatever they might be, feeling sure, that we were obeying a higher and more imperative law. Our children and our servants entered heartily into our sentiments, although some of our Christian neighbors did not.[226]

Elizabeth was obliged to pay a heavy price in her community for her activism and advocacy of other women's activism. She found herself a social outcast. Thankfully, she maintained friendship ties with a small circle of fellow radical abolitionists. In 1858, she hosted such renowned orators as Frederick Douglass, Wendell Phillips, and Sojourner Truth at her home in Central Falls, Rhode Island, where she and Samuel had settled. With the outbreak of the Civil War, they both gave full support to the Union cause, but given their views on immediate abolition, they were disappointed with Lincoln's refusal to emancipate the enslaved at the outset of the war.

Elizabeth's efforts at achieving equality did not end with the emancipation of African Americans. Inequality in education grabbed her attention, and she fought for the integration of schools. She took her militancy to the fight for women's rights next, providing stalwart support for young women denied a college education because of their gender. One of her most noteworthy accomplishments in this realm was her work in the founding of Pembroke College, the women's college associated with Brown University. She failed in her efforts to get Rhode Island to grant women suffrage, but not for lack of trying.

In a great example of making very bitter lemons into lemonade, Elizabeth was somehow able to transform her grief after her first five children died. Instead of feeling hopeless, for which no one could have blamed her, she was instead inspired to convert "the helplessness she felt at the bedsides of her own dying children into activism on behalf of other suffering children who could be helped."[227]

Her vision was of an institution to care for indigent children in Rhode Island where they "would be nurtured and educated by kind, loving adults, where children would receive training in a trade or profession according to their abilities and interests." Her conviction that informed her plan for the State Home and School for Children, was that "Homelessness is not a crime," which she asserted in a newspaper article advocating for the creation of the school.[228]

Here's how she saw the school:

> No girl should be kept peeling potatoes or washing dishes who has the making of a good bookkeeper or fine wood carver or engraver; no boy should spend his minority in cane-seating chairs if he has a genius for architecture or any higher mechanical labor.

There should be a large, plain central building, in which should be kitchen, laundry, dining-room, school-rooms, workshop, hall and sleeping rooms for adult persons employed therein. Then...a circle of cottages around the central house, all facing toward it...In each cottage I would place a good woman and a certain number of children; and this should be their home when not engaged at school, or meals or work. Each household of children should be under the care of the matron of its own cottage, who should, as nearly as possible, supply the place of a mother to them.

The whole establishment should be under the general care of a superintendent and head matron, who should also live in a cottage in the circle, in order to have the whole institution under their eyes.[229]

Failing health, aging—she was almost eighty when the school was finally built in 1885—and her determination to turn her attention to the suffrage referendum caused Elizabeth to take her focus off the school. She ended up directing the campaign to enfranchise women from her bedroom, confined by illness. When a worker at the school informed her that children were being mistreated—corporal punishment and a lack of food—she was outraged. Her daughter Lillian, who wrote about her life, captured her response:

The shock and the horror that the old woman felt can only be imagined. But she bestirred herself at once, and one of the Providence papers said that the mere fact that Mrs. Chace believed there was something wrong in the State School was sufficient reason why an investigation should be made. She girded herself up for what was to be her last great personal conflict with official authorities, but it was difficult, at first, to obtain an investigation into allegations of misdeeds at the newly opened school.[230]

Unfortunately, Elizabeth was too advanced in age to tackle the onslaught of problems that accompany the establishment of an institution such as the State Home and School for Children. She died December 12, 1899, at the age of ninety-three.

Just as Mary Ellen Pleasant has recently been honored for her abolitionist work in her native California, there has been acknowledgment of Elizabeth's work in the quest for freedom and equality in Rhode Island. It took until 2001, but the Secretary of State Edward S. Inman III chose her as the Conscience of Rhode Island for her "tireless championship of the rights of the less fortunate." A bust was created in her honor—so very richly deserved. It was the first time an image of a woman was displayed in the Rhode Island State House.

Elizabeth Buffum Chace was uncompromising in her passion for justice, and she inspired many women, especially young women, to take up the cause. She and Samuel also deserve credit for the outstanding achievements of the children who were their legacy. Elizabeth's son, Arnold Buffum Chace, became the chancellor of Brown University and a renowned mathematician associated with the Rhind Papyrus, the best example of Egyptian mathematics. Their daughter Lillie Chace Wyman became a tireless social reformer and an author, publishing several books and writing regularly for such magazines as the *Atlantic Monthly*.

Two of Elizabeth's grandsons, Richard Chace Tolman and Edward Chace Tolman, became well-known professors. Richard played a crucial role as scientific liaison for the United States Army on the ever-controversial Manhattan Project, which produced the first atomic bomb. Edward, a pioneer in Behaviorism, a systematic approach to the understanding of human and animal behavior, which assumes that the behavior of a human or an animal is a consequence of that individual's history. He successfully sued the University of California, Berkeley, for firing him for refusing to sign the infamous loyalty oath during the McCarthy era.[231] Elizabeth would surely have been proud of her grandson's actions in refusing to kowtow to McCarthy, a modern-day purveyor of discrimination and stigmatization.

Courtesy of Heinz History Center

CHAPTER 16

Jane Swisshelm
Staunch Abolitionist Refusing to Accept Gender Limitations

Jane Swisshelm pursued the quest for equality in numerous arenas during her life, and there were many frontal assaults on equality for her to address, starting with the barriers she confronted as a woman. It almost feels like one is reading about a radical 1960s feminist as Jane's story unfolds. She was the first woman reporter to sit in the House of Representatives, and when she became frustrated by the demise of anti-slavery newspapers, she had so much to express that she started her own. Still, she was not without her own questionable words and actions.

From the start, she faced adversity. She was born on December 6, 1815, in Pittsburgh, Pennsylvania, one of at least six children born to the former Mary Scott and Thomas Cannon. Many of her siblings died at early ages, and no records exist to identify exactly how many there were. Her father was a merchant and real estate speculator.

The first of Jane's encounters with loss and grief occurred when she was eight, during an era when tuberculosis ravaged the population. Then known as consumption, it took her sister Mary and her father, which left the family in dire straits. Jane went to work doing manual labor, making lace and painting on velvet while her mother colored leghorn (made from dried and bleached straw of an Italian variety of wheat) and straw hats. In her autobiography, Jane recalls that earning $5 from a judge who commissioned a portrait in velvet of the Goddess of Liberty was a highlight of her youthful artistic career. Boarding school next beckoned, and she was excited about attending Edgeworth Boarding School in Braddock's Field, Pennsylvania, both to join her cousin and because there were no public schools available for girls at the time.

Soon enough, Jane's tuition payments dried up due to her mother's very difficult circumstances. She was most fortunate to have the headmistress offer her the opportunity to teach the youngest girls in exchange for her continued enrollment at Edgeworth.

Unfortunately, during one of her visits with her family, a doctor thought she was in the first stages of consumption. Her mother had lost four children by then, all to illnesses, so she chose to move to Wilkinsburg, a village outside Pittsburgh, in the hopes that such a move could protect the children—particularly the very possibly symptomatic Jane. What made the year even more traumatic was the death of her older brother, William, whom she deeply loved. He died of yellow fever in New Orleans, a sadly common occurrence at the time.

When Jane was healthy enough to return to teaching, she was fourteen years old. Prior to her having her own classroom, she had resumed her studies with great enthusiasm. She wrote:

> As soon there as possible, she sent me to the city school where I realized my aspiration of studying ancient history and the piano, and devoured the contents of the textbook of natural philosophy with an avidity I had never known for a novel.[232]

She had no difficulty finding pupils at the only school in Wilkinsburg, and she had this to say about her teaching methods:

> I was the first, I believe, in Allegheny County, to teach children without beating them. I abolished corporal punishment entirely, and was soon so successful that boys who were ungovernable at home, were altogether tractable. This life was perfectly congenial, and I followed it for nearly six years.[233]

Jane wrote about discovering that she had become an attractive teenager and we can see her response as a strong indicator of what would become a hallmark of her way of being in the world. Here's what she had to say about the discovery of her outer beauty:

> I was almost fifteen, when I overheard a young lady say I was growing pretty. I went to my mirror and spent some moments in unalloyed happiness and triumph. Then I thought, "Pretty face the worms will eat you. All the prettiest girls I know are silly, but you shall never make a fool of me. Helen's beauty ruined Troy. Cleopatra was a wretch. So, if you are pretty I will be master, remember that."[234]

In 1836, Jane wed James Swisshelm, against the advice of her mother, who saw James as domineering and manipulative. The marriage was problematic from the outset, though there is considerable evidence in her autobiography that Jane loved James in the beginning. Not only did she perceive herself as being "left without support or compensation for my services as tailor, teacher, dress-maker," but she performed these tasks for her husband's family after she was forced to move in with her mother-in-law very soon after her wedding. This proved so difficult that Jane chose to live in self-imposed exile in a hut on her mother-in-law's property. What a start to married life! Given what we already know about her feistiness and her strong will, Jane and her husband quarreled frequently as she was monumentally challenged to fit into the mold of a nineteenth-century married woman.

In the arena of art in which she had sought to excel, she was continually thwarted by the convention of marriage and the expectation that she put aside all other aspirations in deference to her duties as a housekeeper. This never sat well with Jane. As if these sacrifices weren't enough, Jane also wrote about having to give up her love of literature, since it would not be acceptable for her intellectual pursuits to dwarf those of her less well-educated husband. One can only begin to imagine the level of frustration she felt in this marriage.

Two years later, in 1838, the Swisshelms moved to Louisville, Kentucky, so James could join his brother, Samuel, in a business venture.

This is where Jane first encountered enslavement directly. She wrote that from an early age she favored the abolition of slavery, and even described herself as "being brought up an abolitionist." She references a childhood experience of collecting signatures for a petition to outlaw slavery in the District of Columbia where, "in a strictly orthodox Presbyterian community I was everywhere met by the objections: 'Niggers have no souls,' 'the Jews held slaves' and 'Noah cursed Canaan.'"[235] The foundation for a life of active abolitionism was being laid.

Seeing enslavement firsthand caused a life-changing response. She learned of an enslaver at a nearby farm who sold his own mixed-race children. In her autobiography she writes of many such awful incidents, including one in which a young Black woman was forced to have sex with her master, but she is in love with her partner and refuses. In retaliation, the enslaver has the man whipped in front of his beloved until she loses consciousness, and when she awakens she learns that her partner is to be sold, leaving her without an "excuse" to avoid being a victim of rape.

The move to Louisville did not improve the marriage. In 1839 Jane overrode her husband's wishes and moved to Philadelphia to take care of her ailing mother, who died after a year. Jane remained active; she ran a girls' seminary in Butler, Pennsylvania, and also built a successful corset-making business, proving that she was more than capable of succeeding without her husband. During this period of separation, Jane parlayed her love of reading and writing talent into the publication of anonymous articles in a local newspaper. Nevertheless, her troubled marriage persisted, and in 1841 she moved to James's farm, which she called Swissvale, east of Pittsburgh.

Spurred on by a conflict over her mother's estate, Jane was inspired to become an advocate for the property rights of married women. It is likely that Jane's mother, Mary, knowing of her daughter's difficult marriage, stipulated in her will that James would not inherit any part of her estate and bequeathed it to Jane in its entirety. Unfortunately, yet another inequity got in the way of her will, as the laws of the time gave a husband possession of anything and everything his wife owned.

Jane's first forays into the world of writing for an audience was through letters to the editor of the Pittsburgh Commercial Journal. The editor was Robert Riddle who owned other newspapers in Pittsburgh: *Daily Gazette, Daily Morning Post, Mystery, Albatross, Spirit of the Age,* and *Pittsburgh Catholic.* She was far from alone in advocating via her letters for rights to property and child custody. She saw the power of the written word to reach women and Riddle gave her a platform with her letters.

Jane launched her career as a journalist while living at Swissvale, first by writing articles condemning capital punishment and then stories, poems, and articles for the anti-slavery newspaper the *Spirit of Liberty* and other publications in Pittsburgh. She was paid $5 a week for contributions to the *New York Tribune.*

The demise of the *Spirit of Liberty* and of *Albatross,* along with her awareness that she had captured an audience of women, inspired Jane to create her own newspaper, the *Pittsburgh Saturday Visiter,* in 1847, which ultimately had a circulation of six thousand. It was sufficiently successful to be able to merge with the weekly *Pittsburgh Commercial Journal* in 1854, though Riddle was initially exceedingly supportive of her endeavor. She writes, "He had pushed his chair back from his desk, and sat regarding me in utter amazement while I stated the case, then said: 'What do you mean? Are you insane? What does your husband say?'." It took some time, but Jane was ultimately convincing in conveying that her husband's opinion did not matter—at all. Riddle refused to provide Jane with a desk but he finally agreed to create the newspaper together.

Not surprisingly, given how she was denied rights to her mother's estate and was forced to finance her start-up journal by selling her mother's home, many of her editorials, just as her letters had done, advocated for a woman's right to own property. When her husband demanded the money from the sale of the home, Jane joined Lucretia Mott and Mary A. Grew to lobby the Pennsylvania legislature to grant married women the right to own property. The law was passed in 1848.

Two years later, as a reporter for the *New York Tribune,* Jane became the first woman reporter to sit in the US Senate press gallery. It just so happened that on that momentous day, in the middle of a heated debate on the Compromise of 1850, a notorious event took place. Senator Thomas Hart Benton (D-Missouri) charged at Henry Foote (D-Mississippi), who responded by brandishing a pistol. Both were staunchly against abolition, but they differed on certain details, and when Foote insulted President Millard Filmore, that was the last straw. Jane's reporting on the incident received considerable attention and praise. A Wisconsin newspaper subsequently acknowledged her literary gifts, albeit through the lens of gender:

> Nobody but a regular woman could make a description of such a scene so interesting. That jerking, nervous, half breathless excitement which would embarrass the narrative of a man only adds to the piquancy and grace to that of a woman. [236]

While reporting for the *Tribune*, Jane focused her reportorial eye upon Daniel Webster, the powerful Democratic senator from Massachusetts who had become beholden to the slave trade. He had supported the Compromise of 1850, which "admitted California as a free state and abolished the slave trade in the District of Columbia, also included a Fugitive Slave provision which required Northern sheriffs and other officials to cooperate actively in the recapture of escaped slaves."[237]

Jane was outraged by the hypocrisy of Webster, whose upstanding reputation had earned him the nickname "the godlike Dan." This resulted in her accusation that he had sired an illegitimate mixed race family and that he was a habitual drunkard. Neither of the charges were ever refuted as Jane knew there was proof of each. The controversy that resulted was whether the press had the right to delve into the private lives of public figures. Because of the inflammatory nature of such actions, Jane's reputation soared. Ultimately Jane's articles undermined Webster's candidacy for the Democratic nomination for president in 1852.

Some of Jane's most powerful and compelling writing focused on the role of women:

> We have not the slightest idea that women are made of such light material that the breath of any fool or knave may blow them on the rocks of ruin.
>
> When a woman starts out in the world on a mission, secular or

religious, she should leave her feminine charms at home.

Women should not weaken their cause by impracticable demands. Make no claim which could not be won in a reasonable time. Take one step at a time, get a good foothold in it and advance carefully.

If I wrote at all, I must throw myself headlong into the great political maelstrom, and would of course be swallowed up like a fishing-boat in the great Norway horror which decorated our school geographies; for no woman had ever done such a thing, and I could never again hold up my head under the burden of shame and disgrace which would be heaped upon me. But what matter? I had no children to dishonor; all save one who had ever loved me were dead, and she no longer needed me, and if the Lord wanted some one to throw into that gulf, no one could be better spared than I.[238]

Jane's newspaper received numerous comments and reviews. Here are a few that capture the spirit of her writing that were offered as tributes in various obituaries:

Her style was rigorous and caustic and her views of reform radically advanced.[239]

She rebuked advocates of slavery in her own rigorous style, which stung where it hit.[240]

Swisshelm was a rigorous writer, clear, logical and incisive, and she had an inexhaustible armory of ridicule, in the use of which there was not some principle at stake, and then she enlisted on the side where she believed right to be with the whole order of her nature.[241]

In 1851, the birth of her only child, Mary Henrietta, known affection-ately as Zo or Nettie, forced Jane to take a pause from her work and com-mit to being an attentive mother. She gave up her editorial responsibilities but returned to her office a few months later and re-immersed herself in her newspaper endeavors.

Jane was finally able to end her turbulent and unsatisfying marriage in 1857. Soon thereafter she relocated yet again, this time to St. Cloud, Minnesota. With her reputation as a founder of newspapers, she was able to gain control of a string of publications. Using her position as editor, she espoused the causes of abolition and women's rights while also traveling around the area and offering lectures on these topics.

Jane's outspoken and impassioned criticism of the mistreatment of enslaved people and women enraged local Democratic leaders. One of her causes became essentially a "private war" against Sylvanus Lowry, a Southern enslaver and Indian trader who had moved to the area in 1847. He was an influential leader who had held office as a member of the Territorial Council and later served as St. Cloud's first mayor.

Jane was most outraged because Lowry owned slaves in Minnesota, a free state. Using her newspaper as her soapbox, she accused him of "swindling the local Winnebago as a trader, ordering vigilante attacks on suspected land claim jumpers and abusing his slaves."[242] In response, he started a rival paper, *The Union* to offset her influence. He also had his allies break into her newspaper's office, destroy her press and toss the type used for the paper into the Mississippi River. Undaunted and more popular than ever for standing up to such rapacious bullies, Jane appealed to her friends, whose generosity and faith in her enabled her to start over. By 1858 she changed her paper's name to the *St. Cloud Democrat* destined to be her most important newspaper as a result of her feminist views. She was back in business.

When Lincoln was nominated for the presidency in 1860, Jane was a strong supporter. She spoke and wrote on his behalf, and when his election led directly to the outbreak of the Civil War, Jane became a nurse at the front. One of her crowning achievements in a life filled with firsts and breakthroughs was her saving of 182 men. Following the Battle of the Wilderness in March of 1864, Jane had responsibility for the wounded at Fredericksburg for five days. With neither surgeon nor assistant she somehow managed to save each of them.

Her career as a nurse in the hospitals during the war is not the least interesting portion of her life. There, she exhibited the hate of shams, red-tape, and inefficiency which she had shown in all other portions of her life. She defied regulations, she insisted on saving men whom science had given up to die, she revolutionized all with which she came in whom contact, and, after her own convictions, and IN DEFIANCE [our emphasis] of rules, and precedents, she carried on her reforms.[243]

It is apropos that this accomplishment, as close to a miracle as this extraordinary woman was to perform, be followed by what gets her described as a "woman of contradiction" by Tim Post. Reporting for Minnesota Public Radio in 2002 he extolled her outsized accomplishments and then had this to say: "But while she wrote articles advocating more freedom for some, she also pushed for the extermination of the state's Dakota Indian population." The story is quite a bit more nuanced than what that one sentence conveys. Yet it is indisputable that the same woman who wrote this:

> We hold that American Slavery is a combination of all crimes against God and Man – 'the sum of all villainies' - that it is contrary to the revealed will of God and the Constitution of the United States, and as Christians and Patriots all men are in duty bound to labor for its immediate and utter extinction.

...also was almost rabidly in favor of the genocide of another ethnic group, who had been mistreated and oppressed since the arrival of white people on the North American continent.[244]

How did such a dissonant situation arise for Jane? Upon her arrival in Minnesota in 1857, she had envisioned a peaceful relationship between the indigenous people and the settlers. What she likely failed to recognize was that promises and agreements were made to the Dakota Indians for government payments and food. She did not know that the Indians were betrayed.

The war that was fought between the Dakota Indians and the settlers and soldiers of the US military was the largest Indian war in American history. It was fought at the same time as the Civil War battles of Antietam and Second Manassas in 1862. Its causes were, not surprisingly, similar to all of the preceding and subsequent Indian wars. These all too familiar causes explain what occurred and what ultimately led to Jane's abhorrent attitude.

The treaties and agency system that the treaties authorized were not working for the native people. These are the words spoken in 1862 to the Indian agent, Thomas Galbraith, by Chief Little Crow (Taoyateduta), Mdewakanton Dakota, to convey the desperation that led to the war:

> We have waited a long time. The money is ours but we cannot get it. We have no food but here these stores are filled with food. We ask that you, the agent, make some arrangement so we can get food from the stores, or else we may take our own way to keep ourselves from starving. When men are hungry, they help themselves.[245]

Instead of being given either the payment or the food that was desperately needed, they heard in 1862 that Lower Sioux Agency head trader, Andrew Jackson Myrick, had said, "Let them eat grass." An ill-tempered alcoholic who was married to a Dakota woman, Myrick essentially signed his own death warrant with those words. Less than two weeks later the war had begun. Myrick was killed. His mouth was stuffed with grass.

The fighting that followed was ferocious. Two hundred settlers were killed, as were one hundred soldiers. Over two hundred died the first morning, a similar number of lives lost by Custer and his troops at Little Bighorn. Only the deaths resulting from the 9/11 attacks cost the lives of more Americans on our home soil in one single event. Refugees numbered in the thousands and a large part of Minnesota was de-populated, which took many years to recover.

As for Dakota deaths, no number has ever been confirmed. What is known is that hundreds died in the retribution that followed the war. Thirty-eight were hanged at the same time, the largest mass execution in US history. The impact of the war and the executions was the destruction of the Dakota (Sioux) way of life as it had existed for centuries.

None of these facts are intended to diminish the significance of Jane's "contradiction." Her views changed dramatically as a result of the Dakota War, and, given her progressive views on so many subjects, it can be surmised that she just lacked the knowledge that would have enabled her to be less judgmental and condemning. But that may be wishful thinking, because as the NPR report goes on to present:

> Swisshelm spouted a stream of editorials against American Indians during the bloody five week U.S. - Dakota war. In an editorial published in 1862, she called for the punishment of all Indians, whether or not they were involved in the attacks.

> "Exterminate the wild beasts, and make peace with the devil and all his hosts sooner than these red-jawed tigers, whose fangs are dripping with the blood of the innocents! Get ready, and as soon as these convicted murderers are turned loose, shoot them and be sure they are shot dead, dead, DEAD, DEAD! If they have any souls, the Lord can have mercy on them if he pleases! But that is His business. Ours is to kill the lazy vermin and make sure of killing them."[246]

After the Civil War, Jane founded her final newspaper, *The Reconstructionist,* and used it to launch attacks against President Andrew Johnson, whose policies undermined Reconstruction and undid much of what the war had achieved for Black people. Her outspoken opposition to his incompetent leadership led to the demise of the paper and the loss of a government job she had been offered by Edwin M. Stanton, then secretary of war and a Pittsburgh friend. In 1872 she was a delegate to a Prohibition Party, and twelve years later on July 22, 1884, she died at her home in Swissvale. The city of Pittsburgh named the neighborhood of Swisshelm Park in her honor.

Regardless of the basis for her vehement attacks on Native Americans, the words she directed towards the Dakota people are shameful and have led to efforts to remove the plaque in her honor on the campus of St. Cloud University, where her newspaper office had once stood. Some see her racist attitudes as a reason not to honor her other feats. Others want to maintain the plaque along with amended language that includes this very disturbing contradiction while still acknowledging a life of courageous and unflinching efforts to abolish enslavement, advance the cause of women, and use her voice as a journalist to show her fellow Americans the power that resides in a woman of conscience.

We support the latter view. That should be the approach to all of our history and our historical figures. Either denying them their rightful place in the pantheon of those who risked it all for freedom or telling an incomplete story for purposes of glorifying them without revealing the "contradiction" does nothing to further the quest for the truth about our history. Jane Swisshelm deserves recognition for her contributions to undoing racism for African Americans and condemnation for her racism towards Native Americans.

That is the whole story and Don Day, director of the American Indian Center at St. Cloud University when the NPR story was aired and a member of the Leech Lake Band of Ojibwe, says it well. He wants people to know about Swisshelm's views on American Indians, but he doesn't think she should be vilified for them:

> The more history that people know, the more accurate it is. I'm not saying we need to rewrite history or change history, we just need to have a more complete history of everything that goes on around us.

> We can't deny any of the things that she did. She was great—she was an abolitionist, she moved women's rights to points where people never even thought of before. She was actually hated in her time for the progressive thoughts that she had, so we can't deny any of that ... but we also can't deny that she was a racist.[247]

CHAPTER 17

John Gregg Fee
Using Religion to Advance Justice
for the Oppressed

Courtesy of Berea College

A revelation during John Gregg Fee's daily prayers led him to the deep commitment you are about to experience. Here's what he wrote in his autobiography about that moment:

> I saw that to have light and peace from God, I must make the consecration. I said, "Lord, if needs be, make me an Abolitionist." The surrender was complete. I arose from my knees with the consciousness that I had died to the world and accepted Christ in all the fullness of his character as I then understood Him. Self must be surrendered. The test, the point of surrender, may be one thing to one man, a different thing to another man; but it must be made—all given to Christ.[248]

John remained loyal to what he deemed through prayer and biblical understanding to be his life's work: fighting for the liberation of the enslaved and ultimately their full equality.

John was born on September 9, 1816, in Bracken County, Kentucky. His parents, John and Elizabeth, both of Scots-Irish descent, ran a small farm. Here's how Fee described them:

> My mother was industrious and economical; a modest, tender-hearted woman, and a fond mother. I was her first born. She loved me very much, and I loved her in return. Her mother, Sarah Gregg, was a Quakeress from Pennsylvania. Her eldest son, Aaron Gregg, my wife's grandfather, was an industrious free laborer, an ardent lover of liberty, and very outspoken in his denunciations of slavery. This opposition to slavery and his love of liberty passed to his children and children's children, almost without exception.[249]

His father, John Sr., had inherited an indentured servant who completed his indenture. After that John purchased enslaved Africans, ultimately owning thirteen, but eventually he had a change of heart. "He saw that the effects of slavery were bad; that it was a hindrance to social and national prosperity; and consequently invested his money in lands in free States and early deeded portions of these lands to each of his children,"[250] his son later wrote. Despite these significant concerns, John maintained his ownership of the enslaved until he died.

Even as a child, John transcended the prejudices of his environment. He wrote: "I was often scolded for being so much with the slaves, and threatened with punishment when I would intercede for them. Slavery, like every other evil institution, bore evil fruits, blunted the finest sensibilities and hardened the tenderest hearts."[251]

John converted to Christianity at age fourteen and hoped to join the Methodist Episcopal Church, but his father wanted him to wait, given his youth, and together they became members of the Presbyterian Church when John turned sixteen. He began his university education at Augusta College in Kentucky and continued at Miami University in Ohio. With one semester remaining, he returned to Augusta College, from which he graduated.

In 1842, at twenty-six, he entered Lane Theological Seminary, a Presbyterian school in Cincinnati, Ohio. There he met two classmates who changed the direction of his life. In his autobiography John describes John Milton Campbell as "a man of marked piety and great goodness of heart." Campbell had consecrated himself to missionary work in West Africa. Campbell and another classmate, James C. White, formerly of Boston, Massachusetts, later pastor of the Presbyterian Church on Poplar Street, Cincinnati, talked with John and convinced him that there was a means to expressing his anguish about slavery. They inspired John to understand the horror and indignity of enslavement.

> They became deeply interested in me as a native of Kentucky and in view of my relation to the slave system, my father being a slaveholder. They pressed upon my conscience the text, 'Thou shalt love the Lord thy God with all thy heart, and thy neighbor as thy self,' and as a practical manifestation of this, 'Do unto men as ye would they should do unto you.'

At this point, John came to believe that:

> [U]nless I embraced the principle and lived it in honest practice, I would lose my soul. I saw also that as an honest man I ought to

be willing to wear the name which would be a fair exponent of the principle I espoused. This was the name Abolitionist...[252]

Upon committing to the "manifest duty" to "embrace the principle and wear the name," he wrote later, he would face the criticism of "the vast majority of people North and especially South." In addition, he cut himself off "from relatives and former friends."

John was ordained as a minister, but rather than accepting positions he was offered in Indiana or going to Africa as a missionary with his friend John Campbell, he opted to remain in the South. He explained the basis for his choice as: "Then came before me my relation to the slave. I had shared in the fruits of his unrequited toil; he was blind and dumb, and there was no one to plead for him."[253]

But his reason to forgo opportunities to preach elsewhere was even more nuanced and Fee's own words convey the knowledge he had gained of his fellow Kentuckians. He saw slave owners as "willingly deceived by the false teachings of the popular ministry." But he realized that it was the non-slave owners who he needed to reach with his message of "impartial love." They "were by their votes and action the actual slaveholders." This is how he described these people.

> [They] did not see their crime; that they despised the slave because of his condition, and that these non-slave-owners were violently opposed to any doctrine or practice that might treat the slave as a "neighbor," a brother, and make him equal before the law. I knew also that the great body of the people were practically without the fundamental principle of the Gospel, love to God and love to man; that, as in the days of Martin Luther, though the doctrine of justification by faith was plainly written in the Bible, yet the great body of people did not then see it; so now the great doctrine of loving God supremely and our neighbor as ourselves, "on which hang all the law and the prophets," though clearly written in the Bible, was not seen in its practical application by the great mass of the people. Such was my relation to this people, and theirs to God and the world, that I felt I *must* return.[254]

Back in Kentucky, John sought a church that would support his anti-slavery views. Needless to say, this was difficult since pro-slavery sentiment was widespread throughout the state. On top of this, his father intensely disapproved of his abolitionist leanings.

When he did finally get invited to speak at a church in Lewis County, Kentucky, his sermon about the evils of slavery had devastating repercussions. He lost the home he was renting with his wife, Matilda Hamilton, whom he had recently married. Matilda was John's cousin and they had known one another during childhood. It was this very conflict over slavery that caused Fee to leave the Presbyterian Church. He resigned and experienced another religious awakening of equal power. He came to believe that Christianity needed to be non-denominational and non-sectarian.

Starting in 1837 the debate over slavery split the Presbyterian Church in half. The old school that was inspired by Calvinism and did not see value in trying to improve social conditions was in opposition to the new school, which sought spiritual perfection and pursued social justice causes including abolitionism. The new school operated from Lane Seminary, where Fee was a student, and four of the six Presbyterian churches in Cincinnati.

The break between the two schools was complete when the Cincinnati New School Presbytery condemned enslavement in 1841. As a consequence, its churches could no longer have relationships with slave-holding activities. Thus when John arrived in 1842 to the post-radical Lane Seminary, he embraced immediate abolitionism in his first year.

Conflicts were rife within the church, and John was at the center of the great divide. The Presbyterian Synod of Kentucky opposed his stance on refusing fellowship to enslavers. His abolitionist activity ignited difficult conversations at the 1845 Presbyterian Synod of Kentucky. The synod took the position that church doctrine allowed slavery. John held to his belief that it did not, and argued that the Bible was the higher authority. He sent a written appeal to a fellow minister in Pennsylvania, who sent the letter to Lewis Tappan, who published the letter in his Union Missionary journal. The letter would appear in several more journals including the *New York Evangelist*, a new-school publication, and the *Christian Observer* from Philadelphia. The publication of his powerful letter gave him a much wider audience and promoted his abolitionist activity in Kentucky. Fee attained national prominence. But it also aroused even greater resistance to his beliefs.

When the synod met in 1847, it voted to censure John. Members of the assembly went so far as to instruct the Harmony Presbytery to take action to curtail his anti-slavery activities. When he met with his presbytery, he expressed his desire to end their relationship. Somehow, at least in part due to his integrity and grace, he was released "in good standing"—despite what was seen as his terribly misguided abolitionist views.

Thus began John's career as an itinerant preacher, traveling throughout Kentucky and inveighing against the evils of slavery. The work was stressful, and the potential for violence was ever-present. On more than one occasion, John and Matilda were accosted en route to or from a church. Thankfully, their numerous friends were there to rise in their defense.

John also began writing abolitionist tracts. According to Fee, the American Missionary Association (AMA) abridged his book and distributed many copies in Kentucky and other states. The organization also hired him to preach in Bracken and Lewis counties. In the latter, he and his parishioners built a Free Church of Christ. His writing consisted of condemnations of enslavement, the plan to keep slaveholders from church membership, and the absurdity of using colonization as a form of emancipation.

The AMA, which supported John's work throughout his career, was a Protestant abolitionist group founded on September 3, 1846, in Albany, New York, chiefly sponsored by the Congregationalist churches in New England. Its goals were the abolition of slavery, the education of African Americans, the promotion of racial equality, and the spreading of Christian values. Its members and leaders were of both races. As the Civil War approached, the AMA opened contraband camps in the South for African Americans fleeing enslavement. The association also played a major role during the Reconstruction era in promoting education for Black people in the South by establishing numerous schools and colleges.

To say that Kentucky's situation—being a border state as the Civil War approached—was complicated would be a major understatement. The citizens of Kentucky were deeply divided by the issue of enslavement.

Nearly 20 percent of the state's population comprised of enslaved people. Even many Kentuckians who supported remaining in the Union saw no problem with the "peculiar institution." Being a border state, it had strong ties to the South via the Mississippi River, while the railroad had begun to reveal the importance of connections to the North. Ancestors of Kentucky residents came from the bordering Southern states, but many of its children were heading towards work opportunities in the industrializing North.

Politicians also faced a complex road map, and navigating it often resulted in new tensions among leaders. Among the country's most prominent leaders were numerous Kentuckians, including Henry Clay and former vice presidents John C. Breckinridge and Richard M. Johnson. President Lincoln and the Confederate president Jefferson Davis were both Kentuckians as well.

When Lincoln was elected, the state was in political turmoil. The once-popular Whig Party, founded by Clay, was fading in influence and there was a need to find another affiliation. Many chose the Democratic Party, but a few joined the party of Lincoln, the Republicans. In the election of 1860, the Constitutional Union Party, which had nominated Tennessean John Bell as its presidential candidate and Edward Everett of Massachusetts for vice president, won Kentucky. This party was composed of former Whigs and former members of the Know-Nothings, a far-right nativist political party that got its name from their response when asked their affiliation. Notwithstanding the upheaval of the election, Kentucky was prized by both North and South for its agricultural products—tobacco, corn, wheat, hemp, and flax. Were the South to gain the state, it would have a defensible boundary in the Ohio River.

Governor Beriah Magoffin felt that Southern states' rights had been violated by the efforts to limit the continuation and expansion of enslavement, but he nevertheless sought to avoid secession. He tried to broker an agreement with the North via a letter to slave state governors that proposed stricter enforcement of the Fugitive Slave Act Henry Clay had written ten years earlier, as well as Southern veto over any legislation pertaining to enslavement. He wanted to have two conferences—first of slave states and then all states, but events were moving much too fast to allow for such deliberations and compromises. Neither conference took place.

Magoffin was not finished yet. On December 27, 1860, within months of Lincoln's election, he sought a convention of Kentuckians to determine how to proceed regarding secession. Since there was a majority of the General Assembly favoring the Union, the request was declined. The legislators feared the citizens would vote to leave the Union.

The General Assembly was not done either. It sent six delegates to a February 4, 1861, Peace Conference in Washington, DC, and tried to get Congress to call a national convention to try to resolve the secession crisis. Again to no avail. When the group next convened, the following month, the call went out for a border state convention to take place in the capital, Frankfort, on May 27. No response.

As essentially a last resort, the legislature passed a proposed Thirteenth Amendment, also called the Corwin Amendment, to the US Constitution. Though it never mentioned enslavement, it was designed to protect slavery from federal power. Five states ratified it, but it fell far short of what was needed to become law, and within weeks the nation was at war. It is worth remembering Lincoln's fateful words about the possible consequences of secession. In a letter to Orville Browning, written in September of 1861, he wrote:

> I think to lose Kentucky is nearly the same as to lose the whole game. Kentucky gone, we cannot hold Missouri, nor Maryland. These all against us, and the job on our hands is too large for us. We would as well consent to separation at once, including the surrender of this capitol.[255]

With the outbreak of war, the situation intensified. On April 15, 1861, Lincoln requested in a telegram that Magoffin send part of the 75,000 troops to "put down the rebellion." We've already seen Magoffin's Southern sympathies, so his reply will come as no surprise: "President Lincoln, I will send not a man nor a dollar for the wicked purpose of subduing my sister Southern states." Most Kentuckians agreed with the legislator and statesman John Crittenden, who took the position that Kentucky should join neither side and instead mediate the conflict, which inspired the General Assembly to pass declarations of neutrality. Magoffin officially supported this decision.[256]

Of course, maintaining neutrality when chaos and conflict were occurring all around them was impossible. Initially both sides accepted the decision, but each was ready to seize any opportunity that circumstances might afford. The Union established Camp Clay in Ohio, north of Newport, Kentucky, and Camp Joe Holt in Indiana opposite Louisville. The Confederacy constructed Fort Donelson and Fort Henry in Tennessee, just across the border, with troops stationed less than fifty yards from the Cumberland Gap. The locals left Kentucky and signed up with whichever side they supported. Sixty regiments of Kentuckians served in the Union army, but just nine fought with the Confederacy. Interestingly, one brigade of soldiers fighting for the South was called the Orphan Brigade because the soldiers' home counties were under Union control and they couldn't return to their homes until near war's end.

There was one final sign of the struggle to remain neutral. Kentucky's military forces were as deeply divided as its citizens. The state guard leaned towards the Confederacy and the newly formed home guard was sympathetic to the Union. These allegiances came very close to resulting in armed conflict within the military. It was only through the intervention of Simon Buckner, leader of the state guard, and Union General George B. McClellan that neutrality was achieved, but only through the summer of 1861.

Neutrality became increasingly difficult to maintain, and Kentucky's election of 1861 saw considerably more Union than Confederacy sympathizers elected. The latter saw the proverbial handwriting on the ballot boxes and many boycotted, but the results were undeniable. In response a group of disillusioned Southern sympathizers devised a plan to create a Confederate shadow government. Representatives from sixty-eight of the 110 counties gathered on November 18. They passed an ordinance of secession and elected their own governor, George W. Johnson.

President Jefferson Davis had some reservations about the degree to which this Confederate government had usurped the power of the legitimately elected General Assembly, but despite his concerns,

Kentucky was admitted to the Confederacy on December 10, 1861. It was represented by the central star on the Confederate flag.[257] In the end, an estimated 125,000 Kentuckians served as Union soldiers, 35,000 served in the Confederacy and approximately, 24,000 Black Kentuckians, free and enslaved, served as Union soldiers.[258]

What a backdrop for John's abolitionist efforts! By this time, Fee had grown discontented with his ministerial work. He received a land donation from a wealthy landowner and parishioner, Cassius M. Clay, who favored gradual abolition. Nicknamed the Lion of White Hall, the name of his estate, Clay was a Kentucky planter, a politician, and an emancipationist. He freed the enslaved people he had inherited from his father and allowed them to stay on the plantation and earn a wage. During the Civil War, he was appointed by President Lincoln as the United States minister to Russia, and is credited with gaining Russian support for the Union.[259]

It was Mr. Clay, after whom Cassius Clay—before he took his

Courtesy of the National Portrait Gallery

Muslim name, Muhammad Ali—and his father were named. Mr. Clay was well-known to Ali's grandparents as an outspoken opponent of enslavement.

Clay offered to publish John's work in his publication, *The True American*. Between 1845 and 1847, Fee published fourteen articles in Clay's journal. Cassius was a cousin of Henry Clay, which only added to the controversial role he played given Henry Clay's staunch pro-slavery stance. John's articles all focused on answering the question "Is slavery right?" and called for its immediate end as well as for equal rights for emancipated Black people. He built his case with arguments drawn from both the Constitution and the Bible.[260]

In addition to providing John with a platform for his writing, Clay also played the role of protector. John was assaulted more than two dozen times for his outspoken, still controversial views. In one instance, he was almost killed by a sniper whose shot missed him as he sat reading near a window. An attack by a slaveholder who broke a club over his head left him with a permanent scar.

With the land given to him by Clay, John founded the town of Berea, Kentucky, in Madison County in 1853. He aimed for the town to be populated by anti-slavery families. Both John and Clay met with violent opposition from pro-slavery Kentuckians. Clay stood up to his harassers. When it came to defending his newspaper, he used sheet iron to fortify the doors and had two brass cannons loaded with shot and nails behind folding doors. Here is his description of his defenses:

> I furnished my office with Mexican lances, and a limited number of guns. There were six or eight persons who stood ready to defend me. If defeated, they were to escape by a trap-door in the roof; and I had placed a keg of powder, with a match, which I could set off and blow up the office and all my invaders; and this I should most certainly have done.[261]

Clay was eventually forced to move his newspaper to Cincinnati, Ohio, and then to Louisville, Kentucky, where it was renamed *The Examiner*.

In the decade before the start of the Civil War, John faced numerous challenges and threats of violence because of his abolitionist views and his belief in the equality of Black people. In this spirit of freedom and justice, he was moved to found Berea College, the first in Kentucky to be interracial and coeducational. Both were still rare nationally. Oberlin College of Ohio, founded in 1833, had been the first to enroll both Black people and women, so Fee hired some of its teachers and modeled his college after the pioneering institution. Fee and J.A.R. Rogers, the principal, and several others, wrote a constitution and contributed over one hundred acres for the college's campus.

John and his fellow founders had a broad vision of justice and equality. They believed that both slavery and the American caste system needed to be undone in order to achieve social equality. Thus Berea was unique from its beginnings. It provided an interracial, co-educational experience that was in direct opposition to enslavement and caste in the antebellum South. The founders made a commitment to offer a church and free education to *all*.

Under the heading of "no good deed goes unpunished," John visited Boston with his family in 1859 to attend the AMA convention and to fundraise for his school. He was encouraged to seek additional support from Henry Ward Beecher's church in Brooklyn, New York, part of a wide-reaching network that helped to sustain progressive efforts. Sadly, word of Fee seeking and receiving support from Beecher made its way back to Kentucky—of course, in a far less than accurate, "fake news" manner—and aroused pro-slavery sentiment and further condemnation of John's abolitionist work.

As the atmosphere in the country deteriorated, and no doubt influenced by John Brown's raid of Harpers Ferry, as well as John's efforts to gain financial support in the North, a band of armed pro-slavery men came to the town of Berea while John was touring the North. They put J.A.R. Rogers and others on notice and gave them ten days to leave Kentucky. An appeal for protection to Governor Charles Morehead of Kentucky fell on deaf ears, and as a result the town and college were abandoned. Abolitionists were ultimately expelled from both Lewis and Bracken counties. When John went to stay with his in-laws in Bracken Country in 1859, a committee of sixty-two men of "high standing" told him he and his family and supporters had to leave the county.

These threats ultimately forced Fee to move his family north to Cincinnati, where they lived in exile until toward the end of the war in 1864. His attempts to return to Kentucky before then were thwarted as he encountered violent resistance, but Matilda was able to return to their house in Berea for several months with two of their children. John couldn't reach her there so the family returned to Cincinnati. Meanwhile, John had become involved in the evolution of Camp Nelson, located in both Jessamine and Garrard counties on both sides of the Kentucky River.

In 2018, Camp Nelson, was designated a National Historic Monument, finally receiving long overdue recognition for the role it played in US and Civil War history as well as its significance in the history of African Americans. Created as a supply depot and hospital for the Union Army, it eventually became one of the largest recruitment and training centers for formerly enslaved men as well as serving as a refugee camp for their wives and children.

At its peak, Camp Nelson was the country's third-largest recruitment center for US Colored Troops (USCT). It had taken several years for all restrictions on enlistment to be removed. In June of 1864, the number of African American volunteers exploded. Prior to this time these former slaves, at least three thousand, were the camp's primary builders, starting with fortifying Hickman Bridge on May 19, 1863. When they were allowed to enlist, these men had the incentive of fighting for their people's freedom as well as the added inducement provided by their emancipation simply by enlisting.

Still, there were major obstacles in the path of the parents, wives, and children who had accompanied their men to the camp. Early in the war those seeking freedom who made it to Union lines were "contraband of war," and the Union refused to return them to southern slaveholders as the Confederacy demanded. The camp offered them some protection and provided a first step towards a new life, but by 1864 those who had been enslaved in Kentucky were still owned by Kentucky enslavers who had not joined the Confederacy. Enlistment thus provided a path to freedom for those eligible, but anyone such as these enslaved men from Kentucky, along with others unqualified because of their age or sex, had to leave the camp and return to enslavement.

Obviously this was not acceptable to freedmen and their families. When they would not leave on their own, they were removed. In November 1864, four hundred women and children were "forcibly escorted" from the camp and their dwellings were destroyed. When the winter temperatures plunged, 102 refugees died. The tragedy prompted a public outcry and a reversal of this inhumane policy reminiscent of the immigration policy of the Trump administration. Instead of expelling desperate people seeking freedom, the Army began constructing a government-sponsored Home for Colored Refugees, which included a mess hall, a school barracks for single women and the sick, and duplex family cottages. Fee played a major role in establishing the home and raising funds for it.

The home opened in January 1865. Although still not legally free, the wives and children of men fighting for their family's freedom were "legally entitled to sanctuary," but it took until March 3, 1865, for an act of Congress to officially emancipate the family members. This act provided legal protection for the refugees as well as an added incentive for African American men to enlist in the Union Army.

Courtesy of Camp Nelson Civil War Heritage Park

Given the opportunities it afforded to contribute to the cause of freedom, John visited the camp often as a preacher and took up residence as a teacher. He was instrumental in getting the schoolhouse built along with housing and facilities. He persuaded Salmon Chase, secretary of the treasury and one of Lincoln's "team of rivals," to help in obtaining the necessary government funds. John was also able to arrange for teachers and maintained close ties to Camp Nelson until the war ended. He and his wife used their own money to purchase land near the camp that was to be used for home lots, to build a church and a school.

At the war's end, John and Rogers returned with their families to Berea. For years John had been determinedly nonsectarian. When the AMA became aligned with the Congregational Church in 1865, he felt that he no longer could accept their aid, as he believed the AMA, like other sects or denominations, would divide the people of the South into competing denominations. Instead, John and others established the Christian Missionary Association of Kentucky. This organization was made up of individuals, not churches.

John's other major focus was Berea College. After the Civil War, the college resumed and grew. In 1866 it had 187 students—ninety-six African American and ninety-one white. It began with preparatory classes to prepare students for more advanced work at a college level. In 1869 the first college students were admitted, and the first bachelor's degrees were awarded in 1873. Fee was president and headed the board of trustees.

In 1904, thirty-one years after the first student graduated from Berea College, State Representative Carl Day led a successful effort to prohibit interracial education in Kentucky. Berea was the only institution impacted and for four years it fought the capricious and racist "Day Law." The case reached the Supreme Court. The college lost, resulting in the worst crisis in its interracial history. The court's decision created a forty-year hiatus in Black student enrollment.

Forced to segregate, rather than letting the crisis define it, the college divided its endowment and raised sufficient money to found Lincoln Institute, an all-Black boarding high school in Shelby County, Kentucky in 1912. Finally, in 1950, the awful "Day Law" was amended and African American students were once again admitted to Berea College, just four years before the fateful decision in *Brown vs. Board of Education* that established racial segregation in public schools as unconstitutional. That year, the first Black graduate of Berea in fifty years, Jessie Reasor Zander, received her diploma. Here she is on graduation day:

Courtesy of Berea College

In the late 1800s, following Fee's retirement as president of the college, the school's new president, William Goodell Frost, saw the need to educate people in Appalachia. This began Berea's commitment to recruiting students from that region.

John lived to see the dawning of the new century and died on January

11, 1901. He was eulogized by an 1892 Berea graduate, Reverend James Bond, an ancestor of Julian Bond. Julian Bond was a Georgia state senator for 20 years who also was the first president of the Southern Poverty Law Center, and chairman of the NAACP from 1998 to 2010, bringing the institution into the 21st century. John Gregg Fee would have been proud of both Julian's lineage and his determination. James Bond's remarks included these words about Fee as a man who was:

> ...a friend to each and all and sought the highest good of all alike. He loved men, not conditions; humanity, not races or nationalities...John G. Fee was a benefactor of the world. His name and deeds are the heritage of humanity.[262]

The following words about Fee's legacy from an article by Sona Apbasova can be found on the Berea College Hutchins Library website. They encapsulate Fee as both a man of his time and one who would still be seeking justice and equality in this time:

> To this day Berea College serves as a legacy of John G. Fee's hard work, vision, and anti-slavery activism. He was an integrationist who had a vision of an equal and just society that was more than 100 years ahead of his time. Berea College's mission gives equal academic opportunities to individuals of African-American and white Appalachian backgrounds throughout the nation, as well as to individuals of other cultural backgrounds from around the world. Fee's message of impartial love and the equality for all people of the world continues to thrive from one generation to the next.[263]

Fee stayed true to his calling as he experienced it in his youth. He was able to sustain the commitment he made to abolitionism despite enormous obstacles and what he accomplished is the stuff of legend.

CHAPTER 18

Delia Webster
Accepting Imprisonment as the Price for Demanding Freedom

If a book were to be written in today about twenty-first-century people who acted "in defiance," Frances Crowe, lifelong activist who died in 2023 at 100, would surely be included. She appeared in *Called to Serve: Stories of those Confronted by the Vietnam War Draft* in the chapter called "Those Who Loved, Counseled and Supported," but what is relevant to the story about Delia Webster has to do with Frances's response to a simple question: "How many times have you been arrested?" Her answer, which summed up the depth of her commitment to a myriad of social justice causes, was always, "Not enough."

Each of the sources about Delia Webster call her most remarkable achievement the fact that she was the first woman arrested for assisting fugitive slaves—repeatedly. Delia likely would have responded similarly to Ms. Crowe if she'd been asked about her arrest record.

Delia was one of four daughters born to Benajah and Esther Bostwick Webster. Delia, born on December 17, 1817, in Vergennes, Vermont, was clearly a precocious child. Either during or shortly after attending the Vergennes Classical School in her hometown, she began teaching when she was only twelve. From Vergennes she traveled west to attend Oberlin College in 1835. Oberlin features prominently in the lives of several of this book's subjects.[264]

While in various schools, Delia studied art, and when she reached the age of twenty-five in 1843, she headed to Lexington, Kentucky, where she became a teacher of painting. She taught alongside two of her friends, Mr. and Mrs. Spencer. Soon after their lessons began they were asked to start a high school. So began the Lexington Female Academy. The illness of her two colleagues, which necessitated their return to the North, left Delia in full charge of the school.

Delia enjoyed her work as an artist and an educator, but something else was stirring in her. Moving to the South from Vermont and then Ohio, she became increasingly troubled by the enslavement of African Americans. It was during this time that she met Reverend Calvin Fairbank, who would exert a powerful influence upon her life.

Calvin began working to free enslaved people in 1837. He enabled an escaping man to ferry across the Ohio River to free territory. Once he had become known in abolitionist circles for such actions, Levi and Catherine Coffin, Quakers active in anti-slavery efforts, teamed up with him and he delivered escapees to them in Newport, Indiana. The Underground Railroad took them from Indiana to either northern cities or Canada, where their freedom was assured.

In 1842, at age twenty-eight, Calvin became an ordained minister of the Methodist Episcopal Church. He soon traveled to Lexington to assist the wife and children of Gilson Berry, who had already escaped and reached Ohio. While there he met Delia.

Her activities with the Underground Railroad are not known to us, since they were cloaked in secrecy to protect the participants from arrest and prosecution, but we know she learned of Fairbank's success in helping enslaved men and women cross the Ohio River. He claimed to have enabled forty-four to escape by 1844. Delia was already an active abolitionist in Lexington at this time, so it is no surprise that their paths crossed.

By the time the two met, Delia had already established a reputation for assisting those fleeing enslavement. Here's how the Indiana Magazine of History described her work in a 1921 article:

> She came to be hated by the slave masters as well as feared by them. While nothing could be established against her, she was constantly

under suspicion and was subjected to threats intermingled with much persecution. With all this opposition, she continued her work just the same, traveling from one locality to another, always coming in contact with slaves and teaching them the avenues of escape and very frequently aiding them directly in the work herself.[265]

One of the enslaved people they worked together to help escape was Lewis Hayden. Although it cannot be proven, there is some evidence that Delia financed this escape. Delia and Calvin left Lexington on September 28, 1844. They picked up Lewis, his wife, Harriet, and her son, Joseph, whom Lewis adopted as his own. The plan called for the parents to cover their faces and hands with flour and for Joseph to hide under the carriage seat if they were accosted.

Traveling the Maysville-Lexington Turnpike, they arrived at their destination: the home of Reverend John Rankin in Ripley, Ohio. Rankin helped the Haydens get to their next stop in Oberlin, but their owners were in pursuit. They were forced to continue fleeing to Sandusky, Ohio, and eventually to Canada.

With the escapees safely gone from Kentucky, Delia and Calvin were less likely to arouse suspicion, yet, when one of their horses became sick, they had to stop at a tavern. Inside, two Black men from Lexington recognized them. Most unfortunately, these men were unknown to Delia and Calvin, and when they returned to Lexington, the men notified the slaves' master. The livery stable owner then connected the rented carriage with the escaping slaves.

Thus, once the Haydens were on their way to freedom, all was far from well for Delia and Calvin. Likely already quite suspicious of Delia's actions, her landlady conducted a search of her room while she was away assisting the Haydens and uncovered incriminating letters that confirmed her Underground Railroad efforts. This was enough to enable the authorities in Lexington, always alert to those aiding and abetting escaping slaves, to arrest Delia and lock her up in a private room at Megowan's Hotel in the city.

Calvin fared no better. Damning evidence was found, and the authorities, resorting to torture to extract a confession from Israel, the couple's driver, beat him until he admitted what had occurred. As a result, Fairbank was tried in 1845, found guilty, and sentenced to three five-year terms for each of the Hayden family members he helped escape.

Four years later, Lewis Hayden managed to raise the $650 (almost $22,000 today) demanded by his former master, which enabled Governor John Crittendon to issue Fairbank a pardon. Undaunted, Fairbank sought to undo the effects of the dreaded Fugitive Slave Act and was ultimately arrested once again, in 1851, in Louisville. This time he served thirteen years.

Webster's attorneys managed to convince a judge that most of the evidence pointed to Fairbank, so she was tried separately. William Lloyd Garrison and other abolitionists were sympathetic to her plight and raised funds for her defense. She, of course, pled not guilty, but she was convicted and received a two-year sentence of hard labor in the state penitentiary in Frankfort, beginning on January 19, 1845. She was housed in the center of the prison yard in a wooden cottage, since she was the only female prisoner.

The plot thickened rapidly for Delia once she learned that the warden, Captain Newton Craig, was a close relative of several of her enemies. He was the cousin of Parker Craig, who owned the livery stable from which she and Fairbank had rented their carriage. The warden's wife was Peter Craig's sister and a cousin of Delia's first jailer, Megowan. Much too small a world, to be sure.

Craig endorsed enslavement and delivered evangelical sermons to his inmates. Despite this he developed romantic feelings for Delia and sought a relationship with her. Once the word got out that the first woman imprisoned for assisting escaped slaves was in a nearby prison, she became "the idol of Frankfort society," attracting a range of visitors to her cell including leading ministers, state legislators, and even John Greenleaf Whittier, a northern poet who admired her for her courageous abolitionist work.

Persuaded by Newton Craig himself, Governor Crittendon again intervened and granted Delia a pardon. She walked free on February 24, 1845, just five weeks into her sentence. As part of the arrangement, she was obliged to verbally renounce her abolitionist role, which was clearly less important to her than being free—to continue her abolitionist actions! After Webster left prison, she ignored Craig. He was annoyed and wanted to exact revenge on her "for being tricked," but upon her release she headed back to her parents' home in Vermont.

During her three years there, she published a booklet called "Kentucky Jurisprudence: A History of the Trial of Miss Delia Webster" (1845). In her attempt to lay out the legal components of her case and the prejudice that surrounds it as well as the intrigue described above that accompanied her imprisonment, she leaves the questions of who she really was unanswered. One contemporary wondered: Was she, "A young lady of irreproachable character?" Or, according to another she was, "a very bold and defiant kind of woman, without a spark of feminine modesty, and, withal, very shrewd and cunning?"[266]

Following the publication of her booklet, Delia returned to the work she had begun as a twelve-year-old: teaching. She was still active in the abolitionist movement, befriending the Reverend Norris Day, who became her spokesman when bronchitis limited her ability to deliver lectures. While she sat on the stage, he spoke to the crowds who had come to see her. Rumors circulated that they were involved in a romantic relationship.

Eventually Vermont's harsh winters took their toll on Delia's health and she relocated to New York, again to teach and also to become more deeply involved in the women's suffrage movement. She hoped the ocean air would help her heal from chronic bronchitis, but health concerns eventually necessitated her return to the South.

Delia arrived in Kentucky, where none other than Newton Craig, who had sought revenge and then aided in her pardon, became her employer. While she lived in the North, he had written her letters begging her to return, obviously still enamored of her. She moved to Madison, Indiana, a center of Underground Railroad activity, in 1849. For the next several years she was a governess to Craig's family, accompanied them on their travels, and took Craig's son, Dillard, to Vermont, where she became his tutor.

Delia's next endeavor required a quantum leap into land ownership and a plan to start a school. Combining the investments of a group of northern abolitionists and at least $1,000 from Craig, she formed the

Webster Kentucky Farm Association and bought a six-hundred-acre farm in November of 1852 for $9,000 (roughly $363,000 in today's dollars). She hired free Black people to work the farm.

It was not long before slave owners in surrounding communities started reporting that many of their enslaved people had escaped. Given her history, Delia was at the top of the list of suspects enabling the escapes. Once her friends and the laborers realized the threat of being harassed and recaptured, they abandoned the farm, but not Delia. With her refusal to depart, a town meeting was held in February 1854 in Bedford. A resolution was passed that stated:

> Whereas it is known that Miss Delia A. Webster had recently run off numerous slaves from Trimble county, therefore (be it) resolved that it is the will and determination of the citizens of said county that Miss Delia A. Webster leave the State.[267]

It will surprise no one to learn that Delia was not intimidated by such efforts, nor that her refusal to give up her farm led to her arrest. The trial that followed, referred to by Delia as a "mock trial," was brief, and soon she was incarcerated in the Trimble County Jail in Bedford, Kentucky, only to be released on a technicality shortly thereafter.

Another indictment awaited her upon her release. In June 1854 she faced new charges in connection to her Underground Railroad work in 1844. Somehow she managed to escape to Indiana before she was arrested. She was soon found and tried again for what she had done ten years earlier. This time she was acquitted, but the mistreatment she had suffered no doubt contributed to her decision to return to New England, where she remained for four years.

Delia's return to Indiana and her efforts to evade capture failed again. After yet another trial, this time held in Madison in late July of 1859, she was released. As if these recurring arrests and retrials were not enough injury, insult was added in the form of $9,000 worth of destroyed property on her farm. Unable to pay back her loans, she was rescued by friends from the abolitionist movement in Boston, enabling her to hold on to the farm she so cherished.

No matter how hard Delia tried to maintain the farm and to build a school on her land, the opposition to her anti-slavery stance remained intense. In November 1866, arsonists set a series of fires, which resulted in the destruction of seventeen buildings, four barns, and ultimately Delia's home itself. This time she could not obtain the necessary funds to rebuild, and by October of 1869 she was forced to give up her dream.

Forced once more to relocate, Delia returned to Madison and to teaching. With the war over, there were high hopes that Black children could attend public schools, but this did not happen. As a result, Delia taught in a school in an African American Baptist Church on Fifth Street. She also wrote and delivered lectures during this time.

Delia never married. Later in life, she lived with one of her three sisters, Martha Goodrich, first in Wisconsin and then in Le Grand, Iowa. After Martha's death, Delia lived with her niece Alice Goodrich, who was the first woman to graduate from the medical school at the University of Iowa—no doubt at least in part inspired by her heroic aunt.

Delia died in Des Moines, where Alice practiced medicine, at the age of eighty-six in 1904. It took until 1996 for her to begin to receive some of the recognition she so richly deserves both in Kentucky and nationally. She was honored with a watercolor painting along with fifty-nine other Kentucky women for their contributions to their state.

It should now be clear that Delia was a force—a force of nature—for the liberation of people she deeply respected and valued above her own safety and security. She proved time and again that she was a woman of exceptional courage who would not be stopped, no matter what price—including that of her own liberty—she had to pay.

We trust, if there is a heaven, Frances Crowe with whom this chapter began, has warmly welcomed Delia, a soul sister for whom being imprisoned was a small price to pay in the fight for justice.

Sallie Holley (left) and her lifetime companion Caroline Putnam

CHAPTER 19

Sallie Holley
Recognizing the Centrality of Black Women's Freedom

Sallie Hollie's inspiration and dedication to the cause of freedom for Black people arose from a variety of sources, but a single speech by Abby Kelly Foster informed her every waking moment. After hearing the words of this noted abolitionist, Sallie vowed to follow in Foster's footsteps and fight for justice and freedom for all people. Always the trailblazer, Sallie carried out her pledge while educating countless Black students at the school that was eventually named in her honor.

Born on February 17, 1818, Sallie was one of twelve children. Her father's core values included a fierce opposition to slavery and a belief in religious liberalism; his influence was profound. At the age of thirteen she heard her first anti-slavery lecture while attending boarding school in Lyons, New York. But with a father like Myron Holley, this was not Sallie's first exposure to the ideas put forth in the lecture. Myron not only spoke fervently about abolitionism, he was the founder of the Liberty Party, which put the cause of anti-slavery front and center—the first party to make it a political issue. A friend wrote of Sallie's devotion to her father, "No child was ever more imbued with filial reverence." Interestingly, Sallie's mother, for whom she was named, did not share her husband's progressive leanings and remained a lifelong Methodist, a religion that experienced a rift over enslavement. Nevertheless, their marriage endured for many years.

Three experiences of her younger days shed light on the evolution of her race consciousness and confirm her steadfastness with respect to equality. The first involves the five years she was a companion to Louisa Childs. She was an invalid who had owned slaves in North Carolina before relocating to Rochester and bringing one of them, "a pious old personal attendant." Sallie enjoyed her time with both women equally and according to an observer of the family at the time, "She and Aunt Louisa used to talk slavery and anti-slavery over their chess, each with tears in her eyes, so earnest was each."[268]

A second experience that enhanced her growing dedication to justice for all peoples involved General Timothy Childs, Louisa's husband, who had recently fought in the Seminole War. It actually consisted of three separate wars (1817–18, 1835–42, 1855–58). The first of the three began with the purpose of recapturing enslaved people who had run away and sought refuge with the Seminole Indians of Florida. After the third war ended, Seminole land was exploited and settled by whites. Sallie pointed out the immorality of the conflict, and Childs "confessed to its injustice, but pleaded as a soldier that he must obey the commands of his superiors."[269]

Given what Sallie knew about the cruelty of these wars, she gave no credence to his defense. Already she did not believe in war, but, like William Lloyd Garrison, who had been opposed to resorting to violence before 1861, she too wished that those fighting for freedom for the enslaved would emerge victorious.

The third transformative experience in the evolution of her thinking was being in the presence of Frederick Douglass in 1843. He had been asked by the acclaimed women's suffrage advocate Susan B. Anthony to speak at an anti-slavery convention. The cause of abolitionism was so unpopular that no church would host the convention, so he spoke in a warehouse. During a visit to one of her sister's homes in Buffalo, she got to hear one of Frederick Douglass's lectures. His words and his passion had a profound impact on her life.

Upon her father's death in 1841 when she was twenty-three, she taught school in Rochester, choosing "the humblest and arduous position—a primary school consisting of some sixty little Irish girls." She felt "miserably inadequate," and after several false starts, including entertaining a marriage proposal and considering the possibility of working as a nurse in Cincinnati, Sallie spoke with the minister of the Unitarian Society of Rochester, New York, Frederick W. Holland. Rev. Holland's wife's uncle had just returned from England where he had been soliciting support for Oberlin College from British people who were sympathetic to the anti-slavery cause. He pointed out that Oberlin admitted women and African Americans, and persuaded Sallie to apply for admission, and she was accepted. He also gave her an unsolicited gift of $40 ($1400 in today's dollars). With that and a scholarship she had earned, she went off to Ohio in the winter of 1847. Her brother had tried in vain to convince her against going to the "nigger school," as far too many referred to it. Oberlin, more than any other college, embodied "the offspring of the anti-slavery spirit."[270]

Oberlin has been referenced in a preceding chapter as a model for John Gregg Fee's Berea College, and so it is time to give Oberlin its due. Coeducation was an initial purpose of the college when it was founded as Oberlin Collegiate Institute in 1834. As stated in the first circular announcing the college's founding, a primary purpose of the institute was "the elevation of female character, by bringing within the reach of the misjudged and neglected sex all the instructive privileges which have hitherto unreasonably distinguished the leading sex from theirs." Sallie was most assuredly attracted to this mission.

The school became dedicated to serving Black students through a series of what Ms. Holley's biographer calls "happy accidents," the first of which involved students at Lane Theological Seminary near Cincinnati. Thirty of its more vocal anti-slavery students left the seminary due to the repressive actions of the trustees, except for one: Rev. Asa Mahan. The founder of Oberlin, John Shipherd, was on his way to New England to find a president for his new college when he learned of the controversy at Lane and turned around so he could volunteer to become the first president of Oberlin. Mahan accepted the offer and introduced Shipherd to the student protesters.

The second of these "happy accidents" involved a plan conceived by Shipherd and Mahan to ask Theodore D. Weld, the best and the brightest of the protesting students, to become the theological chair of the college. Weld convinced the two men that the man they really needed to recruit for the position was Charles G. Finney, a well-known revivalist minister and theologian. In New York they received a letter from the trustees of Oberlin announcing their refusal to admit students of color. Shipherd, Mahan and the Lane students responded with the simple, unyielding demand: Oberlin must admit African Americans on an equal basis.

For the time, this was a radical and unpopular measure, even dangerous. Previous attempts at "racially" integrated schools, the Noyes Academy and the Canterbury Female Boarding School, had been met with violence that destroyed both schools; refugees from both had enrolled at Oneida Institute in New York. No one anywhere was calling for racially integrated schools, except at Oneida, the first college to enroll Black and white men on an equal basis.

Twenty-four of Oneida's students who left to attend Lane opted to leave Lane in hopes of attending Oberlin. Thus this measure seeking full equality for Black students caused great consternation among the trustees. They had to overcome their own prejudices in order to put forth such a policy. First they tabled it, taking no action until it was made clear that if they did not agree, they would lose the money from the Tappan brothers, fervent abolitionists who had pledged their funds to the school if it enrolled Black students. Mahan, Finney, Shipherd, and the Lane students all threatened to leave without a commitment to educating Black people. The trustees purposefully chose not to hold their meeting and to vote in Elyria instead of Oberlin, hoping to avoid an antagonized and possibly disruptive audience. The vote resulted in a 3-3 tie that was broken by the trustee chairman, John Keep, that meant Black students could be admitted. These were additional results:

- There would be no limit on discussions of slavery or any other topic.
- That Asa Mahan, a Lane trustee who resigned with the students, come as president. The initiative for Mahan becoming president of Oberlin came from the Oneida students, and Weld in particular.
- Professor John Morgan, fired by Lane for supporting the students, would be hired as well.

- Under what Fletcher labeled the "Finney compact," and in sharp contrast with and in reaction to recent events at Lane, the internal affairs of the college were to be under faculty control, which did not sit well with the trustees, presidents and deans through the years.[271]

Sallie was the only Unitarian at Oberlin when she enrolled in 1847, and she often found herself challenged by the dominant belief system as put forth by Finney. She maintained her beliefs, even likening them to dancing, of which she was so fond, but which was frowned upon by some of her teachers as sinful.

Her beloved friend from Oberlin, Caroline Putnam, remembered Sallie's non-conformity on the day of her graduation: "She declined to go with the multitude who kept holiday in white muslin and blue ribbons, yellow being the colour she preferred." Putnam went on to say, "The brave soul was there consecrating itself with lofty enthusiasm to the holy war against slavery. The Divine Voice had called, and with instant, reverent obedience she answered, 'Here am I.'"[272]

Putnam wrote that she and Sallie connected over their shared contempt of slavery. Sallie eventually ran out of money and took on odd jobs, from washing dishes and making bread to tutoring Black Oberlin students who needed help keeping up with their classes. She was mightily challenged by her fellow students and her professors for her Unitarian beliefs, but despite what Putnam called "all the eccentricities at Oberlin, Miss Holley honoured its earnest people, resolute to bless the world by spreading its best light and truth, and especially did she honour it for admitting women and coloured students, alone of all the institutions in our broad land."[273]

Even before her graduation from Oberlin, Sallie had made her views and aspirations to join the abolitionist struggle known. She was opposed by strong forces, including Dr. Hosmer, the minister at her church in Buffalo, who "sought her sister to remonstrate with Sallie to save her from ruining her reputation by joining those hated abolitionists." Her sister answered, "Sallie thinks her salvation depends on not being ashamed of those hated abolition infidels, Parker Pillsbury, Abby Foster and Mr. Garrison." When Millard Filmore signed the Fugitive Slave Act in 1850 and returned to his seat in Hosmer's church, Sallie vowed never to take communion there again.[274]

Another example of Sallie's steadfastness in the cause of equality for Black people occurred towards the end of her time at Oberlin. She was invited to give a speech at the celebration of West India Emancipation on August 1, 1851, by members of Sandusky, Ohio's Black community. This was both a noteworthy recognition of Sallie's reputation in anti-slavery circles and a most significant anniversary for African Americans.

The British Slavery Abolition Act, which became effective August 1, 1834, abolished slavery throughout England and all British possessions. But this didn't guarantee freedom as each West Indian island's government had the power to decide for itself whether or not freedom would happen either immediately or gradually.

In the first year under the act, only Antigua and Bermuda released their enslaved people while the rest of the colonies complied with the act's other provisions. That meant complete freedom for children under six, but enslaved people over that age had to serve an apprenticeship. This was supposed to ensure that they would "acquire all rights and privileges of freedom," but what it really meant was working with no pay for forty-five hours each week for their former masters. The period of these apprenticeships varied from four to six years, and the compensation "was no different from slave provisions: food, clothing, housing and medical treatment. Former owners on the other hand, were compensated for their loss of 'property'. The British government paid West Indian planters a total of £20 million."[275]

Before learning about the loss of freedom that the supposed Abolition Act portended, the enslaved celebrated on August 1, 1834. This included dancing in the streets, thanking God at religious services, and just sharing their happiness with one another. This joy was short-lived, and soon it was replaced by anger and disillusionment. Protests and attempts at rebellion occurred on the islands and in Guyana on the mainland. These uprisings were put down by militia and special guard units. Many "apprentices" were imprisoned and flogged in public squares. Some were hanged. Others managed to run away and fled to maroon communities—settlements of escaped slaves in remote forest or mountainous areas where they were safe.

It wasn't until August 1, 1838, that apprentices in all of the islands and Guyana were granted freedom. This was a major day of celebration in the United States where free African Americans and American abolitionists gathered together—Black and white—in the hopes that West Indian emancipation would lead to freedom for the enslaved everywhere. It would take another twenty-five years for that to become a reality with the Emancipation Proclamation.

Sallie received permission to deliver the address, but when the wife of Oberlin's president, Mrs. Mahan, learned of the upcoming event, she presented one condition: "You will, Miss Holley, please not accept any invitation to stay in a coloured man's house in Sandusky." Sallie replied, "As a matter of truth it had never occurred to me that I should be so invited, but, Mrs. Mahan, now you mention it, I should certainly feel it my duty to accept any such invitation as a testimony to my principles, and, really, to those professed by this Institution."[276]

As her final term of college was about to end, Sallie received a request from Frederick Douglass asking her to become involved in his work with his anti-slavery newspaper, the *North Star*. She turned down his offer because she had already made a promise to Abby Kelley Foster, one that was to provide her with the work of abolition for the next ten years.

Sallie graduated Oberlin in 1851. In 1852, she attended a meeting in Litchfield, Ohio. Abby Kelley Foster made "an eloquent appeal to her audience on behalf of the enslaved woman and asked: 'Who in this great assembly is willing to plead her cause?'" Following the talk, Sallie spoke up and said, "I will take the cause of the slave woman."[277]

Sallie was immediately asked to join the Ohio abolitionist campaign. As Putnam informs us, "From that day all her plans were made with reference to its fulfillment...'I've decided to be an anti-slavery lecturer,' she wrote me, - my first intimation of the event."

Sallie stayed true to her pledge to "take the cause of the slave woman"— and men. She began her speaking tour agitating against enslavement. She also collected funds for William Lloyd Garrison's magazine, the *Liberator*, and the American Anti-Slavery Society. She was determined to provide for her needs and surprised her with these words, "You are to be paid ten dollars a week and your expenses by the Anti-Slavery Society."[278]

Soon after this announcement and recognition of the value of Sallie's services, there was a meeting in Samuel J. May's church that Caroline Putnam referred to as:

> never to be forgotten by me. We had heard Mr. May in the morning. In a burst of eloquence he alluded to the rescue of Jerry, the fugitive slave the previous October. On that morning (of his rescue) no one was so obscure and unknown as Jerry. But when his rights as a man were assailed, before night of the same day there was no one in Syracuse of so much importance as Jerry.[279]

Sallie also spoke that evening. She "told with powerful pathos, the slave's wrongs, and by every motive of humanity and religion urged his cause on the audience."[280] Upon returning to her hotel room, Ms. Foster had been so inspired by the speech that she:

> ...laid her hands on Miss Holley's shoulders and exclaimed, 'Oh, I have been prostrate before the Throne, all this evening, thanking God that when I am so worn and weary and feeble, he had raised up one who can and will speak so nobly and winningly in this holy but hated and persecuted cause.'[281]

The torch was being passed that evening. Sallie traveled by buggy and wagon from village to village speaking eloquently about freedom for the enslaved. She stayed with strangers and dealt with crowds that ranged from "rapt to hostile." Throughout this period she lived, "the rough and tumble kind of a life the anti-slavery lecturer experiences."[282] Sallie was a dedicated letter writer, and this one captures her relentless efforts to promote equality among the races:

> A week or two ago at a common school celebration in this village, the county superintendent invited me to address the children. Accordingly I told them of the slave-children in this country, who are

not allowed to read or write or spell or commit to memory the multiplication table which they had just repeated so well. Whereupon two Buchanan men rose up and left in high indignation that 'an abolition lecture was poked at them.' I am very sorry to even seem rude and 'fanatical' but know not how to avoid it and be faithful to the cause of the slave. In fact, nothing else is so important and proper for all occasions, to be talked of, as the slave and his cause.[283]

Sallie's dedication to the cause of freedom for enslaved people transcended the pacifism of her co-worker, William Lloyd Garrison. She even thanked God for John Brown's Harpers Ferry raid in a prayer before a lecture in Ellsworth, Maine. She joined Garrison in supporting the war that followed soon after Lincoln took office in 1861 and continued to work for the end of enslavement throughout the war.

At the conclusion of the war, Sallie was no less determined to fight for equality. The Thirteenth Amendment (abolishing enslavement except as a punishment for crime) certainly encouraged her, but she was far from satisfied and had this to say when she attended an Oberlin reunion:

They insisted on my relating what I had been about. I said I was afraid they wouldn't care to hear how I had been holding anti-slavery meetings all these years and still 'spoke in public.' Mr. Cooper asked what I lectured upon now. 'Oh,' I said, 'Black folks must vote all through the country.' Helen Finney, who was present with her husband, General Cox, said she thought I wanted women to vote. 'Oh, yes!' I said, 'that's inevitable,' whereupon there was 'immense sensation,' as the newspapers say.

The struggle for equal treatment and equal rights for free Black people was far from over for Sallie. Garrison and his allies were convinced that the American Anti-Slavery Society was no longer needed since the Emancipation Proclamation had achieved its central goal, but for the next five years an internal struggle took place with Sallie as one of the most ardent supporters of the society's need to continue. She was so convinced that she wrote a very strongly worded letter to one woman who favored closing it down. It was published in the *National Anti-Slavery Standard* in 1868. Here is a telling sample:

> It is heartless, cold-blooded, worldly apathy, that can object to the name or the work of an *Anti- Slavery Society*. Since this New Year began, three negroes were seized in Tennessee, bound over logs, and beaten nearly dead, because they voted the Republican ticket. Three thousand black men in Mississippi petition Congress to send them to Liberia. In their touching language, "The white people have all the land, all the money, all the education. Many of the planters refuse to pay us all together, and they work generally to prevent the education of our children." And you tell me there is no need of an Anti-Slavery Society.[284]

> See black men all over the South persecuted, driven from homes, such as they have had, denied work and bread, for daring to vote *loyally*. See them still shot down—killed by all the cowardly, ruffianly means known to the old barbaric days of slavery—and then, if you have a human heart, ask the American Anti-Slavery Society to stop its work, if you can! Are you afraid the Black people will have *too many* friends, *too much* justice, *too much* liberty?[285]

Sallie eventually lost the struggle to keep the Anti-Slavery Society functioning, but she was far from finished with the work she had pledged to perform. In 1870 Sallie began the fight she carried forth until she died. At the age of fifty-two she joined her beloved friend Caroline Putnam in Lottsburg, Virginia. Caroline had started a school there for formerly enslaved people. Thus began a decades-long collaboration at the Holley School, named by Caroline in appreciation for Sallie's purchase of the land upon which the school still stands.

Every year one of them would head north to seek additional funds from friends and former allies in the abolitionist movement to keep the school afloat. They worked tirelessly teaching their students and grew much of the food consumed on campus. Throughout, there was a "near total boycott of any communication by their white neighbors." Sallie took evident pride in the school:

> Though our new schoolhouse is not entirely completed at this date, yet I rejoice to write, the second coat of plaster is this day going on and by November our school will enter triumphantly. These Virginia rebels are fairly confounded to see our schoolhouse spring up so magically, and our fortunes revive from their hostile tread. Like the chamomile bed, the more it is trod upon, the more fragrant and lively it becomes. Our coloured friends are cheered to the very marrow of their bones. Their faces shine as day after day they call on us to exult and crow. Still we know the enemy ever sits with lance in rest to take advantage as often as he can make a deadly thru.[286]

Sallie was not above reproach in her dealings with both white and Black people in her community. Having grown up and been educated in New England Unitarian and Quaker settings, she and Caroline had a particularly challenging time with Southern religion, as can be seen in this letter excerpt:

> The white folks' camp meeting has just ended. Over thirty conversions! The coloured 'protracted meeting' is this week in full blast, making night hideous with terrible noises. All this kind of religion seems to me worthless. It doesn't save from lies and stealing. Nobody's character is elevated or ennobled. Vanity and self-conceit are fostered. People pray and shout and say the Holy Ghost is moving their souls! It is awful.[287]

But whatever class bias and white paternalism are evident in her letters must be measured against her total commitment to the cause of providing a sound education to the Holley School students. She "fought, taught and organized" with fervor despite her discomfort with some aspects of the local culture.

The school itself was unique for its time and location in that it sought not only to instruct in the subjects taught at other freedom schools, but also to empower its students in the world they would encounter upon graduation. They saw knowledge of "letters and figures" as a means to an end. The pedagogy was in service to fostering civically engaged men and women. Thus, while learning their letters, they also studied writing and speaking by investigating the speeches of abolitionists before the war as well as those demanding racial justice during Reconstruction. They celebrated the achievements of African Americans and included in their curriculum John Brown, Frederick Douglass, Lydia Maria Child, Thomas Wentworth Higginson, Oliver Wendell Holmes, Abraham Lincoln, Samuel May, Wendell Phillips, Robert Gould Shaw, Gerrit Smith, Thaddeus Stevens, Charles Sumner, and John Greenleaf Whittier. On occasion, an entire class would spend a day studying a single contributor to the cause of liberation. In an 1882 letter to Louisa May Alcott, who was a supporter of the school, Sallie wrote:

> I wish, Dear Mrs. Alcott—you could have...heard our "Charles Sumner-Class" when they recited the story of his life—Each member of the class reciting some passage of his—biography—It sounded—to my ear—strangely sweet—to hear these poor colored children repeating whole passages from the speeches of their great friend! Then too—we have a "Wendell Phillips' Class"—each member of which will recite some noble paragraph, with a touching effect, quite indescribable—bringing their ever-fearless and faithful defender before us like an inspiring painting! And again, we call our "Old John Brown Class" up to rehearse his grand and ever living testimonies.[288]

We can only conjecture what the impact would have been over the years were all students receiving such an education and exposure to those Sallie and the Holley School saw as role models and inspirations. This book has that purpose.

The obstacles facing these two women educators were enormous and unceasing in late 1892, some twenty-two years after Sallie had begun her career at the Holley School. With Reconstruction in the South on life support, she expressed her frustration in another letter. Her efforts to hold onto Republican majorities in local elections, despite relentless vote rigging by Democrats, had resulted in more disappointment:

> Our Lottsburgh ex-slave-holders boast that they will get the post office in March. One of the most bitter told a white woman that 'That old Yankee,' meaning me, 'has ruined these Lottsburgh niggers, making them think they are as good as anybody.'[289]

Soon after writing this letter, Sallie, on one of the annual New York pilgrimages, caught a chill. Pneumonia developed and Sallie died at age seventy-four on January 12, 1893. She never stopped fighting until the very end. At a memorial service for Sallie before the Women's Suffrage Convention in Washington, DC, Frederick Douglass paid homage to her by recalling their first encounter. The additional commentary is from *A Life for Liberty*, the biography of Sallie Holley written by John White Chadwick.

> "On the third day of our motley meeting, made up entirely of men, I observed with some amazement, as well as pleasure, a stately young lady, elegantly dressed, come into the room, leading a beautiful little girl. The crowd was one that would naturally repel a refined and elegant little lady, but there was no shrinking on her part. The crowd did the shrinking. It drew in its sides and opened the way, as if fearful of soiling the elegant dress with the dirt of toil. This lady came daily to my meetings in that old deserted building, morning and afternoon, until they ended. The dark and rough background rendered her appearance like a messenger from heaven sent to cheer me in what seemed to most men a case of utter despair." The lady was Miss Sallie Holley, and this story illustrates her noble, independent, and humane character. She was never ashamed of her cause nor her company.[290]

What was Sallie's greatest accomplishment then? I echo the sentiment of lao hong han who highlights the thousands of African Americans who were educated at Sallie's and Caroline's Holley School. Some certainly left the South in the Great Migration seeking a safer and less stressful life. But many others stayed in the area and made use of the skills and ideas they'd learned under the expert tutelage of these two women to make their lives and the lives of their families better. As Mr. han states as he ends his tribute to Sallie:

> But many fanned out across the South, like men and women educated at similar schools, taking teaching jobs and ensuring that the white power structure would never again be able to enforce the near-universal illiteracy which had helped keep Black America in slavery's chains.[291]

A worthy legacy, to be sure, and just one more reason this woman requires commemoration. She never stopped believing in the righteousness of empowering women and Black people. Her life is an inspirational testimony to the impact holding to powerful convictions, regardless of the obstacles, and acting upon them can have on so many. As her career unfolded, she kept her eyes consistently on the prize of equality. Did Ruth Bader Ginsberg know about Sallie? If she did, she, too, would have felt a kindred spirit crusading for justice.

CHAPTER 20

Graceanna Lewis
Abolitionist and Natural Scientist

One of the most famous and powerful letters in US history emerged from the Birmingham jail where Martin Luther King Jr. was imprisoned in 1963. More than a century before his impassioned appeal to his fellow clergymen and women, Graceanna Lewis, disillusioned with the silence of her fellow Quakers, wrote a similar letter, "An Appeal to Those Members of the Society of Friends Who Knowing the Principles of the Abolitionists Stand Aloof from the Anti-Slavery Enterprise." In it, she stated with no qualms whatsoever that "the horrors of the southern prison house stand glaring in the light of noon-day sun" while too many Quakers "sat quietly down in the comfort of your own guarded homes, perhaps seeking to avoid every thing that would awaken an interest in the welfare of the slave."[292]

As is often the case with abolitionists in general and most assuredly with several of those we've honored in this book, Graceanna Lewis was raised within a strong abolitionist Quaker household. She was born in 1821 in West Vincent Township in Pennsylvania. After the death of her father when Graceanna was a young child, she was raised by her mother, a schoolteacher who passed on an appreciation for science and a love of nature. Her mother also served as a role model for Graceanna through her social activism, which included offering a safe house to runaway slaves as part of the Underground Railroad.[293]

Graceanna's familial influences were not limited to her immediate family. Her mother's brother, Bartholomew Fussell, was an abolitionist who aided an estimated two thousand runaway slaves as well as the founder of the Women's Medical College of Philadelphia. These three strands—abolitionism, women's suffrage (as represented by her uncle's support of a woman's right to higher education) and science—would be the central endeavors of her life and the means through which she would leave an indelible mark on society.[294]

Graceanna was able to attend the Kimberton Boarding School, where she met and studied under botanist and reformer Abigail Kimber, a well-known plant collector. Kimber's influence—her passions and her career choice—was crucial to Graceanna's decision to teach botany and other sciences. Upon graduating from the Kimberton School in 1842, she became a teacher of botany and chemistry at a boarding school in York,

Pennsylvania. Might she have become a scientist at this point, given her aptitude and fascination? Teaching was one of the very few occupations open to women, so the question is unanswerable.

Graceanna and her sisters, Elizabeth and Mariann, came to despise enslavement at a very early age when they "saw a colored man, Henry, ground with ropes and carried off to slavery with a look of utter agony on his face…They hated slavery from that hour."[295]

Such experiences and the family from which she originated propelled Graceanna into the world of the Underground Railroad. Chester County, where she was born and raised, was an important junction of the Underground Railroad's eastern line. "The free Black community and the Society of Friends formed a strong network of communication, transcending religious and racial barriers that allowed them to guide fugitives to freedom."[296]

The route was well-documented, with sites that ran from Wilmington, Delaware, into Chester County. It then moved onto Montgomery County. Several routes were taken through the county. Those coming to Graceanna's home would follow a path that included stops in Wilmington, Kennett, East Marlborough, Newlin, and Downington. Next was the home of the Vickers family in Lionville and then Graceanna's home, where the fugitives would stay before heading to Phoenixville and eventually Norristown.

One way that Graceanna shared the trauma and fear that was the life of runaway enslaved people was through letters to the editor of the *Friends Intelligencer*.[297] She knew that readers would respond to these powerful lessons, which spoke to the resolve, determination, desperation, and courage of escaping people. She recalled the story of Rachel Moore, "a runaway slave and her six children who arrived at her house 'in a most pitiful condition.'" In the "torrid" weather, "the flapping of the wet garments against their unprotected limbs wore off the skin." Recounting the desperation and urgency of their dangerous situation, she wrote, "They pressed forward with all of the speed possible to them."[298]

Graceanna was very aware of the clothing in which the escapees arrived. The material was coarse and had red stripes in the weave. Neighboring abolitionist families collected a variety of clothes to accommodate the range of ages of those in need so she had a goodly supply at the ready. She then made sure the incriminating clothing was burned.

The story of Rachel and her children was just one of many that Graceanna recounted from her years of harboring fugitive slaves. She shared an anecdote in which she prevented slave catchers from finding those hiding in her house by "imploring them to respect her femininity by not inspecting her bedroom, which she claimed, would invade her privacy." In another incident that occurred in 1855, ten enslaved people stole a carriage from their master and found their way to Graceanna's Underground Railroad station.[299]

With so many lives at stake, including her own, her work as a station master required the utmost secrecy, but Graceanna was not one to keep her abolitionist passion on the shelf. As mentioned earlier in the chapter, she took her fellow Quakers to task in 1848 when she wrote her famous appeal.

One hundred fifteen years later, on April 16, 1963, Dr. King wrote his "Letter from the Birmingham Jail." Though separated by time and place, both were expressions of frustration and chastisement. Graceanna called out her fellow Quakers, just as Dr. King accused his fellow religious leaders of being derelict in upholding the core values of their faiths. She was sick and tired of Quakers who talked a good game, but remained on the sidelines when it came to doing the work of abolitionism. The words that begin her appeal speak to her frustration:

> Dear Friends: Unaided by your efforts, uncheered by your counsel, through many weary yet joyful years of buffeting with the waves of opposition, the advocates of Immediate Emancipation have asked, have implored, have demanded in the name of justice and mercy, that their appeals should be heard.[300]

She goes on to point out, in no uncertain terms, the anguish of enslavement: "Its paralyzing, benighting effects are made known. No longer can the strong cry which is ever ascending from the wrung heart of despair, be by you unheard." She asks a series of questions of her readers:

Are you not verily guilty concerning your brother? Have you not seen him...pining amid the horrors of his captivity until he is sick of hope deferred? What answer comes to the secret of your souls in solemn stillness? Have you done, are you doing your duty?[301]

Dr. King wrote extensively of the inaction and the willingness to wait essentially indefinitely for the "moderates" to whom he addresses his "Letter from the Birmingham Jail." His impatience with such a view is on display:

We will have to repent in this generation not merely for the hateful words and actions of the bad people but for the appalling silence of the good people. Human progress never rolls in on wheels of inevitability; it comes through the tireless efforts of men willing to be co-workers with God, and without this hard work, time itself becomes an ally of the forces of social stagnation. We must use time creatively, in the knowledge that the time is always ripe to do right. Now is the time to make real the promise of democracy and transform our pending national elegy into a creative psalm of brotherhood. Now is the time to lift our national policy from the quicksand of racial injustice to the solid rock of human dignity.[302]

Like Graceanna, King also questions his readers on their commitment to equality:

So the question is not whether we will be extremists, but what kind of extremists we will be. Will we be extremists for hate or for love? Will we be extremists for the preservation of injustice or for the extension of justice?[303]

Once emancipation was guaranteed with the North's victory in the Civil War and the abolition of enslavement with the passage of the Thirteenth Amendment, Graceanna pursued one of her other callings—a commitment to science and more specifically to botany and ornithology. Even with her ongoing commitment to the enslaved during the post-Civil

War years, she was able to devote considerable time and energy to studying with the well-known ornithologist John Cassin at Philadelphia's Academy of Natural Sciences. She met Cassin in 1862 and began a five-year course of study under his expert tutelage. In 1867, Cassin paid homage to the life and work of his protegé by naming *Icterus graceannae*, the white-edged oriole, in Lewis's honor.

Records indicate that in 1865, at the age of forty-four, Graceanna offered "parlor classes" in ornithology while living in Philadelphia. She charged two dollars for each of four sessions, which she conducted in people's homes. Women were not able to participate fully in the life of the mind. Scientific societies granted limited access, but there were few real opportunities to work as a college professor. Despite her serious efforts, Graceanna never taught at the college level. She nevertheless persisted in doing research and publishing her work, earning the respect of many prominent (male) scientists of her time.

In 1868 Lewis published *The Natural History of Birds: Lectures on Ornithology in Ten Parts*. It was to be the first of a multipart series, but the death of her patron, Cassin, put an end to that plan. Without any funding and unable because of her gender to obtain a position offering a significant salary, she could continue no further.[304]

Other factors limited Graceanna's plan to write a definitive work on birds. Her ideas were too complicated for a lay audience, and her critique of Darwin's theory of evolution, which was gaining wide acceptance, made the scientific community unreceptive. Her devout religious upbringing left no room for Darwin. In her view of faith, God was in charge of the universe and had created it intricately from the beginning of time. Thus evolution was not needed. Eventually she began to come around to acknowledging the validity of some aspects of evolution, but that was in the 1890s, well past the point when such a turnaround in her thinking could have earned her a wider audience within the world of science.

Even as her opposition to evolution softened, she still saw it as part of the theist system and rejected Darwin's idea of random variation being connected to natural selection. She persisted in seeing evolution as a "divinely directed process for the perfection of supernaturally created species."[305]

Thus held back by three strikes—lack of a higher education degree, sexism in the scientific community, and her own strongly held religious convictions involving creation—Graceanna was limited to lecturing and working as a freelance scientific illustrator, which did not pay well. In 1870 she took a job at the Philadelphia Friends School to provide a steady income. Teaching, after all, was her first endeavor and a profession at which she excelled, especially in inspiring young girls to become immersed in the sciences. She taught at the Friends School for one year and in 1871 sold family land to help pay for further research. Her next project was to be a set of illustrated charts depicting the relationship of the plant and animal kingdoms, but the new information coming her way was immense and keeping up proved impossible to sustain. She refused to try to publish her charts in an incomplete form, so the project never saw the light of day.

As a result of the perilous state of her finances, Graceanna was obliged to live with a variety of family members throughout her adulthood. This was true of many women of the nineteenth century, who faced discrimination on numerous fronts. She lived with another of her mother's brothers, Dr. Edwin Fussell and his wife, Rebecca, in Media, Pennsylvania, where Dr. Fussell practiced medicine. During her years in Media, she lectured on zoology and was active in the women's suffrage movement, her third major passion. In addition, she was determined to support efforts to prohibit the production and consumption of alcohol and served as secretary of the Women's Christian Temperance Union of Media.[306]

The 1876 Centennial Exposition featured some of Graceanna's botanical drawings. She received very positive comments from the British scientist Thomas Henry Huxley. Seventeen years later her work on a series of fifty paintings for a display at the Pennsylvania Forestry Commissions display at the Chicago World's Columbian Exposition drew much attention. The paintings were subsequently displayed at the 1901 Pan-American Exposition in Buffalo, New York, as well as at the 1904 Louisiana Purchase Exposition in St. Louis.

Graceanna became a member of the Academy of Natural Sciences in Philadelphia and the Delaware County Institute of Science. Thanks to the generosity of her adopted daughter, Ellen, who she had raised since she was nine years old, Graceanna's later years included sharing a summer house by the sea in Longport, New Jersey, with her grateful daughter. Ellen married a wealthy man. This enabled Graceanna to have a much less stressful life without the anxiety of constantly being concerned about having enough money to support herself.

Graceanna died on February 25, 1912, of a stroke. She was ninety. Her pioneering work as a scientist most assuredly distinguishes her, especially overcoming the enormous obstacles she faced as a woman in a closed man's world. We now know how much more she did as a white woman to save countless lives as a station master on the Underground Railroad and as a strong advocate in words and deeds for freedom, thanks to her belief in full equality for African Americans.

Conclusion in Two Voices:

Tom Weiner

Elizabeth Heyrick, 1769-1831

While this book was being written, Sarah Pirtle, a dear friend of the authors and fellow member of our Bridge4Unity anti-racism group located in Western Massachusetts, sent an email. She knew we had been writing a book about ante-bellum anti-racism activists and she had found someone she felt would make a fine addition. She was, of course, correct.

Elizabeth Heyrick certainly could be included in any set of stories about courageous and dedicated anti-enslavement activists. From her position of white privilege in British society she advocated for her fellow Britons to boycott the sugar produced in the Caribbean. Her campaign indirectly led to Sharp's Slave Rebellion on the island of Jamaica in 1831, known as the Baptist War, since her efforts inspired those enslaved laborers on the sugar cane plantations to rebel. The rebellion had a powerful impact:

> But the mere demonstration of military competence – the rebels defeated the island militia in at least one head-to-head confrontation – made an impression like no other uprising had before and helped inspire the British Parliament to pass the Slavery Abolition Act of 1833, which abolished slavery in the West Indies.[307]

When we began this project we considered adding abolitionists from England. It was the discovery of so many Americans who had been neglected or given far too little recognition that resulted in the decision to stay on this side of the "pond." Sarah's email was a reminder of such people as Elizabeth Heyrick, whose stories also merit recognition and commemoration, many of whose words and deeds furthered the cause of freedom and equality in the Americas.

Sadly, as we conclude these profiles "in defiance," there are significant efforts to make it harder to access our nation's true history. The state of Florida is front and center in this systematic endeavor to prevent students from being able to appreciate what our nation has not only done well, but also to acknowledge the harms it has caused. A recent article in the *Washington Post* captures the struggle of four Black citizens seeking to undo this new level of harm emanating from denying facts and manipulating students as a result. Entitled *'We're on the side of righteousness': For these Black Floridians, the fight over what African American history is taught in schools reflects their own experiences and an unwavering commitment,* it features this pronouncement:

> We on the task force worked to come up with the curriculum, with lesson plans and learning activities, so there could be no excuse about what to teach. There's been a lot of hypocrisy in the state to have this law (to teach Black history) on the books for almost 30 years but there are no consequences if the instruction isn't provided.
>
> Recently, that changed. The state of Florida rejected the AP African American studies course, with officials saying that African American history has no educational value. It lit a fire under people. [One consequence was a 2023 law, championed by Thompson and others, that compels school districts to provide evidence that they are teaching Black history and to post lesson plans on their websites.]
>
> So if there is any silver lining to this, it has awakened people that there is a concerted effort to obscure and to sanitize and to whitewash African American history. It validates the belief I have had for decades: We must all work to make sure that (Black) history is part and parcel of American history. People now realize it has to be included intentionally—or it will be excluded intentionally.
>
> I have a lot more support, a lot more energy, a lot more engagement than I've ever had before.

Thankfully, then there are new leaders taking important steps like those in Florida to end systemic racism. In another 100 years, it is altogether possible that someone will be sitting down to write a book about them. Will it be because, in small or large measure, they did not receive the recognition and honor they deserved either in our time or in the unwritten future? It is our hope that books like this one will encourage us to pay more attention to those amongst us who are acting "in defiance" of convention and constraints to bring about a more just, more equitable and more participatory country for Black Americans, which must happen for all of us to be truly free.

Dr. Amilcar Shabazz

The vignettes we have written here are of people only knowable through limited source material along with contextualization by way of the process of historical inquiry. We have focused on key moments in their lives where they acted in defiance of the undemocratic, racist and "maladjusted" norms of their times and climes. Something different than profiles in courage, these are struggles of human hearts. They show up as living, complex beings who at some point refuse to adjust to a normal life in an unjust space, where people are suffering. We have tried to bring before you humans we did not know personally in ways where they become personal to us, symbols of the possibility of radical empathy, of defiance.

These stories about people who lived and struggled to live free before the twentieth century, like the past itself, flow into our present. Thus, the former Evanston, IL, alderwoman Robin Rue Simmons, who led the city to create the first municipal reparative justice program that began making compensatory payments in 2022, stands on the shoulders, as we say, of earlier activists for Black reparations like Callie House, leader of the National Ex-Slave Mutual Relief, Bounty and Pension Association who was imprisoned for her work in 1917, all the way back to the solitary petition of Belinda X. The later activists may have not known about our beloved Belinda at the start of their work, but her spirit was there moving and guiding the hand of history.

One person I met and knew personally who embodied the kind of defiant lives we have chronicled here was Kwame Ture. For more than four decades his example has been a force in my life. He lived and defied the norms of Jim Crow America a generation before I embarked on defying those norms as they operated and oppressed in the 1970s.

Once, we gathered with Ture around a table in the home of Mrs. Dorothy Turner, president of the Black Citizens Task Force, part of a dynamic duo in Austin, Texas, with Ms. Velma Roberts. We were all *ready for revolution*, including undergraduate, college student, twenty-year-old me. At forty, Ture spoke to students as well as to veteran activists. He spoke as a revolutionary theorist and activist who was then organizing on a pan-African basis from his base on the continent of Africa, in Conakry, Guinea. Before I was born he attended Howard University and was known by the name Stokely Carmichael. He became an active leader within the Student Nonviolent Coordinating Committee, learning from the great organizer Ms. Ella Baker and marching alongside Dr. Martin Luther King. His path toward defiance was born of his philosophical orientation (his major at Howard switched from Biology to Philosophy) and his will to go beyond theoretical exercises or thought experiments. His defiance was about making real change in the world.

After beatings and imprisonment, the deaths of comrades and the assassination of Dr. King, Ture, like his comrade and contemporary, Dr. Angela Davis, moved toward revolution as the solution to our subjugation worldwide. Meeting with Ture, however, did not feel like I was rubbing shoulders with the architect of Black Power or someone the head of the FBI a dozen years before worried could become "the black messiah" that might unify and electrify a militant mass struggle for liberation in the U.S. Still a firebrand in his speech that night and still operating on a most advanced intellectual level, in the down-home setting of Ms. Turner's kitchen he mostly listened. He was quiet but warm. If something funny was said his laugh was a roar and his grin wide. I was known then by my comrades and friends as Shabazz, but I had not made the change legal through the courts at that time. Ture, though world famous by the Stokely name, had done so. He was leading me, inspiring me and teaching me and many from my generation, but he did so in his actions and what he embodied, more than what he said.

He was a resolute Pan-Africanist. I was a member of the Southern African Liberation Action Committee working to raise material aid and other forms of solidarity for the independence struggles on the African continent. We shared a similar analysis of imperialism as a driving force in world affairs that would require some form of a revolution inside the USA, the belly of the imperialist beast. Ture, however, had come to feel that political organizing for freedom in the U.S. was secondary at best and perhaps even a futile act of resistance. For Pan-Africanists, he argued, the focus had to be on the freedom and reunification of African people on the continent of Africa in a socialist future rather than the capitalist road most countries officially accepted.

I also agreed with Ture on the necessity of supporting the Palestinian people who faced war, occupation and their destruction in whole or in part. Again, he set an example for us when he and members of the Student Nonviolent Coordinating Committee took up the Palestinian struggle over a decade before. Their study of the situation in Palestine was followed by actually meeting with Palestinians, but this was deemed as controversial. To some Jews who had supported the Black movement for civil and human rights in the U.S., Ture and SNCC coming to support Palestine was a betrayal. In truth, however, it was not.

I was too young to vote when Jimmy Carter was elected president, but I supported his election after the disastrous criminality of Richard Nixon and his Republican Party. As I became active in the fight for the liberation of Southern Africa from white/settler colonial rule I learned of Israel's backing of and deep involvements with those very regimes. While Israel and South Africa's apartheid regime worked closely together, Nelson Mandela and the African National Congress developed close ties with Yasser Arafat's Palestine Liberation Organization (PLO). Mandela would remind the world that "the people of South Africa will never forget the support of the state of Israel to the apartheid regime," and he would state emphatically that "we know too well that our freedom is incomplete without the freedom of the Palestinians." Africa's liberation movement's partisans who we related to and built solidarity with were not caught in the mythical idea of driving Israeli settlers to the sea, but they did recognize Zionism as antithetical to Palestine's right to independence and supported the Palestinians in their fight for land and independence.

Jimmy Carter, who appointed Southern Christian antiracist leader Andrew Young to serve as United States delegate to the United Nations, had several times resisted demands that the outspoken former civil rights leader be dismissed from his post. After thirty months in office, when it was disclosed that Young held a meeting with Zehdi Labib Terzi, the P.L.O. Observer to the United Nations, the Carter administration quickly accepted the ambassador's resignation. While it was not clear whether Young had really violated Washington policy against dealings with the P.L.O. he was nonetheless sacked and I and many others saw it as a lesson about the power of the Zionist lobby in the US.

When Kwame Ture brought this lesson out he was treated as a pariah instead of a hero. The Black community was told to keep quiet and celebrate when President Carter presented the last Medal of Freedom of his presidency "to Ambassador, former Congressman, great American, Andrew Young," on January 16, 1981, just a few days before Ronald Reagan was inaugurated the new POTUS. Some of us did not keep quiet and have never accepted the status quo in Palestine. Our solidarity continued, but so did the well-organized effort to discredit and neutralize us.

As we close this book everything Kwame Ture defiantly called our attention to regarding Israel and Palestine, as well as concerning Africa and imperialism, decades ago, is now showing up in more dead and bloodied bodies as well as bombed out buildings, and millions in forced migration. Being in defiance is not always simple or clear cut, and it always has consequences. Ture's spirit has remained a force in my life even after his transition to the ancestral realm in 1998. If we would have expanded this book to include twentieth-century individuals he is certainly one whose life I would have wanted to grapple with. He was at least fifty years ahead of the world in his thoughts and actions.

There is one other impression Ture made on me that night in Austin in 1981. I call it generational activism. He credited the influence of indigenous people and the Vietnamese during the war that the U.S. government waged on them as how he arrived at this way of thinking. He said we must formulate our response to power dynamics not solely in light of the effect it would have on our current experience, but for what it would mean for seven generations to come. Ture was known for saying that previous generations "had to run, run, run. My generation's out of breath. We ain't running no more." The generation of youth today, from Jackson, Mississippi, to Khan Younis, Gaza, fight for their lives but are also fighting for the lives of the youth who will live there in the 2160s. In this generational way of thinking and organizing one considers how to stay alive in the immediate moment but also how to leave the environment capable of sustaining the lives of your grandchildren's grandchildren. I pray that the study and honor we show to the lives in this book will be generative of this kind of sustainable defiance.

Appendix

Belinda Sutton's Reparations Petition 1783

Commonwealth of Massachusetts

To the Honourable the Senate and House of Representatives in General Court assembled.

The Petition of Belinda an Affrican, humbly shews:

That seventy years have rolled away, since she on the banks of the Rio de Valta received her existence—the mountains Covered with spicy forests, the valleys loaded with the richest fruits, spontaneously produced; joined to that happy temperature of air to exclude excess; would have yielded her the most compleat felicity, had not her mind received early impressions of the cruelty of men, whose faces were like the moon, and whose Bows and Arrows were like the thunder and the lightning of the Clouds.—The idea of these, the most dreadful of all Enemies, filled her infant slumbers with horror, and her noontide moments with evil apprehensions!—But her affrighted imagination, in its most alarming extension, never represented distresses equal to what she hath since really experienced—for before she had Twelve years enjoyed the fragrance of her native groves, and e'er she realized, that Europeans placed their happiness in the yellow dust which she carelessly marked with her infant footsteps—even when she, in a sacred grove, with each hand in that of a tender Parent, was paying her devotions to the great Orisa who made all things—an armed band of white men, driving many of her Countrymen in Chains, ran into the hallowed shade!—could the Tears, the sighs and supplications, bursting from Tortured Parental affection, have blunted the keen edge of Avarice, she might have been rescued from Agony, which many of her Country's Children have felt, but which none hath ever described,—in vain she lifted her supplicating voice to an insulted father, and her guiltless hands to a dishonoured Deity! She was ravished from the bosom of her Country, from the arms of her friends—while the advanced age of her Parents, rendering them unfit for servitude, cruelly separated her from them forever!

Scenes which her imagination had never conceived of—a floating World—the sporting Monsters of the deep—and the familiar meetings of Billows and clouds, strove, but in vain to divert her melancholly attention, from three hundred Affricans in chains, suffering the most excruciating torments; and some of them rejoicing, that the pangs of death came like a balm to their wounds.

Once more her eyes were blest with a Continent—but alas! how unlike the Land where she received her being! here all things appeared unpropitious—she learned to catch the Ideas, marked by the sounds of language only to know that her doom was Slavery, from which death alone was to emancipate her. —What did it avail her, that the walls of her Lord were hung with Splendor, and that the dust troden underfoot in her native Country, crowded his Gates with sordid worshipers—the Laws had rendered her incapable of receiving property –and though she was a free moral agent, accountable for her actions, yet she never had a moment at her own disposal!

Fifty years her faithful hands have been compelled to ignoble servitude for the benefit of an Isaac Royall, untill, as if Nations must be agitated, and the world convulsed for the preservation of that freedom which the Almighty Father intended for all the human Race, the present war was Commenced—The terror of men armed in the Cause of freedom, compelled her master to fly—and to breathe away his Life in a Land, where, Lawless domination sits enthroned—pouring bloody outrage and cruelty on all who dare to be free.

The face of your Petitioner, is now marked with the furrows of time, and her frame feebly bending under the oppression of years, while she, by the Laws of the Land, is denied the enjoyment of one morsel of that immense wealth, apart whereof hath been accumilated by her own industry, and the whole augmented by her servitude.

WHEREFORE, casting herself at the feet of your honours, as to a body of men, formed for the extirpation of vassalage, for the reward of Virtue, and the just return of honest industry—she prays, that such allowance may be made her out of the estate of Colonel Royall, as will prevent her and her more infirm daughter from misery in the greatest extreme, and scatter comfort over the short and downward path of their Lives—and she will ever Pray.

Boston 14th February 1783 the mark of Belinda

Germantown Friends' Protest Against Slavery, 1688

This is to ye Monthly Meeting held at Richard Worrell's.

These are the reasons why we are against the traffick of men-body, as followeth. Is there any that would be done or handled at this manner? viz., to be sold or made a slave for all the time of his life? How fearful and faint-hearted are many on sea, when they see a strange vessel,—being afraid it should be a Turk, and they should be taken, and sold for slaves into Turkey. Now what is this better done, as Turks doe? Yea, rather is it worse for them, which say they are Christians; for we hear that ᵞᵉ most part of such negers are brought hither against their will and consent, and that many of them are stolen. Now, ᵗʰᵒ they are black, we can not conceive there is more liberty to have them slaves, as it is to have other white ones. There is a saying, that we shall doe to all men like as we will be done ourselves; making no difference of what generation, descent or colour they are. And those who steal or robb men, and those who buy or purchase them, are they not all alike? Here is liberty of conscience, ʷᶜʰ is right and reasonable; here ought to be likewise liberty of ᵞᵉ body, except of evil-doers, ʷᶜʰ is an other case. But to bring men hither, or to rob and sell them against their will, we stand against. In Europe there are many oppressed for conscience sake; and here there are those oppressed ʷʰ are of a black colour. And we who know that men must not committ adultery,—some do committ adultery, in others, separating wives from their husbands and giving them to others; and some sell the children of these poor creatures to other men. Ah! doe consider well this thing, you who doe it, if you would be done at this manner? and if it is done according to Christianity? You surpass Holland and Germany in this thing. This makes an ill report in all those countries of Europe, where they hear off, that ᵞᵉ Quakers doe here handel men as they handel there ᵞᵉ cattle. And for that reason some have no mind or inclination to come hither. And who shall maintain this your cause, or pleid for it? Truly we can not do so, except you shall inform us better hereof, viz, that Christians have liberty to practise these things. Pray, what thing in the world can be done worse towards us, than if men should rob or steal us away, and sell us for slaves to strange countries; separating housbands from their wives and children. Being now this is not done in the manner we would be done at therefore we contradict and are against this traffic of men-body. And we who profess that it is not lawful to steal, must, likewise, avoid to purchase such things as are stolen, but rather help to stop this robbing and stealing if possible. And such men ought to be delivered out of ᵞᵉ hands of ᵞᵉ robbers, and set free as well as in Europe. Then is Pennsylvania to have a good report, instead it hath now a bad one for this sake in other countries. Especially whereas ᵞᵉ Europeans are desirous to know in what manner ᵞᵉ Quakers doe rule in their province;—and most of them doe look upon us with an envious eye. But if this is done well, what shall we say is done evil?

If once these slaves (wch they say are so wicked and stubbern men) should joint themselves,—fight for their freedom.—and handel their masters and mastrisses as they did handel them before; will these masters and mastrisses take the sword at hand and warr against these poor slaves, licke, we are able to believe, some will not refuse to doe; or have these negers not as much right to fight for their freedom, as you have to keep them slaves?

Now consider well this thing, if it is good or bad? And in case you find it to be good to handel these blacks at that manner, we desire and require you hereby lovingly, that you may inform us herein, which at this time never was done, viz., that Christians have such a liberty to do so. To the end we shall be satisfied in this point, and satisfied likewise our good friends and acquaintances in our natif country, to whose it is a terror, or fairful thing, that men should be handeld so in Pennsylvania.

This is from our meeting at Germantown, held ye 18 of the 2 month, 1688, to be delivered to the Monthly Meeting at Richard Worrel's.

Garret henderich
derick up de graeff
Francis daniell Pastorius
Abraham up Den graef.

At our Monthly Meeting at Dublin, ᵞᵉ 30—2 mo., 1688, we having inspected ᵞᵉ matter, above mentioned, and considered of it, we find it so weighty that we think it not expedient for us to meddle with it here, but do rather commit it to ^{ye} consideration of ^{ye} Quarterly Meeting; ^{ye} tenor of it being nearly related to ^{ye} Truth.

On behalf of ^{ye} Monthly Meeting,

Signed, P. Jo. Hart.

This, above mentioned, was read in our Quarterly Meeting at Philadelphia, the 4 of ^{ye} 4th mo. '88, and was from thence recommended to the Yearly Meeting, and the above said Derick, and the other two mentioned therein, to present the same to ^{ye} above said meeting, it being a thing of too great a weight for this meeting to determine.

Signed by order of ^{ye} meeting,

Anthony Morris.

Yearly Meeting Minute on the above Protest.

At a Yearly Meeting held at Burlington the 5th day of the 7th month, 1688.

A Paper being here presented by some German Friends Concerning the Lawfulness and Unlawfulness of Buying and keeping Negroes, It was adjudged not to be so proper for this Meeting to give a Positive Judgment in the Case, It having so General a Relation to many other Parts, and therefore at present they forbear It.

Henry Highland Garnet's *Address to the Slaves of the United States of America*, delivered on August 16, 1843

Brethren and Fellow Citizens:—Your brethren of the North, East, and West have been accustomed to meet together in National Conventions, to sympathize with each other, and to weep over your unhappy condition. In these meetings we have addressed all classes of the free, but we have never, until this time, sent a word of consolation and advice to you. We have been contented in sitting still and mourning over your sorrows, earnestly hoping that before this day your sacred liberty would have been restored. But, we have hoped in vain. Years have rolled on, and tens of thousands have been borne on streams of blood and tears, to the shores of eternity. While you have been oppressed, we have also been partakers with you; nor can we be free while you are enslaved. We, therefore, write to you as being bound with you. Many of you are bound to us, not only by the ties of a common humanity, but we are connected by the more tender relations of parents, wives, husbands, children, brothers, and sisters, and friends. As such we most affectionately address you.

Slavery has fixed a deep gulf between you and us, and while it shuts out from you the relief and consolation which your friends would willingly render, it affects and persecutes you with a fierceness which we might not expect to see in the fiends of hell. But still the Almighty Father of mercies has left to us a glimmering ray of hope, which shines out like a lone star in a cloudy sky. Mankind are becoming wiser, and better—the oppressor's power is fading, and you, every day, are becoming better informed, and more numerous. Your grievances, brethren, are many. We shall not attempt, in this short address, to present to the world all the dark catalogue of this nation's sins, which have been committed upon an innocent people. Nor is it indeed necessary, for you feel them from day to day, and all the civilized world look upon them with amazement.

Two hundred and twenty seven years ago, the first of our injured race were brought to the shores of America. They came not with glad spirits to select their homes in the New World. They came not with their own consent, to find an unmolested enjoyment of the blessings of this fruitful soil. The first dealings they had with men calling themselves Christians, exhibited to them the worst features of corrupt and sordid hearts; and convinced them that no cruelty is too great, no villainy and no robbery too abhorrent for even enlightened men to perform, when influenced by avarice and lust. Neither did they come flying upon the wings of Liberty, to a land of freedom. But they came with broken hearts, from their beloved native land, and were doomed to unrequited toil and deep degradation. Nor did the evil of their bondage end at their emancipation by death. Succeeding generations inherited their chains, and millions have come from eternity into time, and have returned again to the world of spirits, cursed and ruined by American slavery.

The propagators of the system, or their immediate ancestors, very soon discovered its growing evil, and its tremendous wickedness, and secret promises were made to destroy it. The gross inconsistency of a people holding slaves, who had themselves "ferried o'er the wave" for freedom's sake, was too apparent to be entirely overlooked. The voice of Freedom cried, "Emancipate yourselves." Humanity supplicated with tears for the deliverance of the children of Africa. Wisdom urged her solemn plea. The bleeding captive plead his innocence, and pointed to Christianity who stood weeping at the cross. Jehovah frowned upon the nefarious institution, and thunderbolts, red with vengeance, struggled to leap forth to blast the guilty wretches who maintained it. But all was in vain. Slavery had stretched its dark wings of death over the land, the Church stood silently by the priests prophesied falsely, and the people loved to have it so. Its throne is established, and now it reigns triumphant.

Nearly three millions of your fellow citizens are prohibited by law and public opinion, (which in this country is stronger than law,) from reading the Book of Life. Your intellect has been destroyed as much as possible, and every ray of light they have attempted to shut out from your minds. The oppressors themselves have become involved in the ruin. They have become weak, sensual, and rapacious—they have cursed you—they have cursed themselves—they have cursed the earth which they have trod.

The colonists threw the blame upon England. They said that the mother country entailed the evil upon them, and that they would rid themselves of it if they could. The world thought they were sincere, and the philanthropic pitied them. But time soon tested their sincerity.

In a few years the colonists grew strong, and severed themselves from the British Government. Their independence was declared, and they took their station among the sovereign powers of the earth. The declaration was a glorious document. Sages admired it, and the patriotic of every nation reverenced the God like sentiments which it contained. When the power of Government returned to their hands, did they emancipate the slaves? No; they rather added new links to our chains. Were they ignorant of the principles of Liberty? Certainly they were not. The sentiments of their revolutionary orators fell in burning eloquence upon their hearts, and with one voice they cried, Liberty or Death. Oh what a sentence was that! It ran from soul to soul like electric fire, and nerved the arm of thousands to fight in the holy cause of Freedom. Among the diversity of opinions that are entertained in regard to physical resistance, there are but a few found to gainsay that stern declaration. We are among those who do not. Slavery! How much misery is comprehended in that single word. What mind is there that does not shrink from its direful effects? Unless the image of God be obliterated from the soul, all men cherish the love of Liberty. The nice discerning political economist does not regard the sacred right more than the untutored African who roams in the wilds of Congo. Nor has the one more right to the full enjoyment of his freedom than the other. In every man's mind the good seeds of liberty are planted, and he who brings his fellow down so low, as to make him contented with a condition of slavery, commits the highest crime against God and man. Brethren, your oppressors aim to do this. They endeavor to make you as much like brutes as possible. When they have blinded the eyes of your mind when they have embittered the sweet waters of life then, and not till then, has American slavery done its perfect work.

TO SUCH DEGREDATION IT IS SINFUL IN THE EXTREME FOR YOU TO MAKE VOLUNTARY SUBMISSION. The divine commandments you are in duty bound to reverence and obey. If you do not obey them, you will surely meet with the displeasure of the Almighty. He requires you to love him supremely, and your neighbor as yourself—to keep the Sabbath day holy—to search the Scriptures—and bring up your children with respect for his laws, and to worship no other God but him. But slavery sets all these at nought, and hurls defiance in the face of Jehovah. The forlorn condition in which you are placed, does not destroy your moral obligation to God. You are not certain of heaven, because you suffer yourselves to remain in a state of slavery, where you cannot obey the commandments of the Sovereign of the universe. If the ignorance of slavery is a passport to heaven, then it is a blessing, and no curse, and you should rather desire its perpetuity than its abolition. God will not receive slavery, nor ignorance, nor any other state of mind, for love and obedience to him. Your condition does not absolve you from your moral obligation. The diabolical injustice by which your liberties are cloven down, NEITHER GOD, NOR ANGELS, OR JUST MEN, COMMAND YOU TO SUFFER FOR A SINGLE MOMENT. THEREFORE IT IS YOUR SOLEMN AND IMPERATIVE DUTY TO USE EVERY MEANS, BOTH MORAL, INTELLECTUAL, AND PHYSICAL THAT PROMISES SUCCESS. If a band of heathen men should attempt to enslave a race of Christians, and to place their children under the influence of some false religion, surely Heaven would frown upon the men who would not resist such aggression, even to death. If, on the other hand, a band of Christians should attempt to enslave a race of heathen men, and to entail slavery upon them, and to keep them in heathenism in the midst of Christianity, the God of heaven would smile upon every effort which the injured might make to disenthral themselves.

Brethren, it is as wrong for your lordly oppressors to keep you in slavery, as it was for the man thief to steal our ancestors from the coast of Africa. You should therefore now use the same manner of resistance, as would have been just in our ancestors when the bloody foot prints of the first remorseless soul thief was placed upon the shores of our fatherland. The humblest peasant is as free in the sight of God as the proudest monarch that ever swayed a sceptre. Liberty is a spirit sent out from God, and like its great Author, is no respecter of persons.

Brethren, the time has come when you must act for yourselves. It is an old and true saying that, "if hereditary bondmen would be free, they must themselves strike the blow." You can plead your own cause, and do the work of emancipation better than any others. The nations of the world are moving in the great cause of universal freedom, and some of them at least will, ere long, do you justice. The combined powers of

Europe have placed their broad seal of disapprobation upon the African slave trade. But in the slaveholding parts of the United States, the trade is as brisk as ever. They buy and sell you as though you were brute beasts. The North has done much—her opinion of slavery in the abstract is known. But in regard to the South, we adopt the opinion of the New York Evangelist—We have advanced so far, that the cause apparently waits for a more effectual door to be thrown open than has been yet. We are about to point out that more effectual door. Look around you, and behold the bosoms of your loving wives heaving with untold agonies! Hear the cries of your poor children! Remember the stripes your fathers bore. Think of the torture and disgrace of your noble mothers. Think of your wretched sisters, loving virtue and purity, as they are driven into concubinage and are exposed to the unbridled lusts of incarnate devils. Think of the undying glory that hangs around the ancient name of Africa—and forget not that you are native born American citizens, and as such, you are justly entitled to all the rights that are granted to the freest. Think how many tears you have poured out upon the soil which you have cultivated with unrequited toil and enriched with your blood; and then go to your lordly enslavers and tell them plainly, that you are determined to be free. Appeal to their sense of justice, and tell them that they have no more right to oppress you, than you have to enslave them. Entreat them to remove the grievous burdens which they have imposed upon you, and to remunerate you for your labor. Promise them renewed diligence in the cultivation of the soil, if they will render to you an equivalent for your services. Point them to the increase of happiness and prosperity in the British West Indies since the Act of Emancipation. Tell them in language which they cannot misunderstand, of the exceeding sinfulness of slavery, and of a future judgment, and of the righteous retributions of an indignant God. Inform them that all you desire is FREEDOM, and that nothing else will suffice. Do this, and for ever after cease to toil for the heartless tyrants, who give you no other reward but stripes and abuse. If they then commence the work of death, they, and not you, will be responsible for the consequences. You had better all die die immediately, than live slaves and entail your wretchedness upon your posterity. If you would be free in this generation, here is your only hope. However much you and all of us may desire it, there is not much hope of redemption without the shedding of blood. If you must bleed, let it all come at once—rather die freemen, than live to be slaves. It is impossible like the children of Israel, to make a grand exodus from the land of bondage. The Pharaohs are on both sides of the blood red waters! You cannot move en masse, to the dominions of the British Queen—nor can you pass through Florida and overrun Texas, and at last find peace in Mexico. The propagators of American slavery are spending their blood and treasure, that they may plant the black flag in the heart of Mexico and riot in the halls of the Montezumas. In the language of the Rev. Robert Hall, when addressing the volunteers of Bristol, who were rushing forth to repel the invasion of Napoleon, who threatened to lay waste the fair homes of England, "Religion is too much interested in your behalf, not to shed over you her most gracious influences."

You will not be compelled to spend much time in order to become inured to hardships. From the first moment that you breathed the air of heaven, you have been accustomed to nothing else but hardships. The heroes of the American Revolution were never put upon harder fare than a peck of corn and a few herrings per week. You have not become enervated by the luxuries of life. Your sternest energies have been beaten out upon the anvil of severe trial. Slavery has done this, to make you subservient, to its own purposes; but it has done more than this, it has prepared you for any emergency. If you receive good treatment, it is what you could hardly expect; if you meet with pain, sorrow, and even death, these are the common lot of slaves.

Fellow men! Patient sufferers! behold your dearest rights crushed to the earth! See your sons murdered, and your wives, mothers and sisters doomed to prostitution. In the name of the merciful God, and by all that life is worth, let it no longer be a debatable question whether it is better to choose Liberty or death.

In 1822, Denmark Veazie [Vesey], of South Carolina, formed a plan for the liberation of his fellow men. In the whole history of human efforts to overthrow slavery, a more complicated and tremendous plan was never formed. He was betrayed by the treachery of his own people, and died a martyr to freedom. Many a brave hero fell, but history, faithful to her high trust, will transcribe his name on the same monument with Moses, Hampden, Tell, Bruce and Wallace, Toussaint L'Ouverture, Lafayette and Washington. That tremendous movement shook the whole empire of slavery. The guilty soul thieves were overwhelmed with fear. It is a matter of fact, that at that time, and in consequence of the threatened revolution, the slave States talked strongly of emancipation. But they blew but one blast of the trumpet of freedom and then laid it aside. As these men became quiet, the slaveholders ceased to talk about emancipation; and now behold your condition today! Angels sigh over it, and humanity has long since exhausted her tears in weeping on your account!

The patriotic Nathaniel Turner followed Denmark Veazie [Vesey]. He was goaded to desperation by wrong and injustice. By despotism, his name has been recorded on the list of infamy, and future generations will remember him among the noble and brave.

Next arose the immortal Joseph Cinque, the hero of the Amistad. He was a native African, and by the help of God he emancipated a whole ship load of his fellow men on the high seas. And he now sings of liberty on the sunny hills of Africa and beneath his native palm trees, where he hears the lion roar and feels himself as free as that king of the forest.

Next arose Madison Washington that bright star of freedom, and took his station in the constellation of true heroism. He was a slave on board the brig Creole, of Richmond, bound to New Orleans, that great slave mart, with a hundred and four others. Nineteen struck for liberty or death. But one life was taken, and the whole were emancipated, and the vessel was carried into Nassau, New Providence.

Noble men! Those who have fallen in freedom's conflict, their memories will be cherished by the true hearted and the God fearing in all future generations; those who are living, their names are surrounded by a halo of glory.

Brethren, arise, arise! Strike for your lives and liberties. Now is the day and the hour. Let every slave throughout the land do this, and the days of slavery are numbered. You cannot be more oppressed than you have been—you cannot suffer greater cruelties than you have already. Rather die freemen than live to be slaves. Remember that you are FOUR MILLIONS!

It is in your power so to torment the God cursed slaveholders that they will be glad to let you go free. If the scale was turned, and black men were the masters and white men the slaves, every destructive agent and element would be employed to lay the oppressor low. Danger and death would hang over their heads day and night. Yes, the tyrants would meet with plagues more terrible than those of Pharaoh. But you are a patient people. You act as though, you were made for the special use of these devils. You act as though your daughters were born to pamper the lusts of your masters and overseers. And worse than all, you tamely submit while your lords tear your wives from your embraces and defile them before your eyes. In the name of God, we ask, are you men? Where is the blood of your fathers? Has it all run out of your veins? Awake, awake; millions of voices are calling you! Your dead fathers speak to you from their graves. Heaven, as with a voice of thunder, calls on you to arise from the dust.

Let your motto be resistance! resistance! RESISTANCE! No oppressed people have ever secured their liberty without resistance. What kind of resistance you had better make, you must decide by the circumstances that surround you, and according to the suggestion of expediency. Brethren, adieu! Trust in the living God. Labor for the peace of the human race, and remember that you are FOUR MILLIONS.

Endnotes

Introduction

1 Sinha, Manisha. "The Forgotten Abolitionists." The *Boston Globe*, February 13, 2016, epaper.bostonglobe.com/BostonGlobe/article_popover. aspx?guid=8618b501-b931-429e-82e0-5e7f99053743&source=prev.

2 Neiman, Susan. *Learning from the Germans – Race and the Memory of Evil.* New York: Farrar, Straus and Giroux, 2019, 276.

3 Neiman, *Learning from the Germans*, 276.

4 Goodheart, Adam. "The Rabbi and the Rebellion." *New York Times* Opinionator, March 7, 2011, archive.nytimes.com/opinionator.blogs.nytimes. com/2011/03/07/the-rabbi-and-the-rebellion/.

5 Walker, David. "Walker's Appeal, in Four Articles; Together with a Preamble, to the Coloured Citizens of the World, but in Particular, and Very Expressly, to Those of the United States of America, Written in Boston, State of Massachusetts, September 28, 1829," 9. Revised and published by David Walker, 1830.

6 Ponti, Crystal. "America's History of Slavery Began Long Before Jamestown." August 14, 2019. www.history.com/news/american-slavery-before-jamestown-16.

7 Guasco, Michael. *Slaves and Englishmen: Human Bondage in the Early Modern Atlantic World*. Philadelphia: University of Pennsylvania Press, 1966.

8 Myers, Kathleen Ann. Translations by Nina Scott. *Fernández de Oviedo's Chronicle of America*. Austin: University of Texas Press, 2007.

9 DuBois, W.E.B. *The Suppression of the African Slave-Trade to the United States of America, 1638–1870*. New York: Longmans, Green, and Co., 1896.

10 Wood, Peter H. "Strange New Land: Africans in Colonial America." Oxford: Oxford University Press, 2003.

11 Wood. "Strange New Land: Africans in Colonial America."

Chapter 1—Belinda X

12   Petition of Belinda Sutton. Massachusetts Anti-Slavery and Anti-Segregation Petitions; Massachusetts Archives Collection. v.239-Revolution Resolves, 1783 iiif.lib.harvard.edu/manifests/view/drs:50257769$4i.

13   Petition of Belinda Sutton.

14   Petition of Belinda Sutton.

15   Petition of Belinda Sutton.

16   Petition of Belinda Sutton.

17   Petition of Belinda Sutton.

18   Petition of Belinda Sutton.

19   DuBois, W.E.B. "The Black North: A Social Study." *The New York Times,* November 17, 1901, archive.nytimes.com/www.nytimes.com/books/00/11/05/specials/dubois-north.html.

20   Green, Lorenzo. *The Negro in Colonial New England, 1620–1776.* New York: Columbia University Press, 1942, 317.

21   Finkenbine, Roy. "Belinda's Petition: Reparations for Slavery in Revolutionary Massachusetts." *William and Mary Quarterly*, Vol. 64 #1, 2007. www-jstor-org.libproxy.smith.edu/stable/4491599.

22   Finkenbine, "Belinda's Petition," 96.

23   Finkenbine, "Belinda's Petition," 96.

24   Finkenbine, "Belinda's Petition," 100.

25   Finkenbine, "Belinda's Petition," 101.

26   Finkenbine, "Belinda's Petition," 101.

27   Various. "Slaves Petition the Massachusetts Legislature." *Social History for Every Classroom: Resources for Teachers*, accessed July 1, 2023, shec.ashp.cuny.edu/items/show/778.

28   Finkenbine, "Belinda's Petition," 102.

29   Finkenbine, "Belinda's Petition," 103

30   Finkenbine, "Belinda's Petition," 103.

31   Finkenbine, "Belinda's Petition," 103–104.

32   Finkenbine, "Belinda's Petition," 104.

33 Finkenbine, "Belinda's Petition," 104.

34 Finkenbine, "Belinda's Petition," 104.

35 "Belinda's Petition," from *The Yellow House on the Corner*, Carnegie-Mellon University Press, Pittsburgh, PA. © 1980 by Rita Dove. Reprinted by permission of the author.

Chapter 2—Paul Jennings

36 James Madison's Montpelier, "The Life of Paul Jennings," www.montpelier. org/learn/paul-jennings.

37 James Madison's Montpelier. "The Life of Paul Jennings."

38 James Madison's Montpelier. "The Life of Paul Jennings."

39 Jennings, Paul. *A Colored Man's Reminiscences of James Madison*. Ithaca, NY: Cornell University Press, 1865. p. 12.

40 Jennings. *A Colored Man's Reminiscences of James Madison*. p.13.

41 Encyclopedia Virginia. "Paul Jennings (1799-1874)" encyclopediavirginia.org/ entries/jennings-paul-1799-1874/.

42 Jennings. *A Colored Man's Reminiscences of James Madison*.

43 Momodu, Samuel. The Pearl Incident, 1848, Black Past, www.blackpast.org/ african-american-history/pearl-incident/.

44 James Madison's Montpelier. "The Life of Paul Jennings."

45 Encyclopedia Virginia. "Paul Jennings (1799–1874)."

Chapter 3—Sarah Mapps Douglass

46 Grayson, Sandra. *Black Women in Antebellum America: Active Agents in the Fight for Freedom*, University of Massachusetts Boston ScholarWorks at UMass, 1996. scholarworks.umb.edu/trotter_pubs/13/.

47 Bacon, Margaret Hope. "New Light on Sarah Mapps Douglass and Her Reconciliation with Friends." *Quaker History*, Vol. 90, Number 1, African-Americans and Quakers, Spring 2001, p. 32

48 Lindhorst, Marie. "Politics in a Box: Sarah Mapps Douglass and the Female Literary Association, 1831–1833." *Pennsylvania History: A Journal*

of Mid-Atlantic Studies Vol. 65, No. 3, African Americans in Pennsylvania (Summer 1998).

49   Douglass, Sarah Mapps. "The Cause of the Slave Became My Own, 1832. abacus.bates.edu/~cnero/rhetoric/Sarah_Douglass.pdf.

50   Bacon. "New Light on Sarah Mapps Douglass and Her Reconciliation with Friends."p. 33)

Chapter 4—Mary Ellen Pleasant

51   Chambers, Veronica, "The Many Chapters of Mary Ellen Pleasant," *NYTimes* Overlooked, January 21, 2019..

52   DuBois, W.E.B. *The Souls of Black Folk – Essays and Sketches.* Chicago: A.G. McClurg, 1903.

53   "Editorial: Mary Ellen Pleasant's Moment," Sonoma Index Tribune, Dec. 9, 2021

54   Hudson, Lynn Maria. *The Making of "Mammy Pleasant": A Black Entrepreneur in Nineteenth-century San Francisco.* University of Illinois Press, 2003.

55   Chambers. "The Many Chapters of Mary Ellen Pleasant."

56   Hudson. *The Making of 'Mammy Pleasant'.* p. 48.

57   Hudson. *The Making of 'Mammy Pleasant'.* p. 48.

58   Hudson. *The Making of 'Mammy Pleasant'.* p. 52.

59   Hudson. *The Making of 'Mammy Pleasant'.* p. 53.

60   *Sacramento Daily Union*, November 14, 1863.

61   "Mammy Pleasant: Angel or Arch Fiend in the House of Mystery?" *The San Francisco Call*, May 7, 1899.

62   Pleasant, Mary Ellen. "I'd rather be a corpse than a coward." www.pinterest.com/pin/360499145148503331/

63   Chambers. "The Many Chapters of Mary Ellen Pleasant."

Chapter 5—Henry Highland Garnet

64   Garnet, Henry Highland and Smith, James McCune, M.D. "A memorial discourse by Henry Highland Garnet, delivered in the hall of the House

of Representatives, Washington City, D.C. February 12, 1865, with an Introduction by James McCune Smith." Philadelphia: Joseph M. Wilson, 1865. p. 18.

65 Sherbondy, Jeanette E. "Reverend Henry Highland Garnet and the Women in His Life." March 28, 2023, www.commonsenseeasternshore.org/rev-henry-highland-garnet-and-the-women-in-his-life.

66 Smith. Introduction to "A memorial discourse..." p. 18.

67 Maryland, on Pennsylvania's southern border, was a slave state as well as a border state. By the eighteenth-century tobacco plantations required great numbers of enslaved laborers. Maryland did not secede.

68 Smith. Introduction to "A memorial discourse..."

69 Smith. Introduction to "A memorial discourse..." p. 20.

70 Smith. Introduction to "A memorial discourse..." p. 23.

71 Sullivan, James. "The New York African Society for Mutual Relief (1808-1860)," *BLACKPAST*, January 2011. www.blackpast.org/african-american-history/new-york-african-society-mutual-relief-1808-1860/

72 Smith. Introduction to "A memorial discourse..." by Garnet p. 24-25

73 Prudence Crandall had encountered the wrath of her white neighbors in Canterbury when she first accepted a Black student to her school. When all of the white families subsequently removed their children from the school, the school became a safe haven for African American girls. This, too, led to hostility and eventually a law was passed in 1833 forbidding schools to teach black girls who were not from Connecticut. This resulted in Crandall being jailed and in two lawsuits—one resulting in a hung jury and one finding her guilty. In 1834, after an angry mob smashed windows and destroyed furniture, Prudence closed the school rather than risk her students' safety.

74 Smith. Introduction to "A memorial discourse..." p. 30.

75 Smith. Introduction to "A memorial discourse..." p. 32.

76 Winkelman, Diana. "The Rhetoric of Henry Highland Garnet." baylor-ir.tdl.org/bitstream/handle/2104/5095/Diana_Winkelman_Masters.pdf?sequence=3.

77 Garnet, Henry Highland. *The Emancipator*, Joshua Leavitt and Elizur Wright, editors, March 4, 1842.

78 Hutchinson, Earl Ofari. Let Your Motto Be Resistance. Boston: Beacon Press, 1972.

79 Hutchinson. *Let Your Motto Be Resistance.*

80 Garnet, Henry Highland. "An Address to the Slaves of the United States" (1843) *BLACKPAST* Posted on January 24, 2007 www.blackpast.org/ african-american-history/1843-henry-highland-garnet-address-slaves-united-states/.

81 "Proceedings of the National Convention of Colored People, and Their Friends, Held in Troy, N.Y., on the 6th, 7th, 8th and 9th of October, 1847." Steam Press of J.C. Kneeland and Co. 1847, p. 17. omeka.coloredconventions.org/ files/original/9380fd8347a91688d93824bab9a4b02f.pdf.

82 "Atrocious Outrage on Henry H. Garnet," *The North Star*, July 7, 1848, Rochester, New York.
Brewer, William. "Henry Highland Garnet." *The Journal of Negro History*, Vol. 13 Number 1. Chicago: The University of Chicago Press, 1928.

83 Peterson, Carla. "A Black Preacher Addresses Congress." *New York Times*, Opinionator. February 11, 2015.

84 Peterson. "A Black Preacher Addresses Congress."

85 Garnet, Henry Highland." "Let the Monster Perish - 1865." *BLACKPAST*, January 2007. www.blackpast.org/african-american-history/1865-henry-highland-garnet-let-monster-perish/.

86 Garnet. "Let the Monster Perish."

87 Garnet. "Let the Monster Perish."

88 Garnet. "Let the Monster Perish."

89 Garnet. "Let the Monster Perish."

90 Garnet. "Let the Monster Perish."

91 Garnet, Henry Highland. "Equal Suffrage: Address from the Colored Citizens of Norfolk, VA to the People of the United States (New Bedford, Massachusetts: 1865)." Copy in New York Public Library; Address also printed in *The Liberator*, Sept. 8,1865. docs.google.com/viewerng/viewer?url=https://omeka. coloredconventions.org/files/original/e9ae5ff32560a8a954a064795e4e7ca6.pdf

92 Garnet. "Equal Suffrage."

93 Pasternak, Martin B., "Rise now and fly to arms : the life of Henry Highland Garnet." (1981). Doctoral Dissertations 1896–February 2014. 1388.

94 Pasternak. "Rise now and fly." p. 221.

95 Pasternak. "Rise now and fly." p. 222.

96   Pasternak. "Rise now and fly." p. 225.

97   Brewer, William. "Henry Highland Garnet."

Chapter 6—Mary Ann Shadd Cary

98   Rhodes, Jane. *Mary Ann Shadd Cary: The Black Press and Protest in the 19th Century*. Bloomington: Indiana University Press, 1999, p. 2

99   Montgomery, Elizabeth. *Reminiscences Of Wilmington, In Familiar Village Tales, Ancient And New (1851)*. Montana: Kessinger Publishing, 2010.

100 Du Bois, W. E. B. (William Edward Burghardt), 1868-1963. "The damnation of women," ca. 1920. W. E. B. Du Bois Papers (MS 312). Special Collections and University Archives, University of Massachusetts Amherst Libraries. p.15-16.

101 Yarhi, Eli. "Mary Ann Shadd Cary American Educator, Publisher and Abolitionist." *Britannica*. 2023. www.britannica.com/biography/Mary-Ann-Shadd-Cary

102 Rhodes,. *Mary Ann Shadd Cary*. p.37

103 Conaway, Carol B. "Racially integrated education: the antebellum thought of Mary Ann Shadd Cary and Frederick Douglass." *Vitae Scholasticae* 27, no. 2. Fall 2010. link.gale.com/apps/doc/A277600910/AONE?u=mlin_oweb&sid=googleScholar&xid=e09872d3.

104 Conaway. Racially integrated education"

105 Conaway. Racially integrated education"

106 Shadd, Adrienne. "The Provincial Freeman". *The Canadian Encyclopedia*, June 7, 2023, www.thecanadianencyclopedia.ca/en/article/the-provincial-freeman

107 Shadd. "The Provincial Freeman".

108 Mitchell, Jerry. "On This Day in 1853, March 24, 2023. mississippitoday. org/2023/03/24/on-this-day-in-1853/

109 Specia, Megan. "Overlooked No More: How Mary Ann Shadd Cary Shook Up the Abolitionist Movement," *NY Times*, June 2018. www.nytimes. com/2018/06/06/obituaries/mary-ann-shadd-cary-abolitionist-overlooked.html.

Chapter 7—Robert Morris

110 Huffman, Robert. "The Life and Legal Strides of Boston Abolitionist Robert Morris." *Courthouse News Service* www.courthousenews.com/the-life-legal-strides-of-boston-abolitionist-robert-morris/

111 Kendrick, Stephen and Kendrick, Paul. *Sarah's Long Walk: The Free Blacks of Boston and How Their Struggle for Equality Changed America.* Boston: Beacon Press, 2004.

112 Peter Snoad, playwrite of "The Draft," April 20, 2020.

113 Kendrick. *Sarah's Long Walk.* p. 16.

114 Kendrick. *Sarah's Long Walk.* p. 19.

115 Kendrick. *Sarah's Long Walk.* p. 8.

116 Kendrick. *Sarah's Long Walk.* p. 70.

117 Kendrick. *Sarah's Long Walk.* p. 97

118 Kendrick. *Sarah's Long Walk.* p. 134.

119 Kendrick. *Sarah's Long Walk.* p. 138.

120 "Freedom from Discrimination (timeline)." *The Annenberg Classroom.* www.annenbergclassroom.org/resource/freedom-from-discrimination/

121 Kendrick. *Sarah's Long Walk.* p. 265.

122 Kendrick. *Sarah's Long Walk.* p. 201.

123 Kendrick. *Sarah's Long Walk.* p. 203.

124 Kendrick. *Sarah's Long Walk.* p. 204.

125 Huffman, Robert. "The Life and Legal Strides of Boston Abolitionist Robert Morris." *Courthouse News Service* www.courthousenews.com/the-life-legal-strides-of-boston-abolitionist-robert-morris/

126 Kantrowitz, Stephen. 'Equality First, Guns Afterward.' *NY Times Opinionator*, March 1, 2013. archive.nytimes.com/opinionator.blogs.nytimes.com/2013/03/01/equality-first-guns-afterward

Chapter 8—John Stewart Rock

127 Contee, Clarence G. "The Supreme Court Bars First Black Member." *The Supreme Court Historical Society*, 1975. Archived from the original on November 20, 2008. Retrieved 20 May 2008. web.archive.org/web/20081120022856/http:/www.supremecourthistory.org/04_library/subs_volumes/04_c01_j.html.

128 Rock, John. "Address to the Citizens of New Jersey." *The North Star*, Rochester NY, Feb. 8, 1850 www.njstatelib.org/research_library/new_jersey_resources/highlights/african_american_history_curriculum/unit_5_antebellum_america/john_rock_address/

129 Rock, John. "I Will Sink or Swim with My Race." *The Liberator*, William Lloyd Garrison Publisher, March 12, 1858, Vol. XXVIII, No. 10 BLACKPAST, January 25, 2007. www.blackpast.org/african-american-history/1858-john-s-rock-i-will-sink-or-swim-my-race/

130 Lanari, Raquel. "How a Harlem Fashion Show Started the 'Black is Beautiful Movement,'" *NY Post*, February 5, 2018. nypost.com/2018/02/05/how-a-harlem-fashion-show-started-the-black-is-beautiful-movement/

131 Lanari. "How a Harlem Fashion Show Started the 'Black is Beautiful Movement.'"

132 Lanari. "How a Harlem Fashion Show Started the 'Black is Beautiful Movement.'"

133 Lanari. "How a Harlem Fashion Show Started the 'Black is Beautiful Movement.'"

134 "Creating a Respectful and Open World for Natural Hair Act of 2021" or the "CROWN Act." *House Resolution 2116.* www.govinfo.gov/content/pkg/BILLS-117hr2116rh/pdf/BILLS-117hr2116rh.pdf

135 Lanari. "How a Harlem Fashion Show Started the 'Black is Beautiful Movement.'"

136 Lanari. "How a Harlem Fashion Show Started the 'Black is Beautiful Movement.'".

137 Rock. "I Will Sink or Swim with My Race."

138 Chief Justice Roger Taney, "Majority Opinion, U.S. Supreme Court," *Scott v. Sanford*, March 6, 1857. *National Archives* www.archives.gov/milestone-documents/dred-scott-v-sandford.

139 Brown, William Wells. "The Black Man His Antecedents, His Genius and His Achievements." Boston: James Redpath, publisher, 1863. www.gutenberg.org/files/64883/64883-h/64883-h.htm#Page_266.

140 Contee, Clarence G. "John Sweat Rock, M.D., Esq., 1825–1866." *Journal of the National Medical Association*, Vol. 68, Number 3, May 1976. www.ncbi.nlm.nih.gov/pmc/articles/PMC2609666/?page=1.

141 Rock, John S. "A Deep and Cruel Prejudice." January 23, 1862, Delivered to the Massachusetts Anti-Slavery Society in Boston, *BLACKPAST*. www.blackpast.org/african-american-history/1862-john-s-rock-deep-and-cruel-prejudice/.

142 Brooks, Christopher. "Historically Speaking: A Tribute to First Black Man Allowed to Argue Before the Supreme Court." *The Morning Call*, Allentown, PA. Feb. 1, 2020. www.mcall.com/2020/02/01/historically-speaking-a-tribute-to-first-black-man-allowed-to-argue-before-supreme-court/.

143 "Salmon Portland Chase, Mr. Chief Justice." *American History: From Revolution to Reconstruction and Beyond*. www.let.rug.nl/usa/biographies/salmon-portland-chase/mr-chief-justice.php.

144 "Salmon Portland Chase, Mr. Chief Justice." *American History: From Revolution to Reconstruction and Beyond*.

145 "The Dred Scott Decision Buried in the Supreme Court – A Negro Lawyer Admitted by Chief Justice Chase." *New York Tribune*, February 7, 1865.

Chapter 9—Sarah Parker Remond

146 Hood, Amy. "Portrait Highlight - Sarah Parker Remond - African American abolitionist, lecturer & physician." www.amyhoodillustration.co.uk/post/portrait-highlight-sarah-parker-remond-african-american-abolitionist-lecturer-physician

147 Porter, Dorothy B. "Sarah Parker Remond, Abolitionist and Physician." *The Journal of Negro History*, Vol. 20, No. 3 (Jul., 1935), The University of Chicago Press on behalf of the Association for the Study of African American Life and History. p. 288.

148 Clay, Sarah. "Letter in The Liberator." William Lloyd Garrison Publisher, November 5, 1858, Vol. XXVIII, November 5, 1858, No. 45 fair-use.org/the-liberator/1858/11/05/the-liberator-28-45.pdf

149 Sterling, Dorothy, ed. "We Are Your Sisters: Black Women in the Nineteenth Century." New York: W.W. Norton and Company, 1984. p. 176.

150 Wilcox-Lee, Naomi. "Sarah Parker Remond." sheroesofhistory.wordpress.com/2017/10/02/sarah-parker-remond/October 2017.

151 "The Anti-Slavery Advocate of March 1, 1859," vol. ii, no. xxvii, p. 211 www.britishnewspaperarchive.co.uk/viewer/bl/0001393/18590301/009/0004.

152 Porter. "Sarah Parker Remond, Abolitionist and Physician." p. 292.

153 Foner, Philip S. and Branham, Robert (editors). *Lift Every Voice: African American Oratory 1787-1901*. University of Alabama Press; Revised edition, (December 11, 1997). p. 388.

154 Johnson, Ben. "The Lancashire Cotton Famine." *Historic UK*, March 14, 2015.
www.historic-uk.com/HistoryUK/HistoryofEngland/Lancashire-Cotton-Famine/.

155 Garrison, Wendell Philips and Garrison, Francis Jackson. "William Lloyd Garrison, 1805-1889. The Story of his life as told to his children." New York Century Company, 1889, vol. iv.

156 Sklar, Kathryn and Stewart, James Brewer. *Women's Rights and Transatlantic Antislavery in the Era of Emancipation* (The David Brion Davis Series). New Haven: Yale University Press, 2007. p. 183.

157 Sklar, and Stewart. *Women's Rights and Transatlantic Antislavery in the Era of Emancipation.* p. 183.

Chapter 10—Abraham Galloway

158 Cecelksi, David. *Democracy Betrayed: the Wilmington Race Riot of 1898 and its Legacy.* University of North Carolina. (1998) p.47

159 Still, William. *Underground Railroad, A Narrative*. Philadelphia: Porter and Coates, 1872. p. 150–152.

160 Franck, Julie. "*Abraham Galloway 8 Feb. 1837   1 Sept. 1870.*" NCPEDIA, North Carolina State University, 2013, Revised September 2022. ncpedia.org/biography/galloway-abraham.

161 Gerard, Philip. "Abraham Galloway: From Cartridge Box to Ballot Box." *Our State, Civil War Series*, www.ourstate.com/abraham-galloway/.

162 Gerard. "Abraham Galloway."

163 Gerard. "Abraham Galloway."

164 Gerard. "Abraham Galloway."

165 Gerard. "Abraham Galloway."

166 Gerard. "Abraham Galloway."

167 Gerard. "Abraham Galloway."

168 Gerard. "Abraham Galloway."

169 Gerard. "Abraham Galloway."

Chapter 11—Francis Pastorius

170 The Pennsylvania Magazine of History and Biography, Volume CXXII, No. 3, (July 1998) www.jstor.org/stable/20093221?seq=1

171 Winberg, Michaela. "William Penn Kept Enslaved People and These Are Some of Their Names," August 17, 2020, billypenn.com/2020/08/17/william-penn-owned-enslaved-people-these-are-some-of-their-names-e/.

172 Froom, Burt. "Pastorius and the Founding of Germantown." *West Mt. Airy: Yesterday and Today* (Article 17), October 2014. vdocuments.mx/pastorius-and-the-founding-of-germantown-by-burt-pastorius-and-the-founding.html?page=1.

173 "The Germantown Friends" Petition Against Slavery, 1688." https://www.loc.gov/resource/rbpe.14000200/?st=text

174 Meggitt, Justin J. "Early Quakers and Islam: Slavery, Apocalyptic and Christian-Muslim Encounters in the Seventeenth Century." *Studies on Inter-Religious Relations 59*. Uppsala: Swedish Science Press, 2013.

Chapter 12—Benjamin Lay

175 Nielsen, Euell A. "Germantown Petition Against Slavery (1688)." *BLACKPAST,* January 13, 2022. www.blackpast.org/african-american-history/germantown-quaker-petition-against-slavery-1688/.

176 "Fearless and Fiery." *Swarthmore College Bulletin.* Issue II, Volume CXV, Winter 2018. bulletin.swarthmore.edu/winter-2018-issue-ii-volume-cxv/fearless-and-fiery.

177 Conliffe, Ciaran. "Benjamin Lay – Outspoken Quaker Abolitionist." *Headstuff,* July 6, 2018. www.headstuff.org/culture/history/terrible-people-from-history/benjamin-lay-quaker-abolitionist/.

178 Conliffe. "Benjamin Lay."

179 Conliffe. "Benjamin Lay."

180 Rediker, Marcus. "The 'Quaker Comet' Was the Greatest Abolitionist You've Never Heard Of." *Smithsonian Magazine*, September 2017 www.smithsonianmag.com/history/quaker-comet-greatest-abolitionist-never-heard-180964401/.

181 Rediker. "The 'Quaker Comet.'"

182 Smith, Thomas R. "The Ghost of William Penn: Ralph Sandiford - Undivided for Humanity," *Daily Times*, Aug 9, 2012. www.delcotimes.com/2012/08/09/ the-ghost-of-william-penn-ralph-sandiford-undivided-for-humanity/

183 Rediker."The 'Quaker Comet.'"

184 Rediker. "The 'Quaker Comet.'"

185 Rediker. "The 'Quaker Comet.'"

186 Rediker. "The 'Quaker Comet.'"

187 Conliffe. "Benjamin Lay."

188 "An Act for the Better Regulating of Negroes in this Province (March 5, 1725– 1726)." Pennsylvania Legislation Relating to Slavery. Adams County History, 2003. dbonus869y26v.cloudfront.net/en/History_of_slavery_in_Pennsylvania

189 Conliffe. "Benjamin Lay."

190 Conliffe. "Benjamin Lay."

191 Conliffe. "Benjamin Lay."

192 Conliffe. "Benjamin Lay."

193 "Fearless and Fiery." *Swarthmore College Bulletin*. Issue II, Volume CXV, Winter 2018. bulletin.swarthmore.edu/winter-2018-issue-ii-volume-cxv/fearless-and-fiery.

194 Conliffe. "Benjamin Lay."

195 Conliffe. "Benjamin Lay."

Chapter 13—Anthony Bénézet

196 Africans in America, "Brotherly Love," Anthony Bénézet. PBS. www.pbs.org/wgbh/aia/part3/3p248.html

197 Vaux, Roberts. *Memoirs of the Life of Anthony Bénézet*. Montana: Kessinger Publishing, LLC, 2007. p. 5.

198 Brookes, George S. *Friend Anthony Benezet*. Philadelphia: University of Pennsylvania Press, 1937. www.encyclopedia.com/people/history/ historians-miscellaneous-biographies/anthony-benezet.

199 Vaux. *Memoirs of the Life of Anthony Bénézet*. p. 17–18.

200 Vaux. *Memoirs of the Life of Anthony Bénézet*. p. 27.

201 Crosby, David L. ed. *The Complete Antislavery Writings of Anthony Benezet, 1754–1783: An Annotated Critical Edition* (Antislavery, Abolition, and the Atlantic World). LSU Press, 2014.

202 Letters of Anthony Bénézet. Internet Archive. archive.org/stream/jstor-2713478/2713478_djvu.txt.

203 Bénézet, Anthony. *A Caution and Warning to Great-Britain, And Her Colonies, In A Short Representation of The Calamitous State of the Enslaved Negroes In the British Dominions.*

204 Vaux. *Memoirs of the Life of Anthony Bénézet.* p. 35.

205 Vaux. *Memoirs of the Life of Anthony Bénézet. p. 140.*

206 "Benjamin Rush, Race, Slavery, and Abolitionism." Dickinson. www.dickinson.edu/info/20043/about/3480/benjamin_rush.

207 Rush, Benjamin. *Biographical Anecdotes of Anthony Bénézet – Essays, Literary, Moral and Philosophical: The Consistent Life Of Bénézet.* Originally published 1798. Republished Syracuse University Press. 2008. p. 314.

Chapter 14—Moses Brown

208 "Rhode Island History," Vol. 23, No. 1, January 1966. Rhode Island Historical Society, 52 Power St., Providence, RI. www.rihs.org/assetts/files/publications/1966_Jan.pdf.

209 "Rhode Island History."

210 Fitzgerald, Frances. "Peculiar Institutions." *The New Yorker*, September 12, 2005. www.newyorker.com/magazine/2005/09/12/peculiar-institutions.

211 "Rhode Island History."

212 "Rhode Island History."

213 Lancaster's ideas were developed simultaneously with those of Andrew Bell in Madras whose system was referred to as the "Madras system of education". The method of instruction and delivery is recursive. As one student learns the material he or she is rewarded for successfully passing on that information to the next pupil. This method is now commonly known as peer tutoring. The use of monitors was prompted partly by a need to avoid the cost of assistant teachers. (Vogler, Pen. "The Poor Child's Friend", *History Today*, February 2015, p. 4–5).

214 Berry, Deborah Barfield. "The US is grappling with its history of slavery. The blueprint for dealing with it? Some say Brown University." *USA TODAY*, Dec. 18, 2019.

215 Simmons, Ruth. "Slavery and Justice: We Seek to Discover the Meaning of Our Past." *Ruth J. Simmons Center for the Study of Slavery and Justice.* Brown University, April 28, 2004. www.brown.edu/initiatives/slavery-and-justice/ op-ed-column-ruth-j-simmons-4-28-04

Chapter 15 - Elizabeth Buffum Chace

216 Chace, Elizabeth Buffum. *Anti-Slavery Reminiscences.* Central Falls, R.I.: E.L. Freeman and Son, 1891. Re-printed by Gemany: Hansebooks, 2017. p. 22.

217 Chace. "Anti-Slavery Reminiscences." 21.

218 "Elizabeth Buffum Chace, Conductor on the Underground Railroad," *New England Historical Society.* www.newenglandhistoricalsociety.com/ elizabeth-buffum-chace-conductor-on-the-underground-railroad/

219 "Elizabeth Buffum Chace: Abolitionist, Suffragist and Philanthropist, History of American Women." www.womenhistoryblog.com/2016/06/ elizabeth-buffum-chace.html

220 Yee, Shirley J. "Black Women Abolitionists: A Study in Activism, 1828-1860." Knoxville: University of Tennessee Press, 1992.

221 Frederick Douglass: "When the true history of the antislavery cause shall be written, women will occupy a large space in its pages, for the cause of the slave has been peculiarly woman's cause." (*The Reader's Companion to U.S. Women's History*, p. 191) William Lloyd Garrison: "The Anti-Slavery cause cannot stop to estimate where the greatest indebtedness lies, but whenever the account is made up, there can be no doubt that the efforts and sacrifices of WOMEN, who helped it, will hold a most honorable and conspicuous position." (Jeffrey, Julie Roy. *The Great Silent Army of Abolitionism: Ordinary Women in the Antislavery Movement.* Chapel Hill: The University of North Carolina Press, 1998. p. 1). Not yet!

222 Earle, Jonathan Halperin. "'Peculiarly Woman's Cause': Feminism, Race, and the Struggle for Equality." *Reviews in American History.* John Hopkins University Press, Vol.28, Number 2, June 2000. muse.jhu.edu/article/29174.

223 Chace. *Anti-Slavery Reminiscences.* p. 20.

224 Chace. *Anti-Slavery Reminiscences.* p. 28.

225 "Runaways Escape to Freedom in Rhode Island." *History of American Women.* www.womenhistoryblog.com/2015/08/underground-railroad-in-rhode-island.html.

226 Chace. *Anti-Slavery Reminiscences.* p. 32.

227 "Elizabeth Buffum Chace." History of American Women.

228 "Elizabeth Buffum Chace." History of American Women.

229 "Elizabeth Buffum Chace." History of American Women.

230 "Elizabeth Buffum Chace." History of American Women.

231 Douglass, John and Thomas, Sally. "Timeline: Summary of events of the Loyalty Oath Controversy 1949–54." www.lib.berkeley.edu/uchistory/ archives_exhibits/loyaltyoath/timeline/short.html.

Chapter 16—Jane Swisshelm

232 Swisshelm, Jane Grey Cannon (1880). *Half a Century.* Chicago: Jansen, McClurg and Co., 1880. Reprinted by Anza Publishing, Chester, NY, 2005. 19.

233 Swisshelm. *Half a Century.* p. 19.

234 Swisshelm. *Half a Century.* p. 34.

235 Swisshelm. *Half a Century.* p. 20.

236 Freeman, Joanne. *The Field of Blood: Violence in Congress and the Road to the Civil War.* New York: Farrar, Straus and Giroux, 2018. p. 173.

237 Worcester Women's History Project, Rediscovered Voices. www.wwhp.org/ Resources/rediscovered.html

238 Jane Swisshelm quotes, AZQuotes, www.azquotes.com/author/63918-Jane_Swisshelm

239 "The Death of Mrs. Swisshelm," *Washington Post*, July 24, 1884, p. 1

240 "Jane Grey Swisshelm" (letter of Rufus Blanchard to the *Chicago InterOcean* [clipping], Harpel Scrapbook, vol. 11, p. 147, Chicago Historical Society).

241 "Death of Mrs. Swisshelm." *St. Cloud Journal Press*, July 24, 1884. p. 2

242 *Pittsburgh Saturday Visiter.*

243 "Mrs. Swisshelm," St. Paul Daily Globe, July 26, 1884, p. 4.

244 Post, Tim. "A Woman of Contradiction." Minnesota Public Radio, September 26, 2002. news.minnesota.publicradio.org/features/200209/23_steilm_ 1862-m/swisshelm.shtml

245 "The U.S. Dakota War of 1862." *Minnesota Historical Society.* www.usdakotawar.org/history/war/causes-war

246 Post. "A Woman of Contradiction."

247 Post. "A Woman of Contradiction."

Chapter 17—John Gregg Fee

248 Fee, John Gregg. *Autobiography of John G. Fee: Berea, Kentucky.* Chicago, Ill.: National Christian Association, 1891. Digital form in Documenting the South, University of North Carolina. docsouth.unc.edu/fpn/fee/fee.html. 9–10. Also muse.jhu.edu/book/60682

249 Fee. *Autobiography of John G. Fee.* p. 9–10.

250 Fee. *Autobiography of John G. Fee.* p. 10.

251 Fee. *Autobiography of John G. Fee.* p. 11.

252 Fee. *Autobiography of John G. Fee.* p. 13–14.

253 Fee. *Autobiography of John G. Fee.* p. 14.

254 Fee. *Autobiography of John G. Fee.* p. 16–17.

255 Basler, Roy P., Pratt, Marion Dolores, Dunlap, Lloyd A. editors. "Collected Works of Abraham Lincoln," Volume 4. (1860-61) Ann Arbor: University of Michigan, 2001. quod.lib.umich.edu/cgi/t/text/text-idx?type=simple;rgn=div2;c=lincoln;cc=lincoln;idno=lincoln4;q1=533;submit=Go;view=text;subview=detail;node=lincoln4:1003.1.

256 Kaller, Seth. "Confederate Governor of Kentucky Seeks Prominent Louisville Editor's Support for Secession in the Summer of 1861." *Historic Documents and Legacy Collection.* Seth Kaller, Inc. www.sethkaller.com/item/2365-26799-Confederate-Governor-of-Kentucky-Seeks-Prominent-Louisville-Editor%E2%80%99s-Support-for-Secession-in-the-Summer-of-1861#:~:text=When%20President%20Abraham%20Lincoln%20called,passed%20declarations%20of%20neutrality%2C%20and

257 Harrison, Lowell H. *The Civil War in Kentucky.* Lexington, KY: The University Press of Kentucky, 1975. p. 64.

258 Quisenberry, A.C. "Kentucky Union Troops in the Civil War." *Register of the Kentucky State Historical Society*, Vol. 18, number 54, 1920. p. 13–18.

259 Richardson, Edward H. *Cassius Marcellus Clay: Firebrand of Freedom.* Lexington: University Press of Kentucky, 1976. p. 89-92.

260 Clay, Cassius, ed. *True American, the Emancipationist Newspaper.* June 1845. *The History Engine.* historyengine.richmond.edu/episodes/view/113.

261 Farrar, Ronald Truman. "Cassius Marcellus Clay – Abolitionist Newspaper Editor," *American Newspaper Journalists: 1690-1872, Dictionary of Literary Biography*, Vol. 43, edited by Perry J. Ashley. Columbia, S.C.: Bruccoli Clark / Detroit: Gale Research, 1985, pp. 98–102. www.encyclopedia.com/people/history/us-history-biographies/cassius-marcellus-clay

262 Apbasova, Sona. "Fee, John Gregg." Berea College Hutchins Library. libraryguides.berea.edu/johngreggfee

263 Apbasova. "Fee, John Gregg."

Chapter 18—Delia Webster

264 Morris, J. Brent. *Oberlin, Hotbed of Abolitionism: College, Community and the Fight for Freedom and Equality in Antebellum America.* Chapel Hill: UNC Press, 2014.

265 Money, Charles H. "The Fugitive Slave Law of 1850 In Indiana (Concluded)." *Indiana Magazine Of History*, Volume 17, No. 3. 1921. p. 281.

266 "Delia Webster and the Underground Railroad." www.perlego.com/fr/book/2536296/delia-webster-and-the-underground-railroad-pdf

267 Tim Talbott, "Petticoat Abolitionist," ExploreKYHistory, accessed September 19, 2024. explorekyhistory.ky.gov/items/show/178.

Chapter 19—Sallie Holley

268 Chadwick, John White. *A Life For Liberty: Anti-Slavery and Other Letters of Sallie Holly.* New York: G.P. Putnam and Sons, 1899. p. 39.

269 Chadwick. *A Life For Liberty.* p. 40.

270 Chadwick. *A Life For Liberty.* p. 45.

271 Fairchild, J. H. "Oberlin: its origin, progress and results." An address, prepared for the alumni of Oberlin College, assembled August 22, 1860. Oberlin, Ohio: Shankland and Harmon.

272 Chadwick. *A Life For Liberty.* p. 51.

273 Chadwick. *A Life For Liberty.* p. 56.

274 Chadwick. *A Life For Liberty.* p. 60

275 "West Indies Emancipation Day, August 1." *The Free Dictionary*. encyclopedia2.thefreedictionary.com/West+Indies+Emancipation+Day.

276 Chadwick. *A Life For Liberty*. p. 65.

277 Chadwick. *A Life For Liberty*. p. 60

278 Chadwick. *A Life For Liberty*. p. 65

279 Chadwick. *A Life For Liberty*. p. 65.

280 Chadwick. *A Life For Liberty*. p. 65

281 Chadwick. *A Life For Liberty*. p. 65.

282 hong han, lao. "Sallie Holley: Inspiration for Anti-Racists" *Daily Kos*, March 26, 2007. www.dailykos.com/stories/2007/3/26/316238/-

283 hong han, lao. "Sallie Holley."

284 "Sallie Holley – She Found Her Place Among the Lowly." *History of American Women*. www.womenhistoryblog.com/2016/01/sallie-holley.html

285 hong han, lao. "Sallie Holley."

286 hong han, lao. "Sallie Holley."

287 hong han, lao. "Sallie Holley."

288 Van Haitsma, Pamela. *African-American Rhetorical Education and Epistolary Relations at the Holley School (1868–1917)*. Taylor & Francis Online, November 14, 2018. www.tandfonline.com/doi/full/10.1080/15362426.2018.1526547?af=R&

289 hong han, lao. "Sallie Holley."

290 Schmidt, Elizabeth. "Sallie Holley (1818–1893)." *Epitaph*, Vol. 12, #2, 1992. fomh.org/wp content/uploads/2021/05/SallieHolley.pdf.

291 hong han, lao. "Sallie Holley."

Chapter 20—Graceanna Lewis

292 Lewis, Graceanna. "An Appeal to Those Members of the Society of Friends Who Knowing the Principles of the Abolitionists Stand Aloof from the Anti-Slavery Enterprise." Cornell University Digital Library. reader.library.cornell.edu/docviewer/digital?id=may869014#mode/1up.

293 Morgan, Barbara. "Graceanna Lewis." Women in World History: A Biographical Encyclopedia: Volume 9, Farmington Hills, MI: Gale Group, 1999.

294 Lukens, Rob. "History's People: Graceanna Lewis – Abolitionist to Natural Scientist" History's People, Daily Local News March 19, 2013. www.dailylocal. com/2013/03/19/historys-people-graceanna-lewis-abolitionist-to-natural-scientist/.

295 Still, William. *The Underground Railroad: A Record of Facts, Authentic Narrative, Letters, etc.* Philadelphia: Porter & Coates (1872). p. 748–753.

296 Lukens. "History's People."

297 The Friends *Journal* began with two earlier publications: *The Friend* from 1827–1955 and *The Friends Intelligencer* from 1844–1955.

298 Lukens. "History's People."

299 Lukens. "History's People."

300 Lewis. "An Appeal to Those Members of the Society of Friends Who Knowing the Principles of the Abolitionists Stand Aloof from the Anti-Slavery Enterprise."

301 Lewis. "An Appeal to Those Members of the Society of Friends Who Knowing the Principles of the Abolitionists Stand Aloof from the Anti-Slavery Enterprise."

302 King Jr., Martin Luther. "Letter from a Birmingham Jail." April 16, 1963. African Studies Center, University of Pennsylvania. www.africa.upenn.edu/ Articles_Gen/Letter_Birmingham.html

303 King. "Letter from a Birmingham Jail."

304 Weidensaul, Scott. *Of a Feather: A Brief History of American Birding.* Boston: Houghton Mifflin Harcourt, 2007. p. 91.

305 Patteson, Daniel, ed. *Early American Nature Writers: A Biographical Encyclopedia.* Westport, CT: Greenwood Press, 2007. p. 256.

306 "Graceanna Lewis: Pioneer Scientist and Abolitionist," *History of American Women.* www.womenhistoryblog.com/2014/12/graceanna-lewis.html.

Conclusion

307 "How one woman pulled off the first consumer boycott – and helped inspire the British to abolish slavery," July 10, 2020, Tom Zoellner Professor of English, Chapman University.

Works Cited

Introduction

DuBois, W.E.B. *The Suppression of the African Slave-Trade to the United States of America, 1638-1870.* NY: Longmans, Green, and Co., 1896.

Goodheart, Adam. "The Rabbi and the Rebellion." NY Times Opinionator, March 7, 2011. archive.nytimes.com/opinionator.blogs.nytimes.com/2011/03/07/the-rabbi-and-the-rebellion/

Guasco, Michael. *Slaves and Englishmen: Human Bondage in the Early Modern Atlantic World,* Philadelphia: University of Pennsylvania Press, 1966.

Mintz, Steven. *African American Voices: The Life Cycle of Slavery.* Chadds Ford, PA: Brandywine Press,1993.

Myers, Kathleen Ann. Translations by Nina Scott. *Fernández de Oviedo's Chronicle of America.* Austin: University of Texas Press, 2007.

Neiman, Susan. *Learning from the Germans—Race and the Memory of Evil.* New York: Farrar, Straus and Giroux, 2019.

Ponti, Crystal. "America's History of Slavery Began Long Before Jamestown." August 14, 2019. www.history.com/news/american-slavery-before-jamestown-16

Pope Alexander VI. "The Doctrine of Discovery, 1493, Papal Bull." www.gilderlehrman.org/history-resources/spotlight-primary-source/doctrine-discovery-1493

Walker, David. "Appeal, in Four Articles; Together with a Preamble, to the Coloured Citizens of the World, but in Particular, and Very Expressly, to Those of the United States of America, in Boston, Massachusetts, on September 28, 1829." Revised and Published by David Walker, 1830.

Wood, Peter H. "Strange New Land: Africans in Colonial America". Oxford: Oxford University Press, 2003.

___. "The Birth of Race-Based Slavery - By the 17th century, America's slave economy had eliminated the obstacle of morality." May 19, 2015. slate.com/human-interest/2015/05/peter-h-wood-strange-new-land-excerpt.html

Chapter 1—Belinda X

Coates, Ta-Nehisi. "The Case for Reparations." *The Atlantic*, June 2014.

Petition of Belinda Sutton. Massachusetts Anti-Slavery and Anti-Segregation Petitions; Massachusetts Archives Collection. v.239-Revolution Resolves, 1783. iiif.lib.harvard.edu/manifests/view/drs:50257769$4i

Or "Petition of an African slave, to the legislature of Massachusetts." From The American Museum, or Repository of Ancient and Modern Fugitive Pieces, Prose and Poetical. For June, 1787. Volume 1. Number 6. Philadelphia: Mathew Cary, 1787.

Dove, Rita. "Belinda's Petition" from The Yellow House on the Corner. Carnegie-Mellon University Press, Pittsburgh, PA., 1980. Reprinted by permission of the author.

DuBois, W.E.B. "The Black North: A Social Study." *The New York Times*, November 17, 1901. archive.nytimes.com/www.nytimes.com/books/00/11/05/specials/dubois-north.html

Finkenbine, Roy. "Belinda's Petition: Reparations for Slavery in Revolutionary Massachusetts." *William and Mary Quarterly*, Vol. 64 #1, 2007. www-jstor-org.libproxy.smith.edu/stable/4491599

Green, Lorenzo. *The Negro in Colonial New England, 1620-1776.* New York: Columbia University Press, 1942.

Royall House and Slave Quarters. royallhouse.org

Various, "Slaves Petition the Massachusetts Legislature," *Social History for Every Classroom: Resources for Teachers*, accessed July 1, 2023. shec.ashp.cuny.edu/items/show/778.

Chapter 2—Paul Jennings

Encyclopedia Virginia. "Paul Jennings (1799-1874)." encyclopediavirginia.org/entries/jennings-paul-1799-1874/

James Madison's Montpelier, "The Life of Paul Jennings." www.montpelier.org/the-life-of-paul-jennings

Jennings, Paul. *A Colored Man's Reminiscences of James Madison*. Ithaca, NY: Cornell University Press, 1865.

Lambert, Lane. *The Other Slave Daniel Webster Freed*. The Patriot Ledger, Feb. 1, 2010. www.patriotledger.com/story/news/2010/02/02/a-forgotten-story-other-slave/40153330007/

"Paul Jennings' 1847 Work Agreement with Daniel Webster." *The White House Historical Association*, March 19, 1847. www.whitehousehistory.org/photos/photo-2-23

"Paul Jennings, Slave, Freedman and White House Memoirist." *The White House Historical Association*. www.whitehousehistory.org/paul-jennings

Paynter, John H. "Fugitives of the Pearl." *Journal of Negro History*, Vol. 16, Number 2, 1916. electricscotland.com/history/america/journalofnegrohistory01.pdf

Paynter, John H. *Fugitives of the Pearl*. Washington, D.C.: The Associated Publishers, Inc, 1930.

"The Paul Jennings Memoir in Context." *Montpelier's Digital Doorway*. digitaldoorway.montpelier.org/project/jennings-annotations/

Chapter 3—Sarah Mapps Douglass

Bacon, Margaret Hope. "New Light on Sarah Mapps Douglass and Her Reconciliation with Friends." *Quaker History*, Vol. 90, Number 1, African-Americans and Quakers, Spring 2001.

Bacon, Margaret Hope. "Sarah Douglass and Racial Prejudice within the Society of Friends." *A Pendle Hill Lecture*, January 1, 2002. Friends Journal. www.friendsjournal.org/2002005/

Britannica, The Editors of Encyclopaedia. "Fanny Jackson Coppin". *Encyclopedia Britannica*. www.britannica.com/biography/Fanny-Jackson-Coppin. Accessed 2 July 2023.

Douglass, Sarah Mapps. "The Cause of the Slave Became My Own," 1832. abacus.bates.edu/~cnero/rhetoric/Sarah_Douglass.pdf

Grayson, Sandra. *Black Women in Antebellum America: Active Agents in the Fight for Freedom*. University of Massachusetts Boston ScholarWorks at UMass 1996. scholarworks.umb.edu/trotter_pubs/13/

"Institute For Colored Youth Historical Marker." ExplorePAHistory.com. explorepahistory.com/hmarker.php?markerId=1-A-37D

Lewis, Jone Johnson. "Sarah Mapps Douglass and the Anti-Enslavement Movement." February 2019. www.thoughtco.com/sarah-mapps-douglass-biography-3530216

Lindhorst, Marie. "Politicis in a Box: Sarah Mapps Douglass and the Female Literary Association, 1831-1833." Pennsylvania History: A Journal of Mid-Atlantic Studies Vol. 65, No. 3, African Americans In Pennsylvania. Summer 1998.

"Sarah Mapps Douglass's Flowers: The First Surviving Art Signed by an African-American Woman." The Marginalian. www.themarginalian.org/2021/06/16/sarah-mapps-douglass-flowers/

Smith, Anna Bustill. "The Bustill Family." *The Journal of Negro History,* Vol. 10, Number 4. Oct. 1925.

Temple, Brian. "Philadelphia Quakers and the Anti-Slavery Movement." North Carolina: McFarland & Company, 2014.

Yee, Shirley. "Sarah Mapps Douglass (1806-1882)." *BLACKPAST* February 15, 2007. www.blackpast.org/african-american-history/douglass-sarah-mapps-1806-1882/

Chapter 4—Mary Ellen Pleasant

Chambers, Veronica. "Overlooked - Mary Ellen Pleasant: Born into slavery, she became a Gold Rush-era millionaire and a powerful abolitionist." The New York Times, 2018. www.nytimes.com/interactive/2019/obituaries/mary-ellen-pleasant-overlooked.html

DuBois, W.E.B. *The Souls of Black Folk—Essays and Sketches.* Chicago: A.G. McClurg, 1903.

Hudson, Lynn. *The Making of 'Mammy Pleasant': A Black Entrepreneur in Nineteenth-Century San Francisco.* Champaign, IL: University of Illinois Press, 2003. www.pulselive.co.ke/the-new-york-times/world/the-many-chapters-of-mary-ellen

"Mammy Pleasant: Angel or Arch Fiend in the House of Mystery?" *The San Francisco Call*, May 7, 1899.

"Mary Ellen Pleasant—Mother of Civil Rights in California." www.mepleasant.com/story2.html

"Mary Ellen Pleasant Becomes a Rich, Black Abolitionist" www.youtube.com/watch?v=FoF3417mQtI

Chapter 5—Henry Highland Garnet

Asplaugh, Jake. "Henry Highland Garnet's 'Address to the Slaves'- The Address and Walker's Appeal." *Colored Conventions Project.* coloredconventions.org/ garnet-address-1843/key-points-of-the-appeal/

"Atrocious Outrage on Henry H. Garnet," *The North Star*, July 7, 1848, Rochester, New York.

Brewer, William. "Henry Highland Garnet." *The Journal of Negro History*, Vol. 13 Number 1.

Chicago: The University of Chicago Press, 1928.

Dunavin, Davis. "Be(a)Man," *WSHU*, April 3, 2020. beman-triangle.research.wesleyan.edu/2012/05/13/history/

"Equal Suffrage: Address from the Colored Citizens of Norfolk, VA to the People of the United States (New Bedford, Massachusetts: 1865)." Copy in New York Public Library; Address also printed in The Liberator, Sept. 8, 1865. docs.google.com/viewerng/viewer?url=https://omeka.coloredconventions.org/files/ original/e9ae5ff32560a8a954a064795e4e7ca6.pdf

Garnet, Henry Highland. "An Address to the Slaves of the United States" (1843) *BLACKPAST.* Posted on January 24, 2007. www.blackpast.org/african-american-history/1843-henry-highland-garnet-address-slaves-united-states/

Garnet, Henry Highland." "Let the Monster Perish - 1865." *BLACKPAST.* January 2007. www.blackpast.org/african-american-history/1865-henry-highland-garnet-let-monster-perish/

Garnet, Henry Highland. "The Past and the Present Condition, and the Destiny, of the Colored Race (1848)." A Discourse Delivered at the Fifteenth Anniversary of the Female Benevolent Society of Troy, NY, Feb. 14, 1848.

Garnet, Henry Highland and Smith, James McCune, M.D. "A memorial discourse by Henry Highland Garnet, delivered in the hall of the House of Representatives, Washington City, D.C. February 12, 1865, with an Introduction by James McCune Smith." Philadelphia: Joseph M. Wilson, 1865.

Garnet, Henry Highland. *The Emancipator,* Joshua Leavitt and Elizur Wright, editors, March 4, 1842.

Hutchinson, Earl Ofari. "Let Your Motto Be Resistance." Boston: Beacon Press, 1972. www.blackpast.org/african-american-history/new-york-african-society-mutual-relief-1808-1860/

Michals, Debra. "Prudence Crandall." *National Women's History Museum, 2015.* www.womenshistory.org/education-resources/biographies/prudence-crandall

Ortiz, Paul. "One of History's Foremost Anti-Slavery Organizers Is Often Left Out of the Black History Month Story." *Time Magazine,* January 31, 2018. time.com/5124917/black-history-month-henry-highland-garnet/#:~:text=Henry%20 Highland%20Garnet%20is%20the,slavery%20organizers%20in%20the%20world

Pasternak, Martin B., "Rise now and fly to arms : the life of Henry Highland Garnet." 1981. Doctoral Dissertations 1896 - February 2014. 1388. doi.org/10.7275/zy0j-rk93

Peterson, Carla. "A Black Preacher Addresses Congress." Sunday, February 12, 1865. *NY Times,* Opinionator. February 11, 2015.

"Proceedings of the National Convention of Colored People and Their Friends; held in Troy, NY; on the 6th, 7th, 8th, and 9th of October, 1847." Steam Press of J.C. Kneeland and Co. 1847. omeka.coloredconventions.org/files/ original/9380fd8347a91688d93824bab9a4b02f.pdf

Sherbondy, Jeanette E. "Reverend Henry Highland Garnet and the Women in His Life." March 28, 2023. www.commonsenseeasternshore.org/ rev-henry-highland-garnet-and-the-women-in-his-life

Schor, Joel. "The Rivalry Between Frederick Douglass and Henry Highland Garnet." *The Journal of Negro History, Vol. 64, Number 1 (Winter, 1979),* University of Chicago Press on behalf of the Association for the Study of African American Life and History.

Sullivan, James. "The New York African Society for Mutual Relief (1808-1860)," *BLACKPAST,* January 2011. www.blackpast.org/african-american-history/ new-york-african-society-mutual-relief-1808-1860/

Winkelman, Diana. "The Rhetoric of Henry Highland Garnet." baylor-ir.tdl.org/ bitstream/handle/2104/5095/Diana_Winkelman_Masters.pdf?sequence=3

Chapter 6—Mary Ann Shadd Cary

"African American Newspapers." *Accessible Archives.* www.accessible-archives. com/2011/02/african-american-newspapers/

Cary, Mary Ann Shadd. "Colored Women's Progessive Franchise Association, Statement of Purpose," 1880.

Conaway, Carol B. *Racially Integrated Education: The Antebellum Thought of Mary Ann Shadd Cary and Frederick Douglass.* Fall 2010. go.gale.com/ps/i. do?id=GALE%7CA277600910&sid=googleScholar&v=2.1&it=r&linkaccess= abs&issn=07351909&p=AONE&sw=w&userGroupName=mlin_oweb& isGeoAuthType=true&aty=geo

Find a Grave, "Mary Ann Camberton Shadd Carey." www.findagrave.com/ memorial/40231747/mary-ann_camberton-cary

Montgomery, Elizabeth. *Reminiscences Of Wilmington, In Familiar Village Tales, Ancient And New (1851).* Montana: Kessinger Publishing, 2010.

Rhodes, Jane. *Mary Ann Shadd Cary: The Black Press and Protest in the 19th Century.* Bloomington: Indiana University Press, 1999.

Shadd, Mary A. *Notes of Canada West: A plea for emigration, or, Notes of Canada West : in its moral, social, and political aspect; with suggestions respecting Mexico, West Indies, and Vancouver's Island, for the information of colored emigrants.* Detroit : G.W. Pattison, 1852.

Shadd, Adrienne. "The Provincial Freeman." *The Canadian Encyclopedia.* June 2023. www.thecanadianencyclopedia.ca/en/article/the-provincial-freeman

Silverman, Jason. "Unwelcome Guests: Canada West's Response to American Fugitive Slaves, 1800–1865." Millwood, N.Y. : Associated Faculty Press, 1985.

Specia, Megan. "Overlooked No More: How Mary Ann Shadd Cary Shook Up the Abolitionist Movement," *NY Times,* June 2018. www.nytimes. com/2018/06/06/obituaries/mary-ann-shadd-cary-abolitionist-overlooked.html

"The Provincial Freeman" "C.V.S." Toronto: 22 July 1854. utc.iath.virginia.edu/africam/afar64dt.html

Yarhi, Eli. "Mary Ann Shadd Cary American Educator, Publisher and Abolitionist." *Britannica.* 2023. www.britannica.com/biography/ Mary-Ann-Shadd-Cary

Chapter 7—Robert Morris

Blaustein, Albert P. and Zangrandro, Robert L. editors. "Civil Rights and the Black American: A Documentary History." Washington Square Press, a Division of Simon & Schuster, Inc., 1968.

"Freedom from Discrimination (timeline)." *The Annenberg Classroom.* www.annenbergclassroom.org/resource/freedom-from-discrimination/

Hisle, Jack. "The Quock Walker Case. Mapping the Great Awakening." people.smu.edu/mappingthega/stories/the-quock-walker-case/

Huffman, Robert. "The Life and Legal Strides of Boston Abolitionist Robert Morris." *Courthouse News Service.* www.courthousenews.com/the-life-legal-strides-of-boston-abolitionist-robert-morris/

Kantrowitz, Stephen. 'Equality First, Guns Afterward.' *NY Times Opinionator,* March 1, 2013. archive.nytimes.com/opinionator.blogs.nytimes.com/2013/03/01/equality-first-guns-afterward/#:~:text=declared%20it%20oblack%20men%E2%80%99s%20duty%20to%20%E2%80%9Cgo%20right%E2%80%9D,of%20the%20same%20prescription%3A%20%E2%80%9CEquality%20first%2C%20guns%20afterward.%E2%80%9D

Kendrick, Stephen and Paul. *Sarah's Long Walk Home.* Boston: Beacon Press, 2004.

"Sarah C. Roberts vs. The City of Boston, 1850." Primary Document. *BLACKPAST.* www.blackpast.org/african-american-history/sarah-c-roberts-vs-city-boston/

The Quock Walker case: "Instructions to the Jury." *PBS, Revolution Part 2, 1750-1805. 1783.* www.pbs.org/wgbh/aia/part2/2h38.html

Chapter 8—John Stewart Rock

"Black is Beautiful: The Emergence of Black Culture and Identity in the 60s and 70s." *National Museum of African American History and Culture.* Retrieved 2022-10-11. nmaahc.si.edu/explore/stories/black-beautiful-emergence-black-culture-and-identity-60s-and-70s

Brooks, Christopher. "Historically Speaking: A Tribute to First Black Man Allowed to Argue Before the Supreme Court." *The Morning Call,* Allentown, PA. Feb. 1, 2020. www.mcall.com/2020/02/01/historically-speaking-a-tribute-to-first-black-man-allowed-to-argue-before-supreme-court/

Brown, William Wells. "The Black Man His Antecedents, His Genius and His Achievements." Boston: James Redpath, publisher, 1863. www.gutenberg.org/files/64883/64883-h/64883-h.htm#Page_266

Buzby, J. H. "John Stewart Rock: Teacher, healer, counselor." Salem, NJ: Salem County Historical Society, 2002.

Chief Justice Roger Taney, "Majority Opinion, U.S. Supreme Court," *Scott v. Sanford,* March 6, 1857. *National Archives* www.archives.gov/milestone-documents/dred-scott-v-sandford

Contee, Clarence G. "The Supreme Court Bars First Black Member." *The Supreme Court Historical Society*, 1975. Archived from the original on November 20, 2008. Retrieved 20 May 2008. web.archive.org/web/20081120022856/http:/www. supremecourthistory.org/04_library/subs_volumes/04_c01_j.html

Contee, Clarence G. "John Sweat Rock, M.D., Esq., 1825-1866." *Journal of the National Medical Association*, Vol. 68, Number 3, May 1976. www.ncbi.nlm.nih. gov/pmc/articles/PMC2609666/?page=1

"Creating a Respectful and Open World for Natural Hair Act of 2021" or the "Crown Act." *House Resolution 2116.* www.govinfo.gov/content/pkg/BILLS-117hr2116rh/pdf/BILLS-117hr2116rh.pdf

"The Dred Scott Decision Buried in the Supreme Court—A Negro Lawyer Admitted by Chief Justice Chase." *NY Tribune*, February 7, 1865. chroniclingamerica.loc.gov/data/batches/dlc_cobol_ver01/data/sn83030213/00206530790/1865020701/0254.pdf

John S. Rock. Black History Now. Sept. 23, 2011. blackhistorynow.com/john-s-rock/

Lanari, Raquel. "How a Harlem Fashion Show Started the 'Black is Beautiful Movement,'" *NY Post*, February 5, 2018. nypost.com/2018/02/05/how-a-harlem-fashion-show-started-the-black-is-beautiful-movement/

Rock, John. "Address to the Citizens of New Jersey." *The North Star*, Rochester NY, Feb. 8, 1850. www.njstatelib.org/research_library/new_jersey_resources/highlights/african_american_history_curriculum/unit_5_antebellum_america/john_rock_address/

Rock, John. "I Will Sink or Swim with My Race." *The Liberator,* William Lloyd Garrison Publisher, March 12, 1858, Vol. XXVIII, No. 10 BLACKPAST, January 25, 2007. www.blackpast.org/african-american-history/1858-john-s-rock-i-will-sink-or-swim-my-race/

Rock, John S. "A Deep and Cruel Prejudice." January 23, 1862, Delivered to the Massachusetts Anti-Slavery Society in Boston, *BLACKPAST.* www.blackpast.org/african-american-history/1862-john-s-rock-deep-and-cruel-prejudice/

"Salmon Portland Chase, Mr. Chief Justice." *American History: From Revolution to Reconstruction and Beyond.* www.let.rug.nl/usa/biographies/salmon-portland-chase/mr-chief-justice.php

"Speech of John S. Rock in The Liberator," William Lloyd Garrison Publisher, August 15, 1862, Vol. XXXII, No. 33, p. 180. fair-use.org/the-liberator/1862/08/15/the-liberator-32-33.pdf

Chapter 9—Sarah Parker Remond

Clay, Sarah. "Letter in The Liberator." William Lloyd Garrison Publisher, November 5, 1858, Vol. XXVIII, November 5, 1858, No. 45. fair-use.org/the-liberator/1858/11/05/the-liberator-28-45.pdf

Crawford, Elizabeth. "Women: From Abolition to the Vote: Women's Suffrage Campaign: 1866-1903. *British History*, BBC, June 20, 2011. www.bbc.co.uk/history/british/abolition/abolition_women_article_01.shtml

Foner, Philip S., and Robert James Branham, eds. *Lift Every Voice: African American Oratory, 1787-1900.* Chapter 66: The Negroes in the United States of America—Sarah Parker Remond. Tuscaloosa: University of Alabama Press, 1998.

Garrison, Wendell Philips and Garrison, Francis Jackson. "William Lloyd Garrison, 1805-1889. The Story of his life as told to his children." New York Century Company, 1889, vol. iv

Hood, Amy. "Portrait Highlight - Sarah Parker Remond - African American abolitionist, lecturer & physician." www.amyhoodillustration.co.uk/post/portrait-highlight-sarah-parker-remond-african-american-abolitionist-lecturer-physician

Johnson, Ben. "The Lancashire Cotton Famine." *Historic UK*, March 14, 2015. www.historic-uk.com/HistoryUK/HistoryofEngland/Lancashire-Cotton-Famine/

Miller Sr., Connie A. *Frederick Douglass American Hero: And International Icon of the Nineteenth Century.* Xlibris, 2008

Porter, Dorothy B. "Sarah Parker Remond, Abolitionist and Physician." *The Journal of Negro History*, Vol. 20, No. 3 (Jul., 1935), The University of Chicago Press on behalf of the Association for the Study of African American Life and History

"Sarah Remond Ejected from Boston Theater—May 4, 1853." mass moments, *A Project of Mass Humanities.* www.massmoments.org/moment-details/sarah-remond-ejected-from-boston-theater.html

Sklar, Kathryn and Stewart, James Brewer. *Women's Rights and Transatlantic Antislavery in the Era of Emancipation* (The David Brion Davis Series). New Haven: Yale University Press, 2007.

Sterling, Dorothy, ed. "We Are Your Sisters: Black women in the Nineteenth Century." New York: W.W. Norton and Compnay 1984.

Wilcox-Lee, Naomi. "Sarah Parker Remond." sheroesofhistory.wordpress.com/2017/10/02/sarah-parker-remond/October 2017

"The Anti-Slavery Advocate of March 1, 1859," vol. ii, no. xxvii, p. 211.
www.britishnewspaperarchive.co.uk/viewer/bl/0001393/18590301/009/0004

Chapter 10—Abraham Galloway

Brown, Norman D. "Stanly, Edward, 10 Jan. 1810 - 12 July 1872." *NCPedia*, 1994.
www.ncpedia.org/biography/stanly-edward

Ceceksi, David. *Democracy Betrayed: the Wilmington Race Riot of 1898 and its Legacy.* University of North Carolina, 1988.

Gerard, Philip. "Abraham Galloway: From Cartridge Box to Ballot Box." *Our State, Civil War Series.* www.ourstate.com/abraham-galloway/

Still, William. *Underground Railroad, A Narrative.* Philadelphia: Porter and Coates, 1872

Franck, Julie (2013). "Abraham Galloway 8 Feb. 1837—1 Sept. 1870." NCPEDIA, North Carolina State University, 2013, Revised September 2022. ncpedia.org/biography/galloway-abraham

Chapter 11—Francis Pastorius

Hamm, Thomas. *The Quakers in America* (Columbia Contemporary American Religion Series). New York: Columbia University Press, 2006.

Weaver, John. *Franz Daniel Pastorius and Transatlantic Culture: German Beginnings, Pennsylvania.* John Weaver, Publisher, 2016.

History of Information. "The First American Public Document to Protest Slavery and One of the First Written Public Declarations of Universal Human Rights." www.historyofinformation.com/detail.php?id=3701

Froom, Burt. "Pastorius and the Founding of Germantown." *West Mt. Airy: Yesterday and Today* (Article 17), October, 2014. vdocuments.mx/pastorius-and-the-founding-of-germantown-by-burt-pastorius-and-the-founding.html?page=1

Gerbner, Katherine. "'We Are Against the Traffik of Men-Body:' The Germantown Quaker Protest of 1688 and the Origins of American Abolitionism." *Pennsylvania History: A Journal of Mid-Atlantic Studies*, Vol. 74, No. 2, April 2007. journals.psu.edu/phj/article/view/59492

"henderich, Garret, up de graeff, derick, Pastorius, Francis daniell, up Den graef, Abraham Germantown Friends' Protest Against Slavery, 1688." www.loc.gov/resource/rbpe.14000200/?st=text

Meggitt, Justin J. "Early Quakers and Islam: Slavery, Apocalyptic and Christian-Muslim Encounters in the Seventeenth Century." *Studies on Inter-Religious Relations 59.* Uppsala: Swedish Science Press, 2013.

Nielsen, Euell A. "Germantown Petition Against Slavery (1688)." *BLACKPAST,* January 13, 2022. www.blackpast.org/african-american-history/germantown-quaker-petition-against-slavery-1688/

Chapter 12—Benjamin Lay

"An Act for the Better Regulating of Negroes in this Province (March 5, 1725–1726)." *Pennsylvania Legislation Relating to Slavery.* Adams County History, 2003. cupola.gettysburg.edu/cgi/viewcontent.cgi?article=1074&context=ach

Conliffe, Ciaran. "Benjamin Lay—Outspoken Quaker Abolitionist." *Headstuff,* July 6, 2018. www.headstuff.org/culture/history/terrible-people-from-history/benjamin-lay-quaker-abolitionist/

"Fearless and Fiery." *Swarthmore College Bulletin.* Issue II, Volume CXV, Winter 2018. bulletin.swarthmore.edu/winter-2018-issue-ii-volume-cxv/fearless-and-fiery

Rediker, Marcus. "The 'Quaker Comet' Was the Greatest Abolitionist You've Never Heard Of." *Smithsonian Magazine,* September 2017. www.smithsonianmag.com/history/quaker-comet-greatest-abolitionist-never-heard-180964401/

Smith, Thomas R. "The Ghost of William Penn: Ralph Sandiford - Undivided for Humanity," *Daily Times,* Aug 9, 2012. www.delcotimes.com/2012/08/09/the-ghost-of-william-penn-ralph-sandiford-undivided-for-humanity/

Chapter 13—Anthony Bénézet

Anthony Bénézet—"1713-1784. Brotherly Love, Part 3—1791-1831." *Africans in America,* PBS. www.pbs.org/wgbh/aia/part3/3p248.html

"Anthony Bénézet, American Educator." www.britannica.com/biography/Anthony-Benezet

Bénézet, Anthony. "A caution and warning to Great Britain and her colonies, in a short representation of the calamitous state of the enslaved Negroes in the British dominions: Collected from various authors and submitted to the serious consideration of all, more especially of those in power." Philadelphia: Henry Miller,1766.

"Benjamin Rush, Race, Slavery, and Abolitionism." Dickinson. www.dickinson.edu/info/20043/about/3480/benjamin_rush

Brookes, George S. *Friend Anthony Benezet.* Philadelphia: University of Pennsylvania Press, 1937. www.encyclopedia.com/people/history/historians-miscellaneous-biographies/anthony-benezet

Crosby, David L. ed. *The Complete Antislavery Writings of Anthony Benezet, 1754-1783: An Annotated Critical Edition* (Antislavery, Abolition, and the Atlantic World). LSU Press, 2014.

"Letters of Anthony Benezet." *Internet Archive.* archive.org/stream/jstor-2713478/2713478_djvu.txt

Rush, Benjamin. *Biographical Anecdotes of Anthony Bénézet—Essays, Literary, Moral and Philosophical: The Consistent Life Of Bénézet.* Originally published 1798. Republished Syracuse University Press. 2008.

Vaux, Roberts. *Memoirs of the Life of Anthony Bénézet.* Montana: Kessinger Publishing, LLC, 2007

Chapter 14—Moses Brown

Berry, Deborah Barfield. "The US is grappling with its history of slavery. The blueprint for dealing with it? Some say Brown University." *USA TODAY*, Dec. 18, 2019. www.usatoday.com/in-depth/news/education/2019/12/16/slavery-reparations-brown-university-antigua-colleges-paying-up/4401725002/

Fitzgerald, Frances. "Peculiar Institutions." *The New Yorker*, September 12, 2005. www.newyorker.com/magazine/2005/09/12/peculiar-institutions

Moses Brown Papers, University of Massachusetts, Special Collections and University Archives. findingaids.library.umass.edu/ead/mums930#:~:text=He%20signaled%20his%20new%20commitments%20by%20manumitting%20the,of%20my%20hand%20was%20to%20give%20them%20liberty.%22

"Rhode Island History," Vol. 23, No. 1, January 1966. Rhode Island Historical Society, 52 Power St., Providence, RI. www.rihs.org/assetts/files/publications/1966_Jan.pdf

Simmons, Ruth. "Slavery and Justice: We Seek to Discover the Meaning of Our Past." *Ruth J. Simmons Center for the Study of Slavery and Justice.* Brown University, April 28, 2004. www.brown.edu/initiatives/slavery-and-justice/op-ed-column-ruth-j-simmons-4-28-04

Chapter 15 - Elizabeth Buffum Chace

Chace, Elizabeth Buffum. *Anti-Slavery Reminiscences*. Central Falls, R.I.: E.L. Freeman and Son, 1891. Re-printed by Gemany: Hansebooks, 2017.

Douglass, John and Thomas, Sally. "Timeline: Summary of events of the Loyalty Oath Controversy 1949-54." www.lib.berkeley.edu/uchistory/ archives_exhibits/loyaltyoath/timeline/short.html

Earle, Jonathan Halperin. "'Peculiarly Woman's Cause:' Feminism, Race, and the Struggle for Equality." *Reviews in American History*. John Hopkins University Press, Vol.28, Number 2, June 2000. muse.jhu.edu/article/29174

"Elizabeth Buffum Chace: Abolitionist, Suffragist and Philanthropist, History of American Women." www.womenhistoryblog.com/2016/06/elizabeth-buffum-chace. html

"Elizabeth Buffum Chace, Conductor on the Underground Railroad," *New England Historical Society.* www.newenglandhistoricalsociety.com/ elizabeth-buffum-chace-conductor-on-the-underground-railroad/

"Runaways Escape to Freedom in Rhode Island." *History of American Women.* www.womenhistoryblog.com/2015/08/underground-railroad-in-rhode-island.html

Stevens, Elizabeth C. "Elizabeth Buffum Chace and Lillie Chace Wyman: Motherhood as a Subversive Act in Nineteenth Century Rhode Island." *Quaker History* Vol. 84, No. 1, Nineteenth-Century Feminist Strategies for Nonviolence, Spring 1995.

Yee, Shirley J. "Black Women Abolitionists: A Study in Activism, 1828-1860." Knoxville: University of Tennessee Press, 1992

Chapter 16—Jane Swisshelm

Blakemore, Erin. "How the First American Woman to Be a Political Journalist Got Her Start." *TIME on line*, January 12, 2017. time.com/4627868/ first-female-political-journalist/

Freeman, Joanne. *The Field of Blood: Violence in Congress and the Road to the Civil War*. New York: Farrar, Straus and Giroux, 2018.

Gorman, Kathleen L. "The U.S. Dakota War." *Essential Civil War Curriculum.* www.essentialcivilwarcurriculum.com/the-us-dakota-war.html

"Jane Gray Swisshelm, Editor, Journalist and Newspaper Publisher." *History of American Women.* www.womenhistoryblog.com/2007/02/jane-grey-swisshelm. html#:~:text=With%20the%20financial%20support%20of,because%20of%20 her%20feminist%20sentiments.

Post, Tim. "A Woman of Contradiction." *Minnesota Public Radio,* September 26, 2002. news.minnesota.publicradio.org/features/200209/23_steilm_1862-m/ swisshelm.shtml

"Rediscovered Voices." Worcester Women's History Project. www.wwhp.org/ Resources/rediscovered.html

Stoler, Mark. "Things Have Changed" 2019. havechanged.blogspot.com/2019/04/ senator-foote-draws-his-pistol.html

Swisshelm, Jane Grey Cannon (1880). *Half a Century.* Chicago: Jansen, McClurg and Co., 1880. Reprinted by Anza Publishing, Chester, NY, 2005.

Swisshelm, Jane. "The St. Cloud Visiter," Vol. 1 No. 9, May 13, 1858. chroniclingamerica.loc.gov/lccn/sn85025584/1858-05-13/ed-1/seq-1/

"Sylvanus Lowry. Minnesota Legislators Past and Present," accessed 4 July 2012. www.lrl.mn.gov/legdb/fulldetail?id=13707

"Thomas Hart Benton." *Historic Missourians.* historicmissourians.shsmo.org/ historicmissourians/name/b/bentonsenator/

"The U.S. Dakota War of 1862." *Minnesota Historical Society.* www.usdakotawar.org/history/war/causes-war

Chapter 17—John Gregg Fee

Apbasova, Sona. Fee, John Gregg, Home. Berea College. libraryguides.berea.edu/johngreggfee

Basler, Roy P., Pratt, Marion Dolores, Dunlap, Lloyd A. editors. "Collected Works of Abraham Lincoln," Volume 4. (1860-61) Ann Arbor: University of Michigan, 2001. quod.lib.umich.edu/cgi/t/text/text-idx?type=simple;rgn=div2;c=lincoln;cc=lincoln;idno=lincoln4;q1=533;submit=Go;view=text;subview=detail;node=lincoln4:1003.1

Berea College, "Our Inclusive Mission." www.berea.edu/our-inclusive-mission

Clay, Cassius, ed. "True American, the Emancipationist Newspaper." June, 1845. *The History Engine.* historyengine.richmond.edu/episodes/view/113

Farrar, Ronold Truman. "Cassius Marcellus Clay—Abolitionist Newspaper Editor," American Newspaper Journalists: 1690-1872, Dictionary of Literary Biography, Vol. 43, edited by Perry J. Ashley "Cassius Marcellus Clay" by Ronald Truman Farrar, in *American Newspaper Journalists: 1690–1872, Dictionary of Literary Biography*, volume 43, edited by Perry J. Ashley (Columbia, S.C.: Bruccoli Clark / Detroit: Gale Research, 1985, pp. 98–102. www.encyclopedia.com/people/history/us-history-biographies/cassius-marcellus-clay

Fee, John Gregg. *Autobiography of John G. Fee: Berea, Kentucky*. Chicago, Ill.: National Christian Association, 1891. Digital form in Documenting the South, University of North Carolina. docsouth.unc.edu/fpn/fee/fee.html

Harrison, Lowell H. *The Civil War in Kentucky*. Lexington, KY: The University Press of Kentucky, 1975.

Kaller, Seth. "Confederate Governor of Kentucky Seeks Prominent Louisville Editor's Support for Secession in the Summer of 1861." *Historic Documents and Legacy Collection*. Seth Kaller, Inc. www.sethkaller.com/item/2365-26799-Confederate-Governor-of-Kentucky-Seeks-Prominent-Louisville-Editor%E2%80%99s-Support-for-Secession-in-the-Summer-of-1861#:~:text=When%20President%20Abraham%20Lincoln%20called,passed%20declarations%20of%20neutrality%2C%20and

Quisenberry, A.C. "Kentucky Union Troops in the Civil War." *Register of the Kentucky State Historical Society*, Vol. 18, number 54, 1920.

Richardson, Edward H. *Cassius Marcellus Clay: Firebrand of Freedom*. Lexington: University Press of Kentucky, 1976

Chapter 18—Delia Webster

Cottman, George Streiby, Esaray, Logan, Coleman, Christopher Bush. "Indiana Magazine of History," Volumes 17-18, 1921. Re-published Charlestown, SC: Nabu Press 2012.

"Delia Webster." History of American Women. www.womenhistoryblog.com/2015/01/delia-webster.html

Eisan, Francis K. *Saint or Demon? The Legendary Delia Webster Opposing Slavery*. New York: Pace University Press, 1998.

"Lewis Hayden." New Bedford Historical Society. nbhistoricalsociety.org/portfolio-item/lewis-hayden

Money, Charles H. "The Fugitive Slave Law of 1850 In Indiana (Concluded)." *Indiana Magazine Of History*, Volume 17, No. 3. 1921. p. 281.

Morris, J. Brent. *Oberlin, Hotbed of Abolitionism: College, Community and the Fight for Freedom and Equality in Antebellum America*. Chapel Hill: UNC Press, 2014.

Runyon, Randolph Paul. *Delia Webster and the Underground Railroad*. Lexington: University Press of Kentucky, 2015.

Talbott, Tim. "Petticoat Abolitionist." *Explore KY History*, accessed July 8, 2020. explorekyhistory.ky.gov/items/show/178?tour=9&index=4

Chapter 19—Sallie Holley

Chadwick, John White. *A Life For Liberty: Anti-Slavery and Other Letters of Sallie Holly*. New York: G.P. Putnam and Sons, 1899.

Greenfield, Nathan. "At Oberlin, Long Tradition of Shared Governance is Ended." University World News. December 4, 2022. www.universityworldnews.com/ post.php?story=20221203065247323

Higgins, Jimmy. "Sallie Holley, Inspiration from our History." *Fire From the Mountain*. March 26, 2007. firemtn.blogspot.com/2007/03/sallie-holley-inspiration-from-our.html

"History of Holley School." Holley Graded School. holleyschool.weebly.com/ about-holley-school.html

hong han, lao. "Sallie Holley: Inspiration for Anti-Racists" *Daily Kos*, March 26, 2007. www.dailykos.com/stories/2007/3/26/316238/-

Johnson, James E. "Charles Grandison Finney: Father of American Revivalism." *Christian History Institute*, Issue #20, 1988. christianhistoryinstitute.org/ magazine/article/charles-grandison-finney

Oneida Institute. "Oneida County Freedom Trail, The History of the Underground Railroad in Central NY." www.oneidacountyfreedomtrail.com/ oneida-institute.html

"Sallie Holley—She Found Her Place Among the Lowly." *History of American Women*. www.womenhistoryblog.com/2016/01/sallie-holley.html

Schmidt, Elizabeth. "Sallie Holley (1818-1893)." *Epitaph*, Vol. 12, #2, 1992. fomh.org/wp-content/uploads/2021/05/SallieHolley.pdf

"Seminole Wars." *Encyclopedia Britannica*. www.britannica.com/topic/Seminole-Wars

Van Haitsma, Pamela. *African-American Rhetorical Education and Epistolary Relations at the Holley School (1868–1917)*. Taylor & Francis Online, November 14, 2018. www.tandfonline.com/doi/full/10.1080/15362426.2018.1526547?af=R&

"West Indies Emancipation Day, August 1." *The Free Dictionary.*
encyclopedia2.thefreedictionary.com/West+Indies+Emancipation+Day

Chapter 20—Graceanna Lewis

Cassin, John. "Proceedings of the Academy of Natural Sciences, 1867."
Philadelphia. www.biodiversitylibrary.org/page/26288905#page/7/mode/1up

"Graceanna Lewis: Pioneer Scientist and Abolitionist," *History of American
Women.* www.womenhistoryblog.com/2014/12/graceanna-lewis.html

King Jr., Martin Luther. "Letter from a Birmingham Jail." April 16, 1963.
African Studies Center, University of Pennsylvania. www.africa.upenn.edu/
Articles_Gen/Letter_Birmingham.html

Lewis, Graceanna. "An Appeal to Those Members of the Society of Friends Who
Knowing the Principles of the Abolitionists Stand Aloof from the Anti-Slavery
Enterprise." Cornell University Digital Library. reader.library.cornell.edu/
docviewer/digital?id=may869014#mode/1up

Lukens, Rob. "History's People: Graceanna Lewis—Abolitionist to Natural
Scientist" *History's People,* Daily Local News March 19, 2013. www.dailylocal.
com/2013/03/19/historys-people-graceanna-lewis-abolitionist-to-natural-scientist/

Morgan, Barbara. "Graceanna Lewis." Women in World History: A Biographical
Encyclopedia: Volume 9, Farmington Hills, MI: Gale Group, 1999.

Patteson, Daniel, ed. *Early American Nature Writers: A Biographical Encyclopedia.*
Westport, CT: Greenwood Press, 2007.

Still, William. *The Underground Railroad:A Record of Facts, Authentic Narrative,
Letters, etc.* Philadelphia: Porter & Coates (1872).

Weidensaul, Scott. *Of a Feather: A Brief History of American Birding.* Boston:
Houghton Mifflin Harcourt, 2007.

Acknowledgements

Tom Weiner

Where to begin the list of those who have contributed to the concept, the creation, the editing, and the publication of *In Defiance*? I have wanted to write this book for over forty years, since I discovered the dearth of resources about people like the ones portrayed between this book's covers. I was inspired by the creators of *Meeting the Challenge: Biographies of Black Americans* which I shared with my sixth-grade students to explore, honor, and appreciate. That workbook gave me both hope and impetus to dig deeper and discover others whose contributions to American culture need to be explored and celebrated.

My two younger children, Madeline and Stefan, deserve much credit for the next step in my coming to *In Defiance*. Having encountered Black people who were little known and whose contributions were immense, I began the search for their white counterparts, and here, too, I ran into obstacles. But when Maddie and Stefan heard that I was considering writing a book that would center white people, they both strongly urged me to reconsider. My thought had been that white people, especially as I witnessed the waning of their commitment to Black Lives Matter, needed to be inspired, and how better to do so than with stories of white people from early in American history who fought back against the horrors of enslavement? My children's thought was that our country did not need another book that appeared to elevate white people by themselves in the effort to emancipate Black people. There were more than enough white savior stories already.

So the book evolved to include little-known but hugely significant Black and white women and men. Early on, when I had only discovered a few of the book's subjects, I had the good fortune to discuss the project and share several of the profiles with students sin a multi-cultural education class at Smith College, thanks to Dr. Lucy Mule, their professor. The feedback they provided was invaluable and made the book better.

It was in sharing this book with Dr. Shabazz that I was gifted with my other major revelation—from writing it myself with my white voice to co-authoring it with a preeminent scholar of African American history. Our paths had initially crossed through our participation in Brid for Unity, B4U, which included white and Black men and women from Western Massachusetts, Letcher County, Kentucky, and several communities in South Carolina. Our group's goal—to conduct dialogues and develop trust across various divides, especially racial divides, brought Shabazz and myself together with upwards of thirty kindred spirits. I acknowledge each of their contributions to the evolution of my consciousness and my openness to others whose stories have enriched me.

Dr. Shabazz saw the project's potential as well as where he could contribute his knowledge, experience, and perspective, which has immeasurably added to the work. Once the book began to take shape, I sought out the expert editing assistance of my dear friend David Perkins, who encouraged me to think of ways to grab reader interest from the opening paragraph of each profile. His contributions to our conversation and his editing improved the book. It also deepened our friendship as I sought to return the favor by offering my take on his deeply researched and compelling biography of Leontyne Price, which will hopefully soon be joining *In Defiance* in the publishing world.

Next up is a member of the Smith College Campus School class of 2015, the second to last of my forty years teaching at the school (most recently known as the Campus School of Smith College). Auden Cote-L'Heureux came back into my life in the summer of 2023 via a LinkedIn message from his father, who had been my student teacher in the '90s and who wrote to me about Auden's work teaching computer skills to rural Ghanaians ranging in age from five to seventy. Once Auden and I met for lunch, I got a firsthand glimpse at his diverse set of skills, which ultimately manifested in his taking on the challenge of getting permissions for the many photos in our book as well as making sure they were the right size and pixelation. Auden did this because he instantly believed in the value of *In Defiance* and because he knew he could do it, even when I was voicing my doubts. He did it, and I am eternally grateful for his efforts and successes.

We next needed a publisher who also believed in the value of the book, and such a publisher is Michel Moushabeck. Knowing his integrity through witnessing his commitment to the Palestinian House of Friendship, on whose board I have sat for the past eight years, and having long followed his announcements of the outstanding books he has published by Middle Eastern authors and others whose work we admire, I was convinced that he should be the first publisher to approach. The result of that decision is evident in the book you've now read.

Michel enlisted the herculean efforts of our editor, David Klein, who encouraged us to make the book more user-friendly by "killing our darlings," the phrase he shared with us pertaining to the necessity of letting go of less-than-key components that the book initially contained. It was an arduous process, and David demonstrated restraint and patience as well as expertise in getting the best from us.

Finally, my wife, Susan, gets a shout-out for supporting my writing efforts and being willing to enable me to spend the requisite time and energy to churn out another book. Knowing that she not only wants my various projects to succeed but that she also shares the values each one puts forth is yet another source of inspiration and commitment.

A final blue note from Dr. Amilcar Shabazz ...

In 1964, John Coltrane released *A Love Supreme*, a musical expression of gratitude for having overcome an addiction to heroin seven years earlier and his subsequent spiritual awakening. The album's first song, "Acknowledgement" says, in a musical way, behold my gratitude to the forces that have awakened me to live a new life, in a new way. In the way of my ancestors, let us first acknowledge the "twenty and odd" lives that we remember here in this book. Thank you to their spirits, and may the remembering of them here be acceptable in their sight and a blessing to all of us who are because they were.

Let me also be grateful to my personal ancestors, especially Coincoin Marie Thérèse, who was born in 1742, in what we today call Louisiana. She was the child of François and Marie Françoise (aka Francisque), a "full black slave couple," as genealogist Elizabeth Shown Mills referred to them. My work on this book would not have been possible without my love, Demetria Rougeaux Shabazz, who is now with the ancestors. Her defiant fight against cancer inspires me to support research that can lead to better detection, prevention, and treatment of this awful disease.

And always, as Nikki Giovanni says, there are the children ...

we feed the children with our culture
that they might understand our travail

we nourish the children on our gods
that they may understand respect

we urge the children on the tracks
that our race will not fall short

but children are not ours
nor we theirs they are future we are past

My children, Mandela, Amilcar II, and Ursa Sekou, the "very sea-mark of my utmost sail," face a future that requires a humanity that will act in defiance. May they, their generation, and those yet unborn have the courage, fortitude, and wisdom to win the battle not yet truly won. Uhuru sasa, freedom now!